SEAMANSHIP FOR DIVERS

Also available

Sport Diving – The British Sub-Aqua Club Diving Manual
Safety and Rescue for Divers
Advanced Sport Diving
Snorkelling for All

SEAMANSHIP FOR DIVERS

The British Sub-Aqua Club

Stanley Paul

London

First published 1986
Reprinted 1990, 1993

1 3 5 7 9 10 8 6 4 2

First published in the United Kingdom in 1986 by
Stanley Paul & Co Ltd
Random House, 20 Vauxhall Bridge Road, London SW1V 2SA

Random House Australia (Pty) Limited
20 Alfred Street, Milsons Point, Sydney,
New South Wales 2061, Australia

Random House New Zealand Limited
18 Poland Road, Glenfield,
Auckland 10, New Zealand

Random House South Africa (Pty) Limited
PO Box 337, Bergvlei, South Africa

Random House UK Limited Reg. No. 954009

A CIP catalogue record for this book is available
from the British Library

ISBN 0 09 166291 5

Set in 9 on 10pt Rockwell Light

Printed in Great Britain by Scotprint Ltd,
Musselburgh, Scotland

Contents

Seamanship for Divers

Before the advent of the inflatable boat, sport diving was generally confined to the immediate shore line with long surface swims being the order of the day. Nowadays, inflatables and other small craft, with improved design and more powerful and reliable outboard engines, are widely used by divers to explore hitherto inaccessible dive sites. Diving from larger vessels is also growing in popularity, bringing within range some of the most remote and challenging diving sites like St. Kilda, the Outer Hebrides and the Shetland Islands.

Seamanship for Divers has been planned to bring together those aspects of boat handling and seamanship specifically relevant to divers, in an attractive and illustrative form. At the same time, basic information relating to Buoyage, Charts, Tides and Meteorology has been included. The coverage of these subjects should not be considered as definitive by the reader but should form the basis for further study. Real experience is gained by hands-on use and the reader is advised to attend one of the BSAC's popular Boat Handling Courses.

Mike Holbrook
National Diving Officer

Acknowledgements

The British Sub-Aqua Club gratefully acknowledges the efforts of the following persons who have contributed to this publication:

Editors:
Mike Busuttili
Mike Holbrook

Gordon Ridley
Mike Todd

Contributors:
Mike Busuttili
Don Collier
Deric Ellerby
Mike Holbrook
Gordon Ridley
Dave Shaw
Mike Todd
Barry Winfield

Basic Seamanship

Ropes

For divers there are a number of quite specific uses for ropes underwater, but users of boats of all sizes find that they inevitably handle rope on almost every trip they make. Rope is used for many different purposes on boats, some of them essential to the running of the boat, some associated with the work for which the boat is used, and some traditional or even decorative. We want to concentrate here on the main purposes for which seagoing divers will use rope.

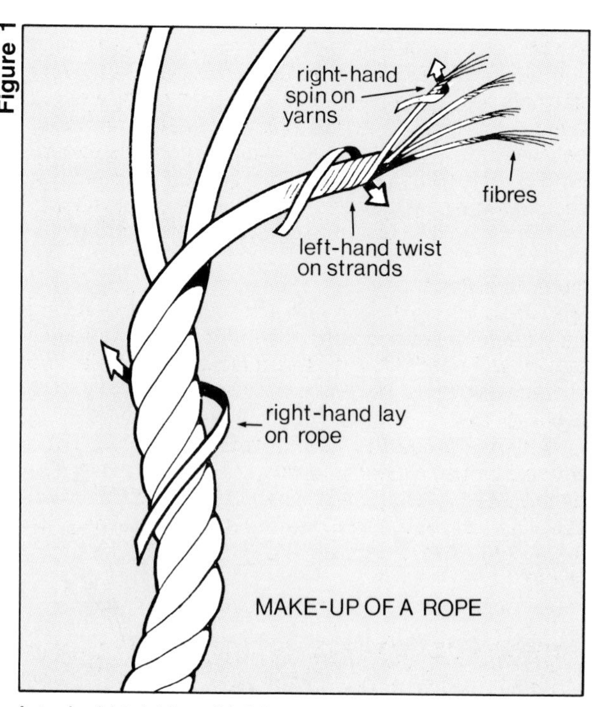

A typical 'right-hand laid' rope

The Construction of Rope

The first thing that you will notice about a rope is that it consists of a number of strands, usually three, which are twisted together and yet seem to stay firmly together. If you look more closely at just one strand, you will see that it is twisted in the opposite direction to that of the main rope and this is what makes the rope hold together.

The direction in which the strands are twisted is called the 'lay' of the rope. If you hold the rope so that it points away from you, the strands will go to the right. This is known as 'right-hand-laid', 'plain-laid' or 'hawser-laid' rope and is by far the most common type. In a right-hand-laid rope the strands go to the right but the yarns making up each strand go to the left. The yarns are, in turn, laid up right-handed.

In a rope made from synthetic fibre the individual filaments will run the length of the rope and leave a smooth surface. The hairy appearance of rope made from natural fibres is caused by the ends of the shorter, natural fibres projecting beyond the rope's surface. Synthetic material can be used to make 'hairy' rope by cutting the filaments into shorter lengths during the rope-making process.

Other types of rope include: cable-laid (three strands laid up left-handed); shroud-laid (four strands laid up right-handed around a heart); and plaited or braided ropes.

Material used for Ropes

Traditional ropes were made from a variety of vegetable fibres including manilla, hemp, sisal, coir and cotton. Natural ropes have some disadvantages: they swell when wet, rot, mildew, jam, freeze in cold weather, are slow to dry, and have a low strength-to-weight ratio. The fact that they sink when wet is a possible advantage for diving purposes, but generally the high maintenance requirement has led to their being largely replaced by synthetic-fibre ropes.

The principal synthetic fibres employed in rope making are nylon, polyester and polypropylene. They display different strength characteristics in the ratio 5:4:3 respectively. Nylon, apart from being strongest, has the greatest elasticity, a quality which can be useful when towing or mooring. Polyester, usually found under the trade name of Terylene, is not so strong but far less elastic and is used where a steadier permanent tension is required. Polypropylene floats and this, combined with its relative cheapness, makes it popular in boating. Other fibres such as polyethylene (trade name Courlene) are also quite common for lighter ropes.

Synthetics have high strength-to-weight ratios and excellent rot resistance; they perform well when wet and require far less care. They can be made in different colours and their ends can be easily heat-sealed. However, their smooth surface, which makes them pleasant to handle, also makes them less good at holding a knot than a hairy natural-fibre rope.

Sizes of Rope

The size of modern ropes, particularly synthetic ropes with which we are mainly concerned, is measured across the diameter in millimetres, at the widest part. If you hear a size quoted in inches, then beware, for it *used* to be common to describe a rope by its circumference in inches.

It is worth stating the obvious: a rope must be long enough for the purpose for which it is intended. It is, of course, possible to join two or more ropes together, but the strength of the resulting line is never as good as that of one continuous length, and the bends used to join the ends may jam in pulleys, cleats, etc.

When deciding upon a suitable rope for a particular job, both the strength and the size have to be considered. However, with modern synthetic ropes, which are very strong, it is usually the handling characteristics which dictate the size. For example, a 25-kg shot weight would require only a 3-mm diameter rope, but it would be very difficult to haul up; consequently a 12–15-mm rope would be more suitable. In practice most ropes used on diving boats will be at least 10–12 mm, with the possible exception of a line designed to store on a reel such as that used on a surface marker buoy. In this case compactness is the first requirement and less strength is needed.

Choosing a Rope

If you need to select a rope for a specific job on a diving boat, then you have to consider the particular qualities that you will need. Cost is often a factor when selecting synthetics as the range is quite wide.

Disposability

Does the rope need to have a long life, as would be required for permanent lines such as mooring lines? For this purpose a quality nylon line would represent good value. For short-term work in which the rope may be cut or lost (surveys, salvage, etc.) lower-cost fibres will suffice.

Stretch

Is it desirable or not? While useful in a mooring line, it is unsuitable for shrouds and other standing lines.

Handling

The most pleasant line to handle may be a braided line but it is expensive and can be difficult to coil. Natural fibres give good grip, but can also give a bad rope burn if allowed to run through the hand.

Stowability

In a small boat it may not always be easy to stow a line neatly, particularly an anchor line, so for this purpose consider its stiffness or suppleness.

Lines

For the sake of clarity, a line is a rope used for a particular purpose, and it will usually be described as such: e.g. lifeline.

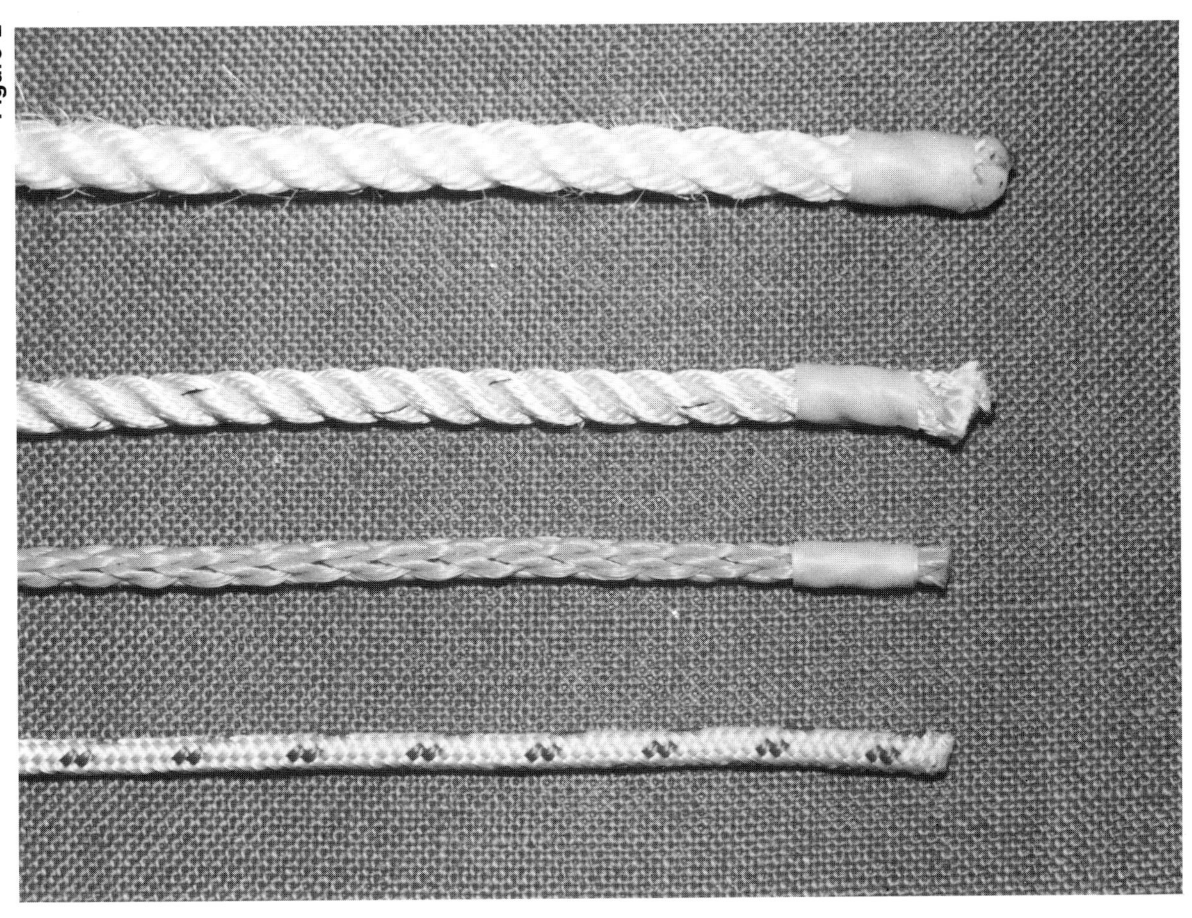

Figure 2

Four types of synthetic rope (from the top down): 'hairy' finish, hawser-laid polypropylene; hawser-laid polyester; plaited polypropylene; braided nylon

Knots

Over the years a vast number of knots has evolved as people have found new jobs to be done with ropes and cords of all sizes. We want to concentrate here on a selection of the most useful and simple knots, those which are likely to find a use on and around a diving boat.

Knots can be further classified into knots, bends and hitches. Knots are used to form a stopper in the end of a line or to make a noose or a loop. Bends are used to join two ropes of equal or near equal thickness. Hitches are used to join a line to a ring, a post, a bollard or a substantially thicker rope.

Strength and Security

Knots will generally reduce the strength of the rope in which they are tied. The simpler the knot, the more likely it is to be harmful to the rope as the tension will be spread over fewer turns. Knots which use more turns will be less harmful as the increased friction will absorb the load more gradually and jam less readily.

A knot which is strong under load may not be secure if it slips when the load is released. A secure knot will hold well under varying conditions and is, therefore, preferable. It is obviously best to choose a knot which is easy to undo, since most rope needs to be repeatedly re-used and it is wasteful to have to cut off jammed knots.

Some Useful Knots

Remember that there is no one universal knot that is best in all situations. In this small selection we cover a useful set of knots which are well worth learning to tie.

Figure 3

A 'slip' bowline

Bowline

A popular knot amongst divers due to its suitability for tying a lifeline to a diver. It forms a fixed loop in the end of a line, will not jam and is easy to undo. When tied correctly the end will lie inside the loop, otherwise it is known as a left-handed bowline which, in practice, seems to work just as well. A useful derivative is the bowline on a bight, tied in the middle of a line and useful for making a sling or a bosun's chair when the pull is on both ends of the line.

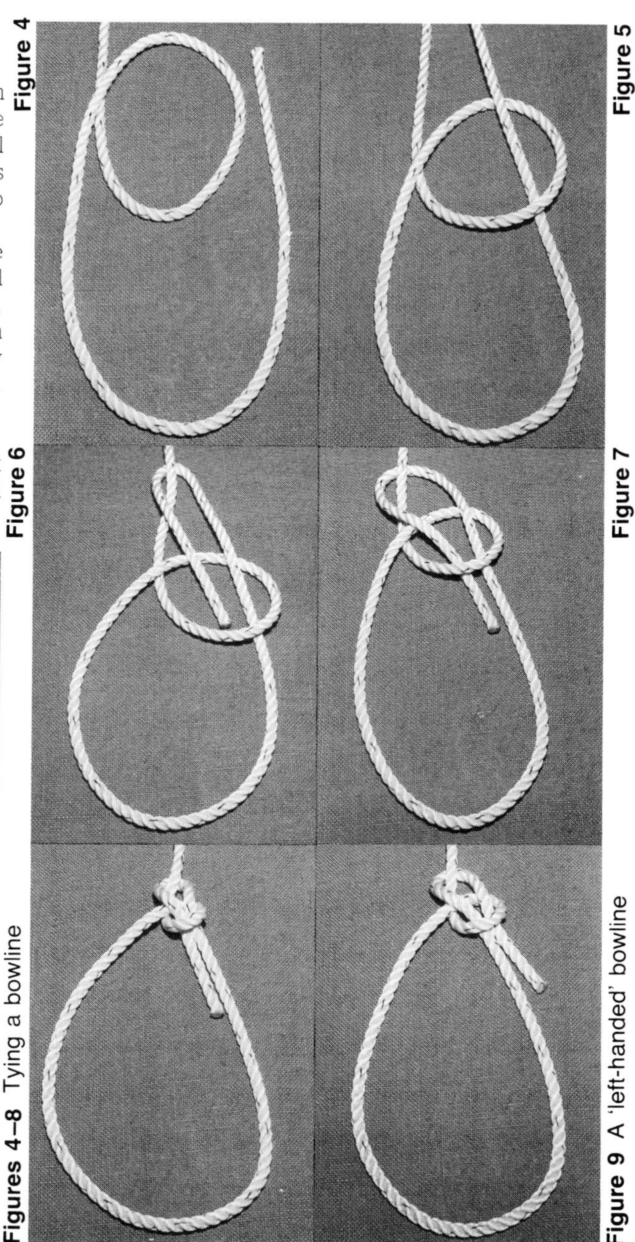

Figures 4–8 Tying a bowline

Figure 9 A 'left-handed' bowline

Figure 10

The reef knot

Reef Knot
Principally used to tie together the two ends of the same line, as round a parcel. It requires constant tension with the knot pressed against a solid object. It is not a bend. It consists of two overhand knots, one left-handed and one right-handed, otherwise it becomes a granny knot which will slip or jam.

Figure 11

The granny knot

Figure of Eight
A simple and useful stopper knot. Can be used to stop a line from fraying or to prevent it from passing through a narrow lead or hole.

Figure 13

Figure 13

The bowline on-a-bight

Figure 14

Bowline used to attach a line to an anchor

Bends

Should you need to join two lines together, then use a proper bend because the join will become the weakest part of the line.

There are, of course, more permanent methods of joining two lines, by splicing or seizing, which are described later in this section.

Sheet Bend

A useful bend for joining together two lines which are not very different in diameter. Start by taking a bight in the larger of the two lines, then pass the thinner end through the loop from the underside, around the back and across the front of the loop under its own standing part (the main part of the line). If the first line is stiff, this can be counteracted by taking an additional turn around the neck of the bight to make a double sheet bend.

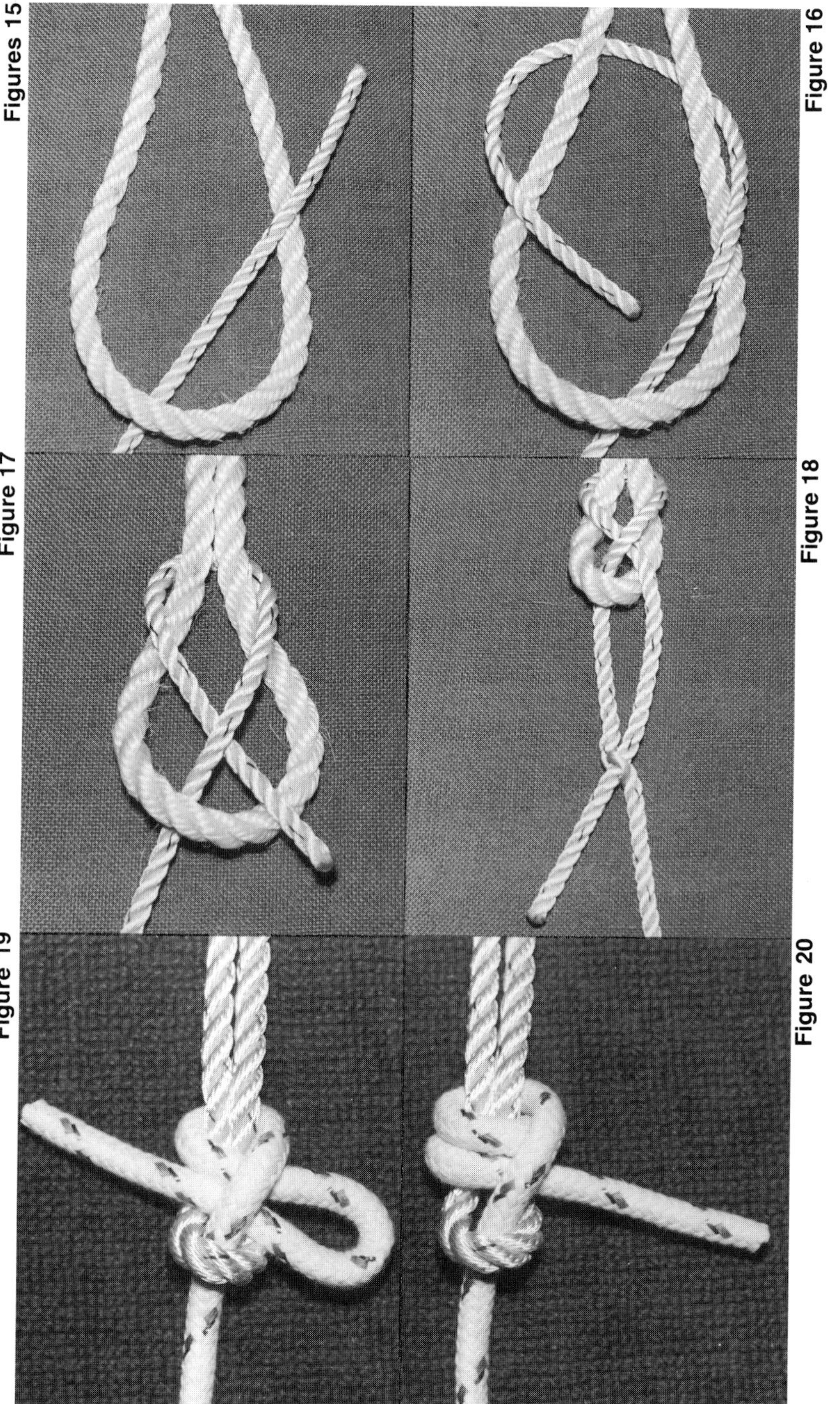

Figures 15–17
Tying a sheet bend

Figure 18
Securing the free end by passing through the lay, as a temporary measure

Figure 19
Sheet bend with a 'slip'

Figure 20
Double sheet bend (note this does not increase the strength of the bend, merely the security of the free end)

Fisherman's Knot
This is called a knot because it is usually tied in small lines or cord, but since it joins two lines its function is that of a bend. It consists simply of two overhand knots tied around the standing part of two lines, each knot enclosing the other line's standing part. When pulled tight they hold well and are relatively easily separated.

Figure 21

Figure 22

Figure 23

The 'truckers' bend' is used to secure cargo, in this case, a boat on a trailer. It can be pulled tight, and is easily released. This bend, which depends upon the block and tackle principle, is easily tautened by one person

Hitches

Whenever we tie off a line to something other than another line we use a hitch. If the other object happens to be a rope fixed at both its ends, then we also use a hitch. Let us first of all look at the hitches we would use to tie off a line to a spar, a rail, a ring or a bollard, as would occur when mooring a boat.

Clove Hitch

There are several ways of tying this hitch, but to start with we will consider tying on to a horizontal rail. First pass the end over the top of the rail and bring it to the left of the standing part. Then pass it over again, to the right of the first turn, and then bring the end back up between the two turns so formed. When tying up to a bollard it is easy to throw the first loop over, perhaps holding the strain with the loop's friction, until you can throw a second loop. In each case keep the loose end under the standing part. In either case the hitch cannot be considered permanent unless the end is stopped, usually with a couple of half hitches.

Figure 24

Figure 25

Figure 26

Figure 27

Figure 28

A clove hitch can be 'thrown' over a mooring bit or bollard by putting the first loop over and then reversing the second

Two Half Hitches
To tie off a line temporarily, pass the end over the spar and make two half hitches, both in the same direction.

Figure 29

Anchor Bend
So called as it is suitable for securing a line to the ring of the anchor. Start with two round turns through the ring or over the rail, then take the end through the turns, and finish with two half hitches or some other method of stopping the end.

Figure 30 Figure 31 Figure 32 Figure 33

Round Turn and Two Half Hitches
This is far better since the extra turns around the rail give added friction and reduce the wear. Pass the end over the rail twice then proceed as for two half hitches. A single half hitch will suffice if the end is then seized or spliced to the standing part.

Figure 34

Slips
With the above hitches and with other knots and bends it is easy to improve the speed with which they can be undone by finishing them with a slip. This consists of taking the end back through the last part of the knot so that it needs only to be pulled to undo or 'spill' the knot. Of course, this immediately reduces the permanence and security of the knot but may prove useful in situations such as a short-term mooring.

Splices

The most permanent and strongest method of joining two similar ropes is to splice their ends together. Unless the rope has to run through a sheave or pulley block, the short splice will be the best choice. The long splice has the advantage of not increasing the diameter of the rope but is less strong.

Short Splice

Undo the strands of each rope a little way and seal or whip the ends. Bring the ends together so that they intertwine and temporarily stop or whip this join. Take one strand of either rope and tuck it alternately under and then over the strands of the other rope, going against the lay. Repeat for the other two strands, then repeat with the strands of the other rope. Tuck the remaining ends under and over, as before, until only the whipped ends remain. Cut them off fairly close to the rope, but not so that they slip back between the strands. Smooth out the splice by rolling it under foot.

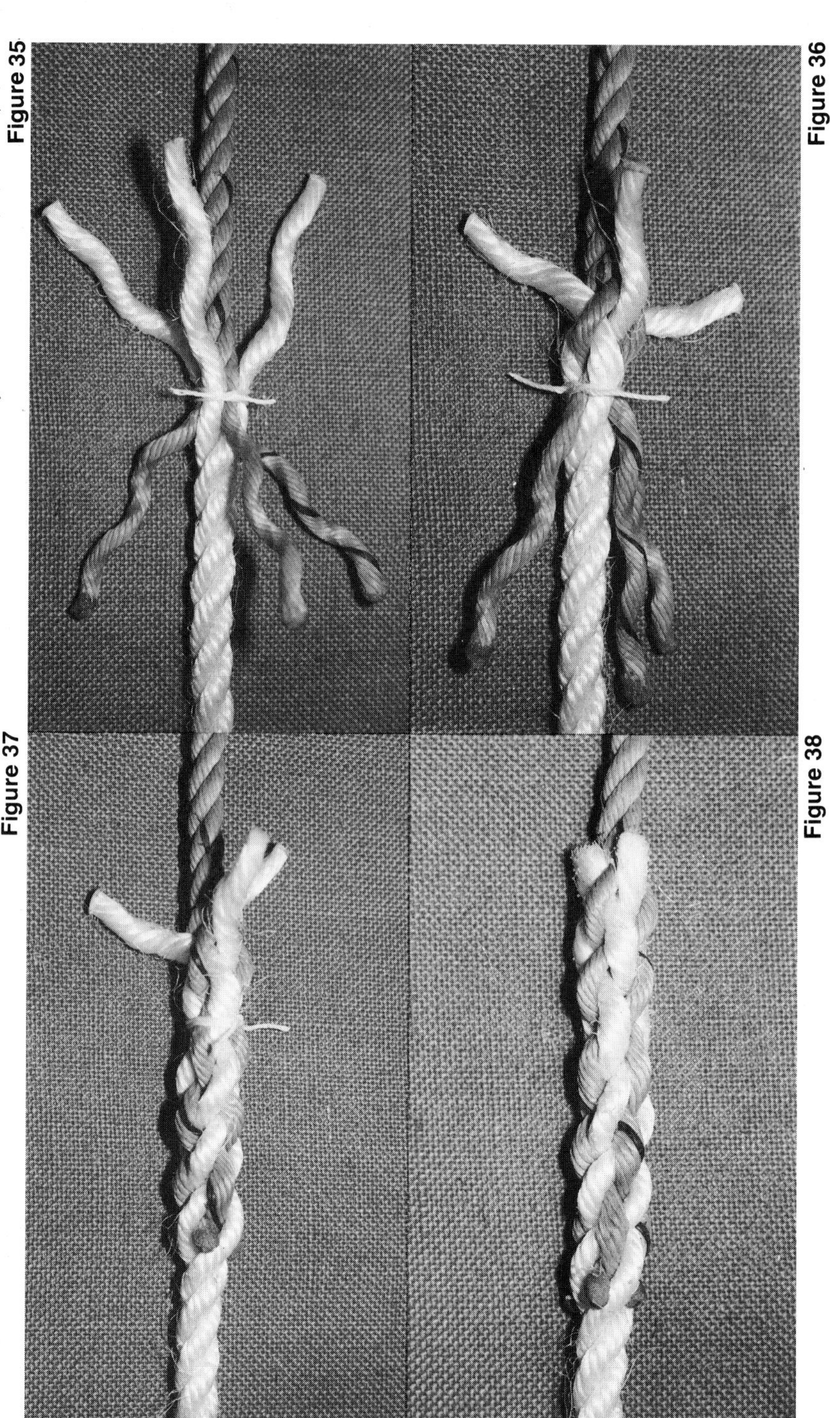

Figures 35–38

Making a short splice. Note that the free ends are each tucked three times through the lay of the rope

(A long splice requires more rope as the strands are unlaid further than in the short splice and each strand is then laid in the groove vacated by the matching strand in the opposing rope; the strands are halved then tucked once)

Eye Splice
Used for forming a permanent loop in the end of a line. Determine the size of the loop and undo the strands to that point. Tuck the first strand through a strand of the rope against the lay. Then tuck the strand to its left through the next strand of the rope. Turn the loop over and tuck the remaining strand through the last strand of the rope. Repeat the procedure until you have made three tucks with each strand, then trim off the remaining ends, but not too short.

If the rope is stiff or heavy a marlin spike or a fid will prove useful in prising the strands apart. In synthetic rope the remaining ends can be heat-sealed to prevent further fraying, but aim for a smooth finish with no sharp edges.

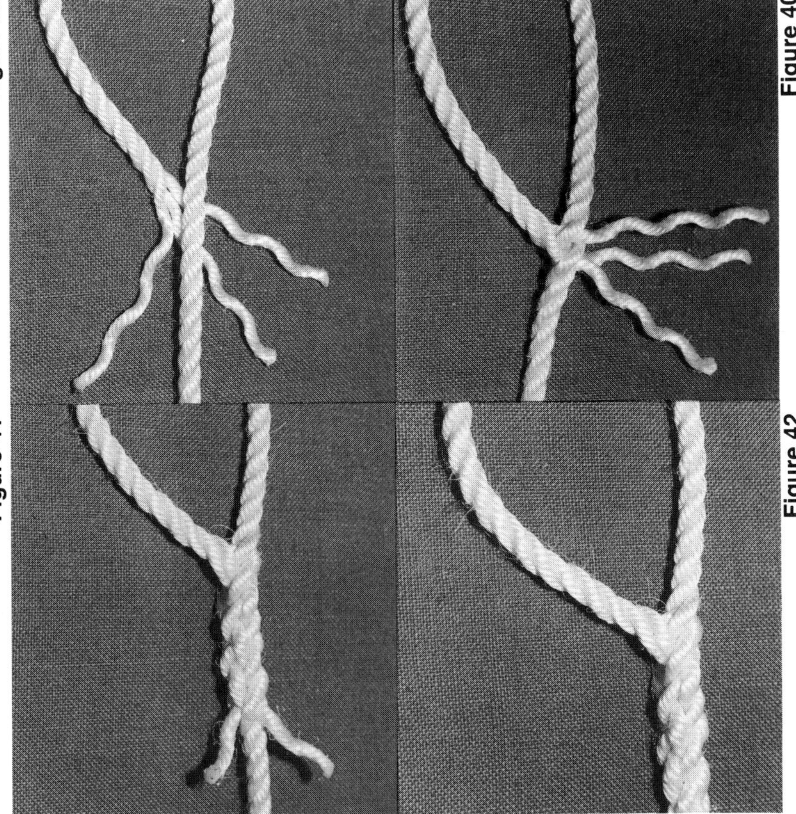

Figures 39–42
Making an eye splice

Coiling

Rope has the ability to form itself into the most hopeless tangles if it is not handled properly. Due to its being a right- or a left-handed lay, rope will coil naturally in one direction only. The coil must follow the direction of the lay. If you go against this rule you will produce a twist in every bight, unless you twist the rope as you make the coil, in which case the twists appear as you pay it out later. If you are pulling a line in and want to make a coil on the deck or ground, simply form the coil in the direction of the lay. If you are collecting the line in your hand, then the same applies. If you want to stow the coil it should be bound so that it will be possible to handle it as a coil when next needed. Take it in the hand and, using the last metre or so of line, make three turns around the coil and finish by passing the end through the coil above the turns. The coil can then be hung up by the loose end for storage and drying.

If, instead of the end, a fairly long bight is passed through the coil, then another line can be bent to the loose end without the need to re-coil the two lines into one new coil.

Coiling a rope

Whipping

If a rope is cut then the end will work loose and start to undo. To prevent this the end of a rope is finished off in some way, depending on the job it will have to do. Not all whipping involves the use of other cordage; we will look at the range of possibilities available to us.

Constrictor Knot
The quickest and simplest way to prevent the end of a line from coming apart is to tie a constrictor knot around it. This knot will serve well until a more permanent method can be used but will not be expected to come undone before that time. Start by tying a clove hitch and then pass the loose end across and then through the first turn. This knot has many other uses, particularly as a temporary clamp.

Figure 44

Figure 45

Figure 46

Figure 47

Heat Sealing
The end of a synthetic rope can be sealed with a hot knife or a flame to fuse the filaments together. It is considered a temporary solution and does not replace a plain whipping since the sealed end will eventually crack and fray once more. Avoid building up a hard ball of material or forming sharp edges which could cut the hand.

Plain Whipping

Also known as a common whipping, it uses twine or 'small stuff' to bind the end of a rope tightly. Start by laying a short loop of twine near the end of the rope and wind the twine around the rope against the lay. Pass the last turn through the end of the loop so that by pulling on the first end the second end will be trapped under the final strand. Cut the two ends off short.

The whipping should be as long as the diameter of the rope. Use natural twine on a natural-fibre rope and synthetic twine on a synthetic rope.

Figure 48

Figure 49

Figure 50

Sleeves

Sleeves are short tubes of material which fit over the end of the rope. They contract to fit the rope either elastically or from the application of heat. They are quick and simple but may lack flexibility.

Palm and Needle Whipping

An even more permanent form of whipping, normally used on sailing vessels, where the appropriate materials will also be available.

Figure 51

Stowage

On a larger diving boat there will be a number of different lines that are used for a variety of purposes, some regularly and others much less frequently. Those that are in relatively constant use will be stored where they are used. Mooring lines will normally be found ready for use, or in use, at the bow and at the stern. The anchor warp will be attached to the anchor and stored nearby. All other lines are best kept coiled and ready in suitable storage. The best way to store rope is to hang it up in coils in a place where it can benefit from ventilation to assist drying. Ideally, in order to prevent rot and mildew, rope should be allowed to dry before being stowed away. The problem is less serious with synthetic ropes but they also will benefit from being stored hung up as a coil.

Figure 53

Pass the final loop through . . .

Figure 52

Coils can be easily stowed

Figure 54

. . pull it down and tighten

New Rope

New rope is usually supplied in the form of a fairly tight coil and will take a degree of 'set' from this form of storage. Before use it should be unrolled, stretched and re-coiled into the looser coils described previously. A method which can be employed in areas of little traffic is to pay the line out behind the boat while travelling, allowing it to straighten out in the wake, and then haul it in to make a new coil, being careful to avoid the propeller. This system is also useful for a line which has collected twists and tangles during use. Some types of rope that have not yet been used under load can be expected to stretch when first used. This may make them unsuitable for use as standing lines or shrouds.

Maintenance

Ropes are subject to wear and abrasion when in use and this can weaken them considerably. It is very important that ropes are inspected periodically to check whether wear has taken place and to judge the extent to which it may render the line unsuitable for its planned use. It is possible that a worn line can be downgraded to a use which will put it under less load.

Often it is the ends of lines which suffer most and these may have to be trimmed back to give good ends. Avoid taking a short length off the end of a good line for some little job as this may make an expensive coil of rope quite unsuitable for its original purpose. A line that has worn sections is by far the most suitable for cutting up into shorter lengths.

Inspections should look for cuts and abrasions, which weaken a particular strand of the rope. They need not go right through the rope to render it unsafe. Remember, the whole rope is only as strong as its weakest part.

If the line has knots jammed into it, this also will serve to weaken it. If the knots can be unjammed and released, then the rope can be rated at its original strength provided no damage is caused by the unjamming.

Accessibility

Certain lines may need to be located and paid out swiftly. In this case it is useful to keep them on a reel or drum, which will rotate to allow the line to be paid out. This technique is essential for the deployment of jackstays in survey work, and can be useful for setting a shot line. The reverse procedure should be considered for recovering the line if it is planned to use it again soon. Alternatively it can be recovered conventionally and flaked into a basket, to be loaded back onto the reel later. On a large boat, lines will normally be recovered by means of a winch, which allows easier handling of the rope to be stored.

In smaller boats it is often easiest to carry the main lines in plastic baskets or buckets. If the lines are laid into the bucket as they come aboard then they will pay out just as easily when needed. This avoids the need to make coils and to take up extra space in the boat. For light lines a hand reel or winding board is useful.

Figure 55

Using a power winch to recover a line

Figure 56

Pass the line first over a mooring cleat . . .

Figure 57

. . . and then over alternate horns, followed by a final locking turn

Rules of the Road

The International Regulations for Preventing Collisions at Sea, 1972, is the mariners' Highway Code. As the rules that apply to motorists are essential to safety on our roads, so the rules governing the conduct of vessels are fundamental to safety at sea. The most important rules relating to small vessels can be found in Appendix 2. Where possible, reference to the appropriate rule is made in the following text.

If you are driving your vessel in a narrow channel or shipping lane, keep as far to the starboard side of the channel as possible (Rule 9a). Avoid trying to cross a traffic lane or channel where larger vessels usually have to keep to a well-defined route. They are unlikely to alter course if you get in their way. If you have to cross, cross at right angles to the direction of flow and keep well clear at all times (Rule 9b). If a vessel is approaching you from your starboard side and there is a risk of a collision, then you must give way (Rule 15), just like at a traffic island, where you give way to vehicles coming from the right. Slow down and allow the vessel to cross, or bring your vessel around and behind him. This area is referred to as the 'give-way arc', which is defined as an imaginary line drawn from the bows of your vessel, extending to 2 points abaft of the beam 112° 30′. A point represents 11.25°.

Occasionally you will meet another vessel which is coming straight for you head-on or nearly head-on. In this situation you must turn your vessel to starboard (Rule 14a). The other vessel should do the same, so that each

Figure 58

Large unmanoeuvrable craft are unlikely to alter course and additionally have limited visibility close to their bows

Figure 59

Give way to a vessel approaching from the starboard and pass to the rear of the vessel

Figure 60

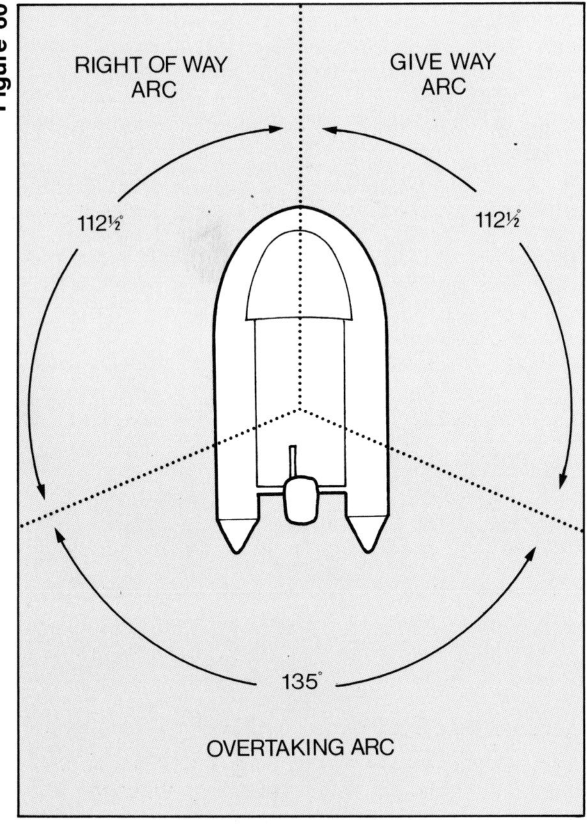

The 'give-way arc' showing sector priorities

vessel passes on the port side of the other. You should always keep a good lookout for other vessels (Rule 5) in your area and be prepared to take avoiding action in plenty of time.

Give other water users plenty of room, especially sailing vessels (Rule 18a), which may have to tack suddenly. Normally power gives way to sail, unless the powered vessel can only safely follow a channel. Fishing vessels may have their nets out, so do not approach them, or any moored vessels not under command. When you overtake another vessel, keep well clear and allow plenty of sea room (Rule 13a).

High-speed inflatables are very manoeuvrable and should not find themselves in situations in which they are unable to keep clear of other water users. However, with speed it is easy to misjudge distance.

Figure 61

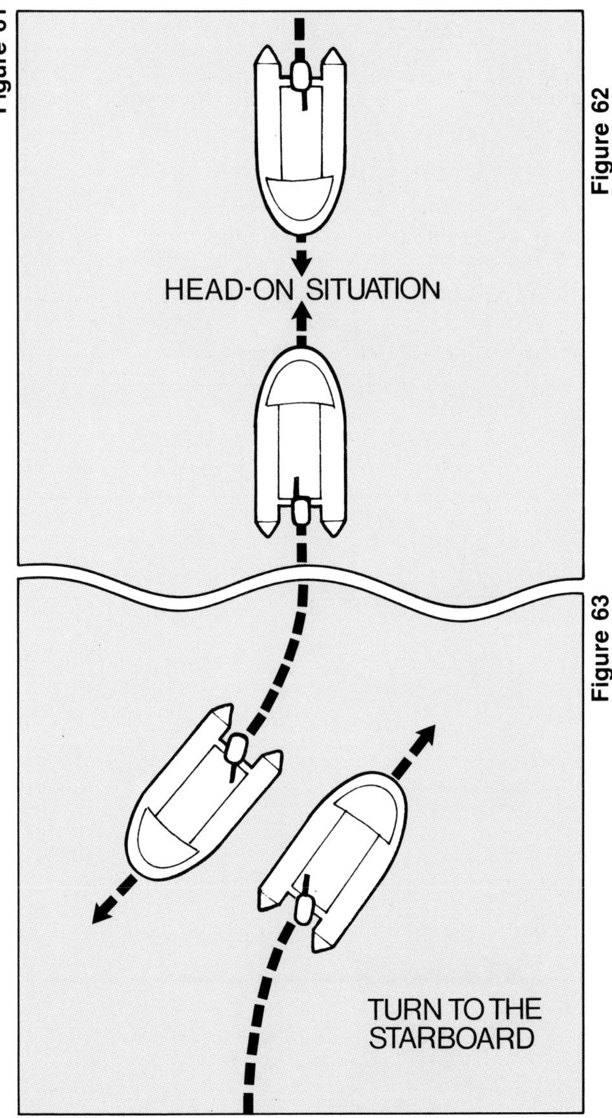

When two vessels are approaching each other head-on or nearly head-on, both must turn to starboard. If any doubt exists, then assume that this manoeuvre is required

Figure 62

Power boats generally give way to boats under sail

Figure 63

When overtaking, keep well clear

Lights

From sunset to sunrise or in restricted visibility, vessels of 12m or more in length but less than 50m are required to carry lights with the following visibility. For example:

> **masthead light, 5 miles (3 miles for below 20m)**
> **sidelights, 3 miles**
> **sternlight, 2 miles**
> **towing light, 2 miles**
> **white, red, green or yellow all-round light, 2 miles**

In vessels of less than 12 m in length the light intensity of the masthead light is 2 miles and of the sidelights 1 mile. In vessels under 20 m both sidelights can be combined into one lamp.

Vessels of less than 7 m in length whose maximum speed does not exceed 7 knots are not obliged to carry fitted lights, but it is a requirement that you carry a flashlight or handlamp if you are at sea in the dark or in restricted visibility.

Figure 65 shows clearly the arcs of visibility that the individual lights must have, and a few examples of the lights displayed by vessels at night which indicate their type and situation.

Shapes

In daylight, lights are not very effective and are difficult to see. Therefore vessels usually display various shapes from their mast to indicate the activity in which they are engaged. Six common examples of the use of shapes are shown in Figure 66.

Figure 65

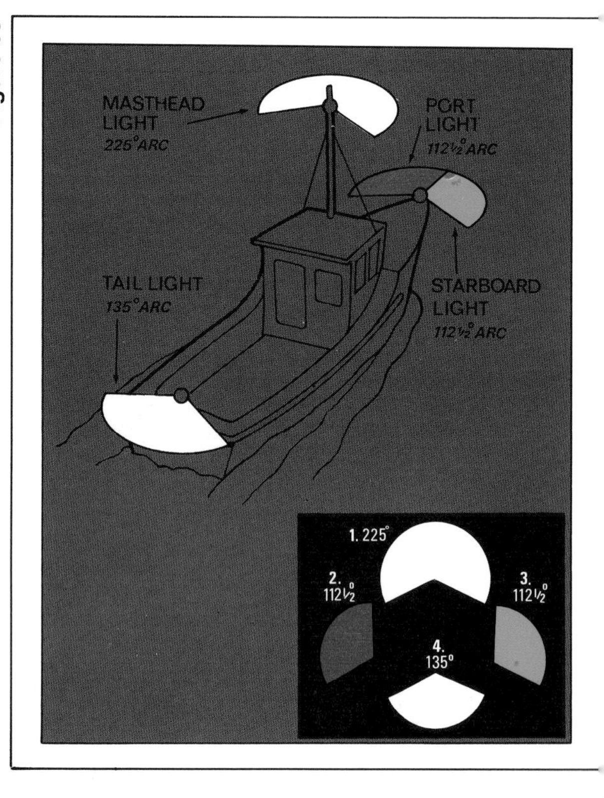

Figure 64

Lights for sailing vessels underway
1. Sailing boat under 7 m shows white light to prevent collision. If practicable she should show sidelights and sternlight
2a. Combined sidelights plus sternlight
2b. Masthead tricolour lantern
3. Separate sidelights and sternlight for sailing vessel over 20 m
4. Alternate to 2b

Lights for power-driven vessels underway
5. Motor boat under 7 m, less than 7 knots
6. Motor boat under 12 m (combined masthead and sternlight)
7. Motor yacht under 20 m (combined lantern for sidelights)
8. Motor yacht over 20 m
9. Larger vessel, over 50 m, with two masthead lights – the aft one higher

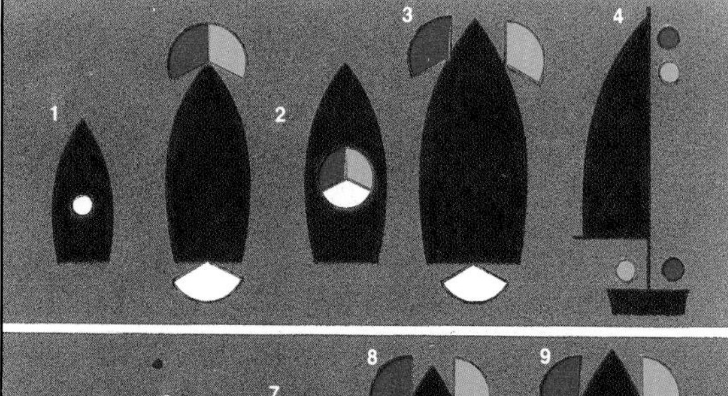

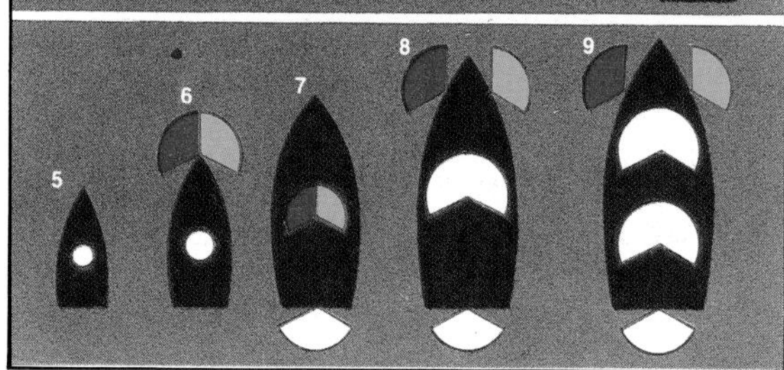

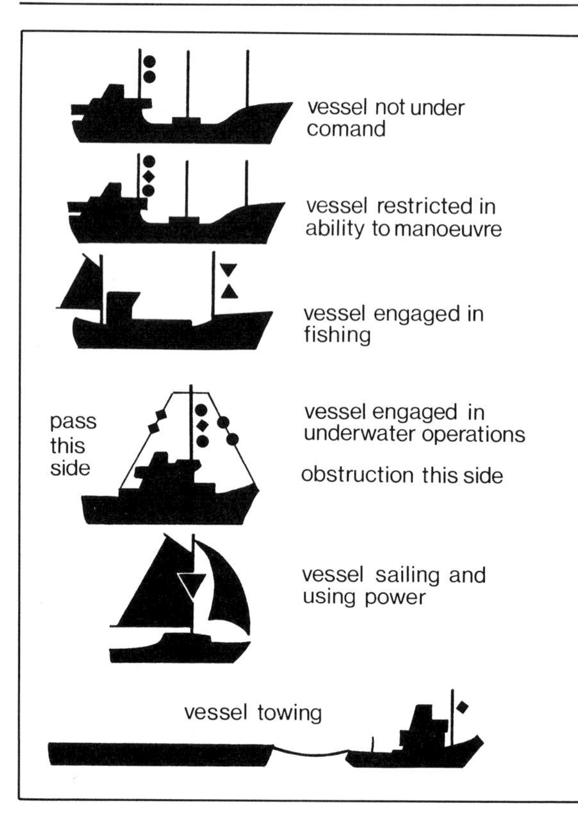

Vessels at anchor

Hovercraft

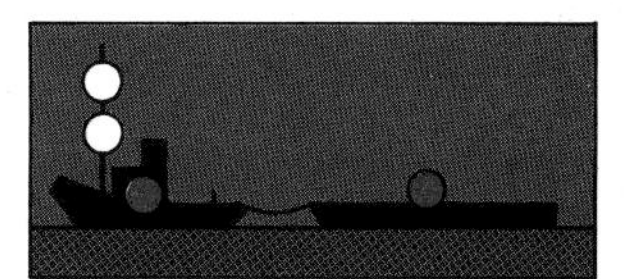

Vessel towing where: (a) length of tow less than 200 m

Power-driven vessel under 50 m

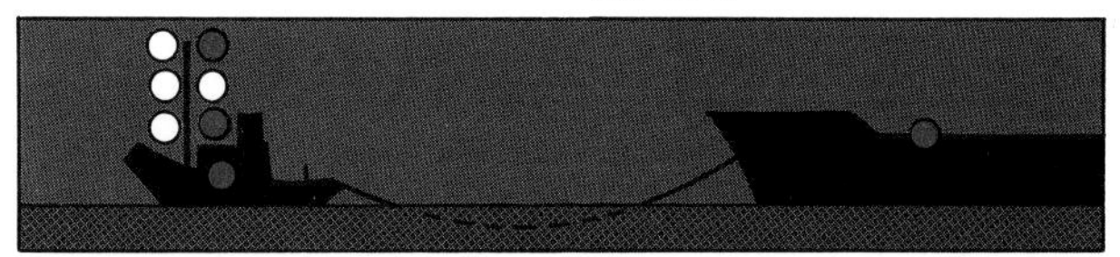

(b) length of tow exceeds 200 m. Towing vessel unable to manoeuvre shows additional red/white/red lights

Fishing vessel other than trawler with gear extended more than 150 m horizontally

Trawler

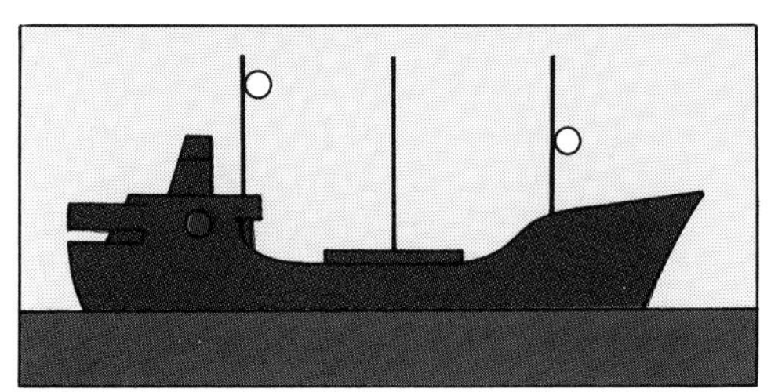

Power-driven vessel 50 m or over

Not under command making way. When not making way no sidelight shown

Vessel at anchor 50 m or more in length

Sound

Sound signals are used to call attention to an intended manoeuvre or warn other vessels in the vicinity of a boat's presence in poor visibility or fog. These signals should be understood by divers in small craft which may be operating near to busy shipping lanes (see Figure 68).

Figure 67 A hand-held fog horn powered by compressed gas

Figure 68

In fog these are signals you may hear

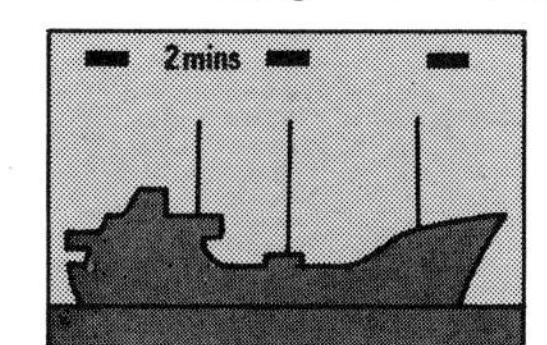

Power-driven vessel underway and making way

2mins

Power-driven vessel underway, but stopped

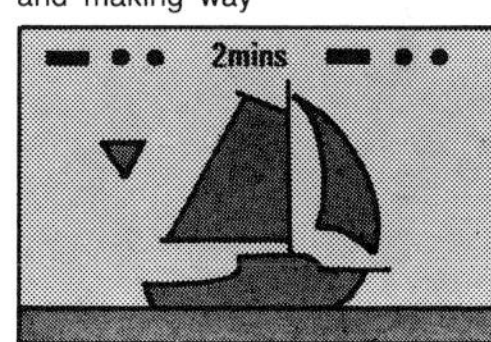

Sailing vessel under power

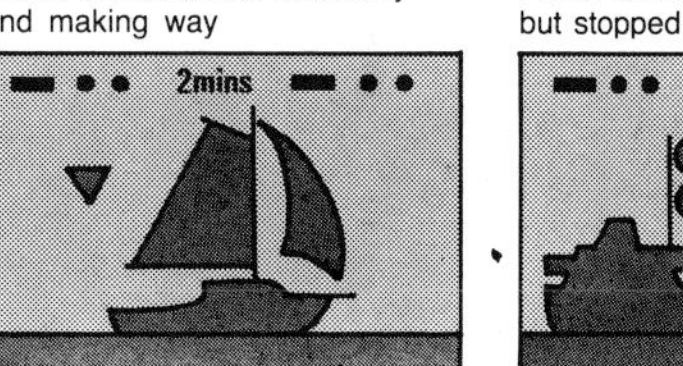

Vessel not under command

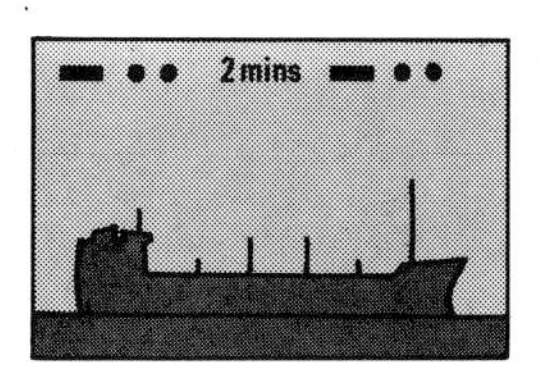

Vessel constrained by her draught

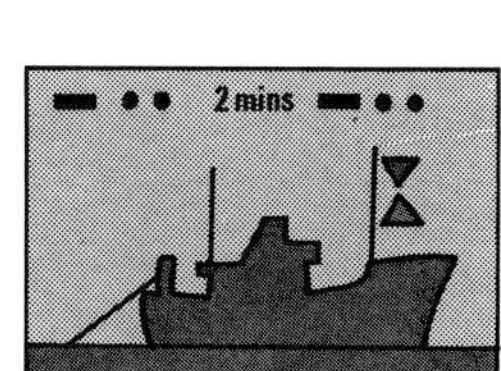

A vessel fishing

Buoyage

The system of buoyage, like charts, is mainly designed for commercial shipping. However, an understanding of buoyage, used in conjunction with charts, can provide divers with valuable information for position fixing, wreck location and pilotage.

Buoys and Beacons

Buoys are moored, floating marks that indicate the sides of navigable channels; mark the boundaries between safe and unsafe water; show where danger lies; give the deepest water; or indicate special features. They have four basic shapes: Can, Cone, Sphere and Pillar, while some floating marks are spar-shaped for reasons of economy.

Beacons of wood or metal can often be found erected in shallow water or on the shore and these serve the same purpose as buoys. Beacon towers are usually built on rocks to make them more visible.

The shape of a buoy is the clue to its meaning. However, the colour, the topmark and the lights combine with the shape to indicate the safe route.

Figure 70

Alternative buoy shapes

Figure 69

The four basic buoy shapes

Figure 71 Figure 72

A Port hand buoy　　A Starboard hand buoy

Systems of Buoyage

The system of buoyage used in all European waters is the International Association of Lighthouse Authorities' Maritime Buoyage System 'A' which combines Cardinal and Lateral marks. The lateral marks in System A differ significantly from the lateral marks still in use in North and Central America, Japan, South Korea and the Philippines where the old lateral system, referred to as System B, is still in use.

Combined Cardinal and Lateral System A

System A provides five types of buoy markings which can be used in any combination. However, the topmark is the important feature, especially with cardinal marks (see page 28). The significant features by night are the colour and rhythm of the light. By day, they are the colour, shape and topmark.

Lateral Marks

Lateral marks are used in conjunction with local or general direction of buoyage to indicate well-defined channels, and the port and starboard sides of the route to be followed. Port-hand can-shaped buoys are coloured red and starboard-hand cone-shaped buoys are green. The purpose of the lateral system is to indicate the general direction to be taken by the mariner when approaching a harbour, river or estuary from seaward, the rule being that when approaching from seaward, you should keep the can-shaped red port buoys on your left and the cone-shaped green starboard buoys on your right. In other areas the conventional buoyage direction usually follows a clockwise direction around land masses.

Figure 73

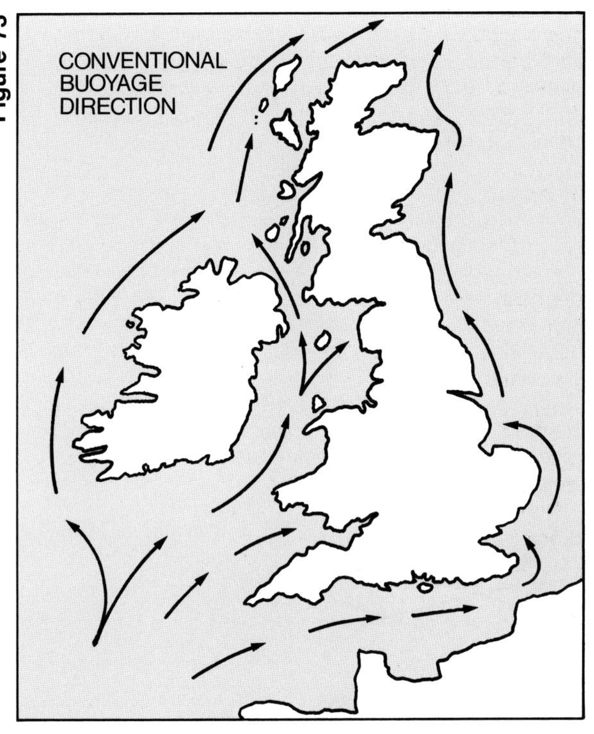

The lateral system assumes the mariner is travelling in the direction indicated, which is that of the main flood tide

Figure 74

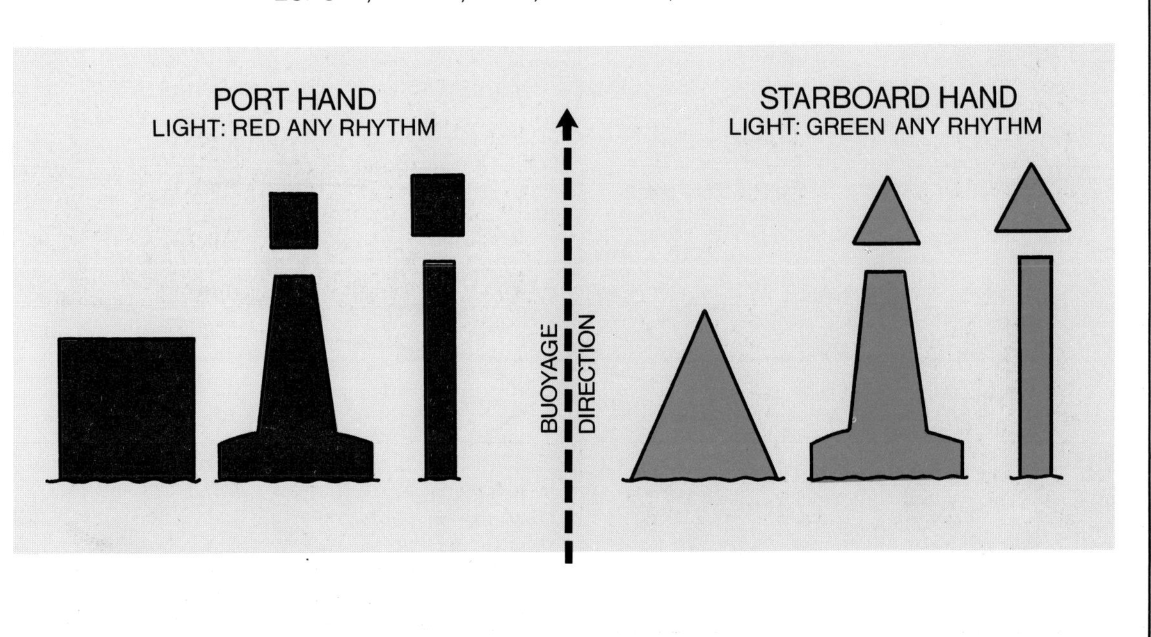

Cardinal Marks
Cardinal marks are pillar- or spar-shaped buoys coloured black and yellow. Four different colour patterns and topmarks indicate in which 'sector' a buoy stands, North, South, East or West. They are used in conjunction with a compass heading to indicate where the best navigable water can be found. A north-sector buoy, for example, indicates that clear water is to the north of the buoy.

Figure 75

A North sector Cardinal buoy

The Cardinal Marks. These are named after the quadrant in which they are placed. Take careful note of the colour patterns, topmark shapes and light sequences

Figure 76

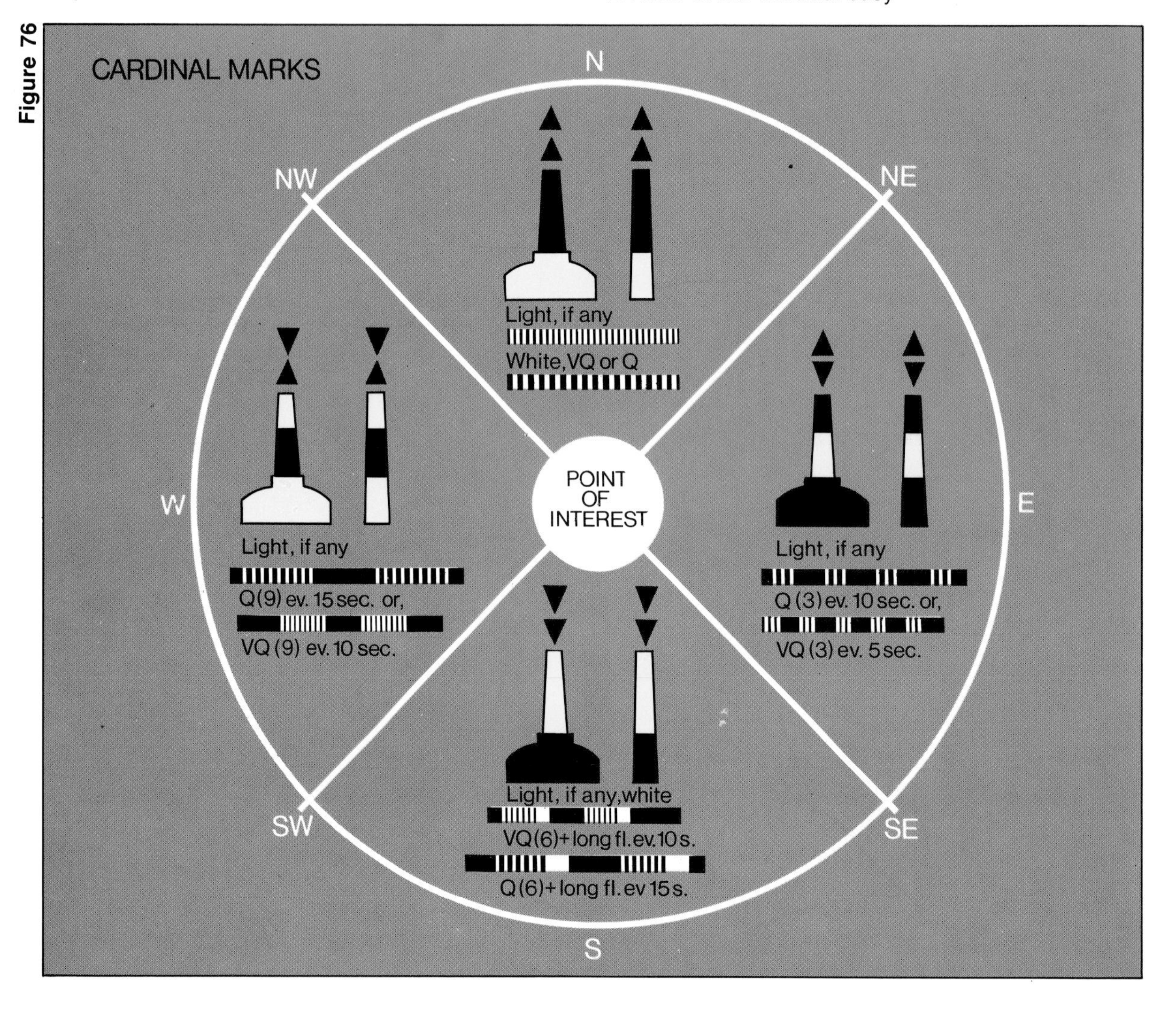

Isolated-Danger Marks
These buoys are pillar- or spar-shaped, with black and red bands. They are used to mark an isolated danger which has navigable water all around.

Figure 77

Safe-Water Marks
These are spherical, pillar- or spar-shaped buoys, with red and white vertical stripes. They indicate that there is navigable water all around the mark. They are used mainly to mark the mid-channel or as an alternative landfall mark.

Figure 78

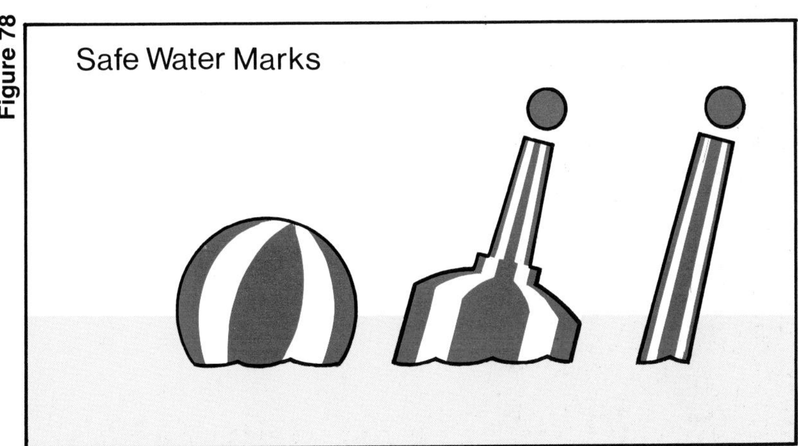

Special Marks
Special marks are yellow and the shape is optional. They are not primarily intended for navigation but indicate special areas or features, for example spoil grounds, military exercise zones and sewer outfalls.

Figure 79

Overleaf:

Figure 80
A typical buoy pattern in a channel entrance illustrating the combined use of Lateral and Cardinal buoys

Figure 81
A section of a typical chart showing the location of Cardinal buoys around a shoal

Figure 80

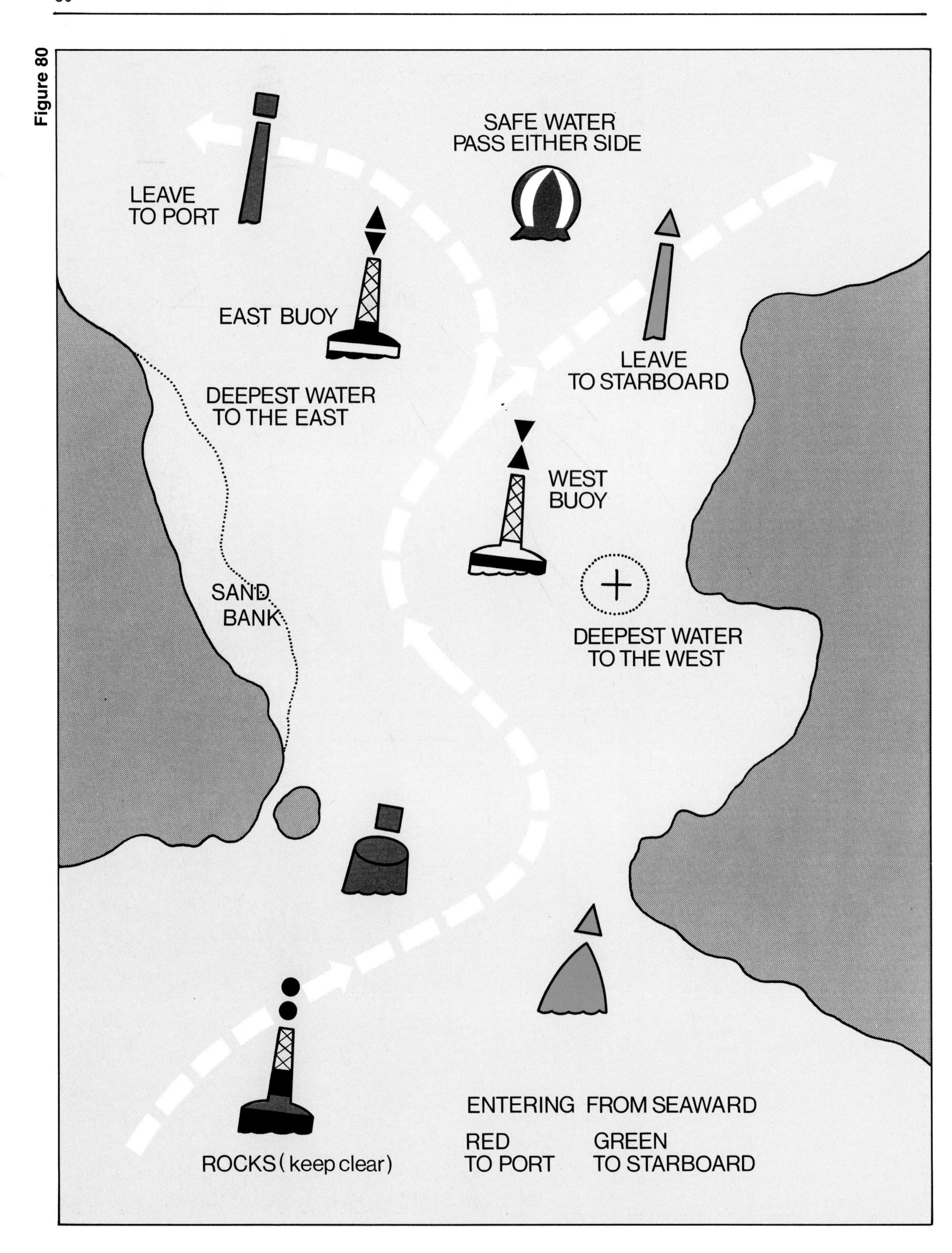
SAFE WATER
PASS EITHER SIDE
LEAVE
TO PORT
EAST BUOY
LEAVE
TO STARBOARD
DEEPEST WATER
TO THE EAST
WEST
BUOY
SAND
BANK
DEEPEST WATER
TO THE WEST
ENTERING FROM SEAWARD
RED
TO PORT
GREEN
TO STARBOARD
ROCKS (keep clear)

Figure 81

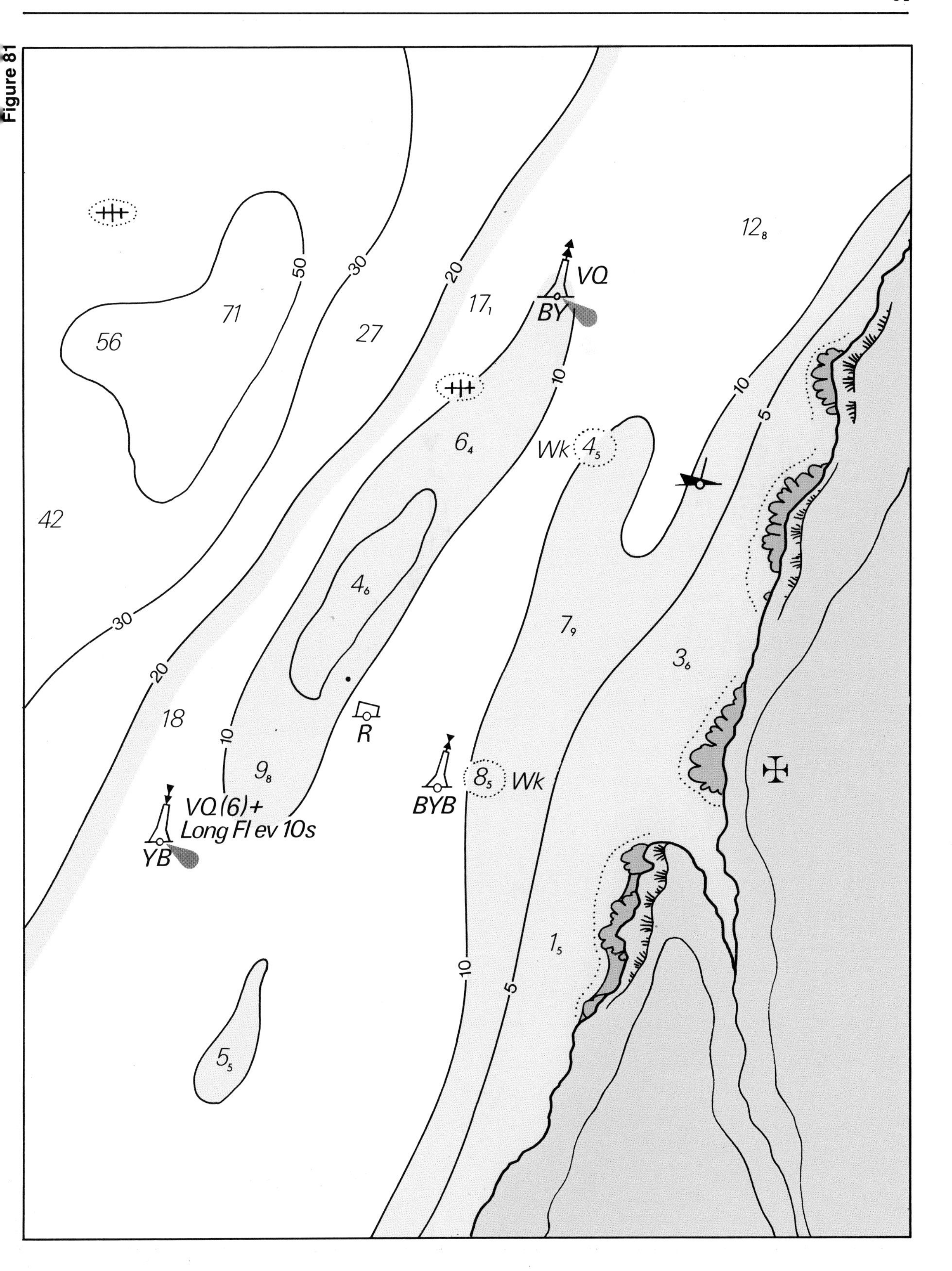

VQ
BY
VQ (6)+
Long Fl ev 10s
YB
BYB
R
Wk
Wk
56
71
27
17_1
12_8
42
6_4
4_5
4_6
7_9
3_6
18
9_8
8_5
1_5
5_5
50
30
20
10
5

SUZUKI
71
BSAC
EVINRUDE
40
GWYNEDD BSAC

Small Boats

Small Dive Boats

In order to reach many of the sea's more interesting sites, the diver needs more than just fin power. One solution to this problem is to use a small boat, an answer which can provide the diver with a great deal of flexibility in the choice of diving sites.

Selecting a Small Boat

As a generalization, the type of boat used by divers ranges between 3 and 6 m. in length, and may take from two to eight divers and their equipment. These craft are powered by engines which vary between 5 and 150 hp. In most instances the diver's boat is essentially a work boat. Its task is to transport divers and their equipment as safely, quickly and comfortably as possible to and from the dive site, and to act as a stable platform from which to conduct diving operations while on site. Add to this the requirement that the boat be easy to move by road, to be launched and recovered, and you will understand why there has to be a degree of compromise in the selection of most diver's boats. Any compromise should not be at the expense of adequate seaworthiness, however. The boat must be capable of transporting divers and their equipment, in safety, through any weather and sea conditions they might reasonably expect to meet in carrying out sport diving.

With the range of sea conditions experienced by divers, it is not unknown for boats to become swamped. In these circumstances a large amount of buoyancy is desirable – at least enough to support the boat, its engine and fittings, and all the divers. Even in these extreme conditions there should be sufficient reserve buoyancy to avoid having to jettison any equipment.

As a diving platform, the greater the boat's deck space, the easier it is for the divers to organize themselves and kit up. Stability is a great advantage at this stage, and also when the fully kitted divers enter the water and are recovered at the end of the dive. The construction of the boat will also affect the method by which the divers enter the water, and the ease with which they come aboard after a dive.

For travelling to and returning from the launch site, ease of transporting the boat by road must be considered, plus the number of divers needed to launch and recover the boat. At many sites a lighter craft can be man-handled into the water, whereas a heavy boat will have to be launched from a trailer down a well-constructed slipway. A four-wheel drive vehicle much simplifies difficult launches.

Once afloat the speed at which a laden boat can travel, how this is affected by various sea states, and the comfort of the divers during the passage are important factors. Fuel consumption of any given boat/engine combination will affect the boat's potential range as well as the divers' pockets.

Types of Craft

Inflatables

Although portability was once the major attraction of this type of boat, nowadays stability and buoyancy are the inflatable's most significant features. Typically the diver's inflatable boat will consist of two airtight side tubes which meet at the bow, a flexible hull with either a solid or an inflatable keel, and a solid transom. On the transom will be mounted an outboard engine with either direct controls or remote controls. The side tubes will usually be subdivided into a number of independent compartments to minimize loss of buoyancy in the event of a puncture.

Unfortunately the inflated tubes which make this type of craft so safe and stable encroach on valuable floor space. They also present a considerable barrier to recovering divers from the water, although they pose no real difficulty for divers entering the water. A further problem is the relative difficulty in gluing 'customizing' fittings to the tubes, especially when the boat has been in use for some time.

Because these boats are collapsible the hull is rather flexible. This can be advantageous given the rough handling they sometimes suffer, but is not a desirable feature. The lack of rigidity, especially of the keel, adversely affects the boat's handling. This drawback makes small-radius high-speed turns difficult, and to try to rectify this some inflatables are fitted with a rigid keel. However, even the best inflatables suffer from a tendency to skid in high-speed turns and can hardly be described as responsive at low speeds.

The rigidity of the inflatable is provided by putting sufficient air into the tubes – until they are hard. If the tubes then heat up in the sun, the air pressure will increase, possibly to a level that can cause damage; so either keep the boat cool or release some of the air to prevent this. Conversely, when the boat is launched the water can have a cooling effect, thus lowering the pressure and making the boat too soft. In this case the tubes should be topped up before setting off, otherwise the handling of the boat may be adversely affected, even to the extent of floor sections jumping out of place and the boat folding while underway.

Riding in an inflatable can be an exhilarating, if rather wet and often uncomfortable, experience. Most inflatables are designed to 'plane'. that is, to ride on top of the water at a relatively high speed, rather than cut through the water like a displacement hull. A consequence of this is that the most comfortable ride is at the stern, whereas the bows tend to bounce. Despite these drawbacks the modern inflatable boat has proved to be an excellent workhorse for many divers. Its continued popularity hinges on its portability, stability and inherent safety, and also its forgiving nature when controlled by an inexperienced cox. If properly cared for an inflatable will give many years of sterling service.

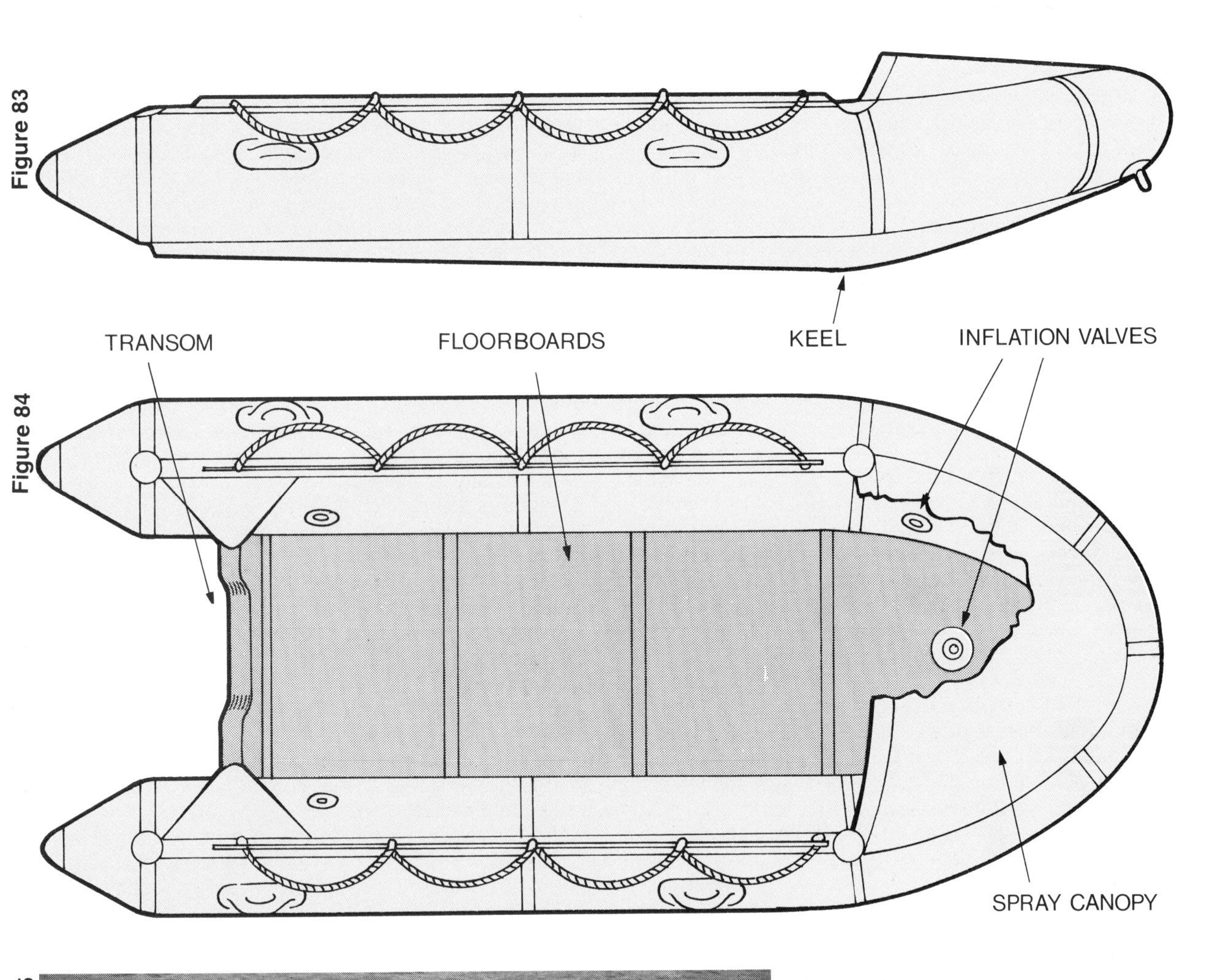

Figure 83
A side elevation of an inflatable

Figure 84
A plan of an inflatable showing a conventional layout

Figure 85
Inflatables are justifiably popular amongst divers and provide a versatile diving platform

Rigid-hull Inflatables

These craft are essentially a marriage between a rigid hull and an inflatable. The hull is usually a strong V-shaped construction made out of glassfibre reinforced plastic (GRP), with flexible inflatable side tubes. This combination gives the superior handling characteristics of the rigid hull, with the buoyancy of the inflatable. As with the inflatable, these tubes are usually divided into separate compartments for added safety. It is usual for such craft to have forward controls, either based on a dashboard bridging the tubes, or mounted on a centre console which may incorporate seating for the cox and possibly some crew members. Fuel tanks are frequently fixed out of the way in the bows, or even under the deck, in the keel.

Although the tubes can be deflated, these boats are not designed to fold away and are generally either moored or moved on a trailer. The increased weight makes them more difficult to launch and a trailer is normally required. However, the stronger hull means that they can be used for transporting diving equipment, although they must not be overloaded.

In the water they are fast, manoeuvrable craft, providing a more comfortable ride than the inflatable, though some are prone to rolling when stopped in a swell. Designed to plane for economic fast cruising, their weight and design leaves more of the rigid keel in the water, enabling them to be used for spectacular high-speed manoeuvres in the hands of an expert. At low speeds they act as a rigid displacement hull, which again gives a big improvement in handling characteristics over the inflatable. As a class they suffer the same disadvantages as the inflatable as regards space for kitting-up and ease of recovering divers.

It is worth noting that from their earliest development the Royal National Lifeboat Institution has had a strong interest in rigid-hull inflatables, and their present-day inshore rescue boats are excellent examples of what this class can achieve. One military derivative of this type of boat has the capability to flood itself and deflate the tubes: then, with its waterproof outboard engine sealed, to proceed underwater as a submersible, powered by electric motors. The crew are, of course, divers.

Solid hulls

There are innumerable types of craft within this category, but the one currently of most interest to divers is the dory. This class of boat has a large working deck area relative to its overall size. It achieves this by having fairly steep sides and a blunt bow. Being fairly beamy in comparison to its length, it is a more stable diving platform than the narrower ski or speed boats, which also belong in this size and price bracket. The underwater hull is often of a multi-keel design, with descriptive terms such as 'gull wing' and 'cathedral' being applied to the shape. As with the previous two classes, these boats are also meant to plane for maximum comfort and economy.

Their solid construction means that they almost invariably have to be launched from a trailer, and the need to save weight is not quite as crucial as in the two previous types. For not too large a penalty divers can therefore benefit from some form of superstructure designed to shelter them from the more unpleasant effects of wind and waves. This may be little more than a windshield, or a small forward cabin or cuddy, possibly equipped with a couple of berths and simple cooking facilities. Undoubtedly the ride is drier, and this has the side effect of making the fitting of various navigational, safety and diving aids much easier. Solid hulls are also easier to fit with echo-sounder transducers, and radio and electronic navigation aid antennae can be fitted away from engine interference.

As these boats do not have bulky buoyancy tubes, unless other means are provided, there is often a lack of inherent buoyancy should they be holed or even swamped, as a number of divers have discovered to their cost. Usually some buoyancy compartments are built in, and sometimes the hull is constructed from a rigid foam-core sandwich between two GRP layers, which also provides some buoyancy. However, this is often barely sufficient to float the flooded hull itself, apart from the added weight of the engine, equipment and divers. It is therefore recommended that sufficient extra buoyancy is added, even if this means sacrificing some of that valuable deck space.

One special case worth mentioning here is the aluminium assault craft which can be found on the surplus military equipment market. Remember that divers use them in very different conditions from those in which they were intended to operate, away from close support, and with very different expendability criteria! For safety, extra buoyancy is essential in these otherwise good workhorses.

Figure 86

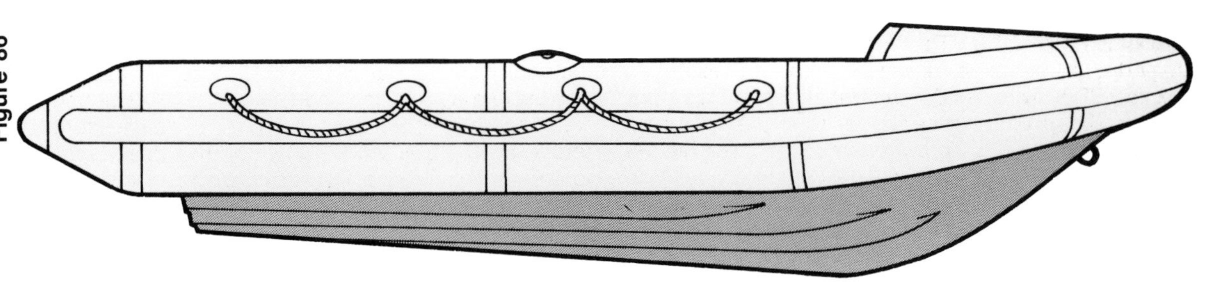

Side elevation of a rigid-hull inflatable

Figure 87

The rigid-hull inflatable offers excellent handling characteristics. These craft are becoming increasingly popular for offshore diving and for diving in remote areas

Loading

Various pieces of equipment have to be carried in a diving boat, and it can be quite a problem deciding where to put them. A good plan is to consider the purpose of each item and how and when it might be used.

Positioning of the crew, unless the boat is fitted with fixed seats, is usually left till last, but it is well to remember that hanging on in the bow of a wildly bucking inflatable can be very tiring, so the cox should drive considerately. The ability to move the crew's weight around can be very useful in encouraging the boat over the 'hump' and onto the plane, but even distribution of the equipment load is equally important. When taking out an unladen boat it is important to have sufficient weight, in the form of crew, to hold the bows down and prevent the boat being flipped over by wind and waves. Take careful note of the manufacturer's specification for the boat and do not exceed the load that the boat was designed to carry.

Wind and Current

When travelling as a displacement hull, apart from the engine's propulsive force, the other major effect on the direction in which the boat is moving is that of the water it is travelling through. If the water is moving in the same direction as the boat, its speed will be added to that of the boat's. If it is moving in the opposite direction, it will reduce the effective speed of the boat over the ground. When the water is moving across the boat's line of travel, the boat will naturally be displaced sideways at the speed of the water's flow. Generally speaking, even off the plane, the speed of the boat will typically be ten times that of the water and the effect is therefore minimal, particularly over short distances.

Once on the plane the effects of water flow are minimized even more, and the effects of wind become more important. With so little of the boat in the water, the wind is able to have much more effect on the boat's hull and strong sideways gusts can be quite noticeable. Travelling into the wind and coming over the top of a wave allows the wind to exert quite a lifting force on the boat's hull, giving the crew lots of excitement and some excellent photographic opportunities. However, unless the situation is carefully judged, it is easy to loop the boat in these conditions, so take care! Similarly, high-speed turns in these conditions can be spectacular, but can also allow the wind to get under the hull and capsize the boat.

Propulsion and Steering

Dive boats are normally powered by outboard petrol engines, though a few of the larger rigid hulls may be fitted with inboard/outboard engines.

Figure 88

An inflatable performs best when not overloaded and with heavy equipment stowed as low as possible

Anchors

In the event of engine failure your boat will be subject to the forces of nature. Inflatable boats not under power can travel significant distances over the surface of the sea. This can be particularly hazardous when there is an offshore wind. Another complication may well be your inability to keep the boat's head into the oncoming waves. Therefore an anchor is an essential part of your boat's safety equipment.

Although the main function of the anchor is to arrest the boat's progress in an emergency, divers often use it to locate a wreck site or other points of interest by dragging the anchor and snagging the submerged obstacle.

It is inadvisable to anchor the boat while diving is taking place as this reduces its mobility in the event of a diver surfacing in difficulties. Try to avoid anchoring, unless there is more than one boat available and the anchored boat is acting as a diving platform, unless the anchor can be jettisoned quickly and has a buoy attached to mark its position.

The Main Components

A typical anchor comprises a length of rope, followed by a short length of chain and then the anchor itself. On larger vessels the rope is usually replaced by chain.

Figure 89

A small boat anchor is made up of the anchor, a warp consisting of a length of chain and line, the addition of an anchor buoy, allowing jettisoning of the anchor in an emergency, and a bucket or basket to ease rope stowage

Rope

Modern synthetic fibres such as nylon are extremely strong and durable, but for ease of handling the diameter is important. Thin nylon rope can be impossible to handle with wet and cold hands. Choose a rope of around 10–12 mm diameter.

To calculate the length of rope you need, consider the deepest point over which you may wish to anchor the boat, taking into account the depth of the site at high water springs. A minimum length of twice the water depth is necessary for the anchor to hold a boat safely in good weather. A minimum length of 100 m is considered adequate for most small boats used for diving.

Chain

You will also require 5–6 m of galvanized chain connected to the anchor by a galvanized shackle, with a galvanized ring or shackle connecting the chain and rope. The rope should be secured to this shackle with an anchor bend or a permanent eye splice (see pp. 15 and 17). A useful size of chain (short link) is 6–8 mm diameter.

Anchor

Choose your anchor with care as different shapes have different holding capabilities for mud/sand or rock. The CQR (Figure 90) is better in mud and the Danforth (Figure 91) is better in sand. The Clyde anchor is a variant of the Danforth. The Bruce anchor (Figure 92) has an advantage over the CQR as it is lighter in relation to its holding power.

The fisherman's anchor and the folding grapnel have poor holding capabilities (Figure 93–94) on sand and mud, since they can only dig in with one fluke. This means that their holding surface area is relatively small. However, on wrecks and rocks they are more effective – sometimes too effective!

Although excellent in terms of compactness, the folding grapnel should be checked carefully as it is prone to close if the locking ring has not been properly located. Caution also applies to the use of the fisherman's anchor (any anchor with sharp points) in an inflatable boat, as the points can, if not correctly stowed, puncture the tubes.

A common fault is to use too small an anchor for the size of boat. Small boats of 3–4 m in length should find an anchor weight of 5 kg adequate. However, boats over 5 m will require up to 10–kg anchors to hold the boat in moderate sea conditions.

How an Anchor Works

It is important to appreciate how an anchor holds on a sandy, muddy or rocky bottom.

If the pull on the anchor is parallel to the bottom, or slightly downward, the effect will be to increase the anchor's holding power by spreading the load over an increasing cross-section of seabed. An upward pull will decrease its ability to hold. As the distance from the anchor increases so the cross-section of seabed decreases (see Figure 95).

The effect on a muddy bottom will be for the anchor to pull out at the fluke or at some point along the reducing cross-section. On a rocky or boulder-strewn bottom the effect will be similar. A boulder can be lifted out, or an overhang of rock broken off, with the tension (see Figure 95).

To be effective the anchor needs to lie on the seabed so that the pull at the anchor is horizontal (see Figure 96). The length of chain between rope and anchor should remain on the bottom from its own weight and not be lifted by the pull of the boat. Obviously the longer the chain or rope, the heavier it will be to handle. However, more rope in the water will reduce the angle between the front of the boat and the anchor on the bottom, so reducing the upward pull caused by the effect of waves or wind.

Figure 90 Figure 91

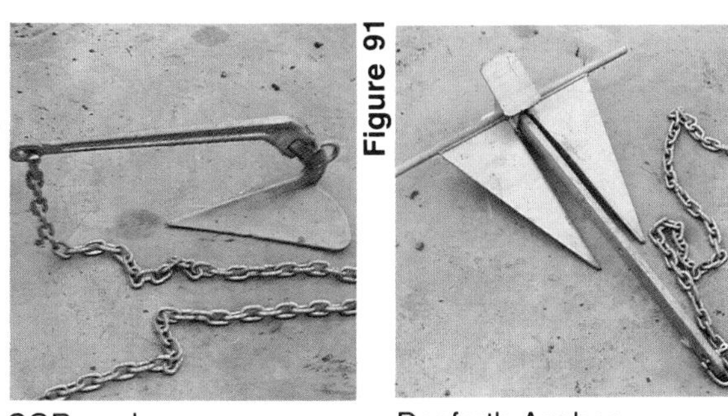

CQR anchor Danforth Anchor

Figure 92

Bruce anchor

Figure 93

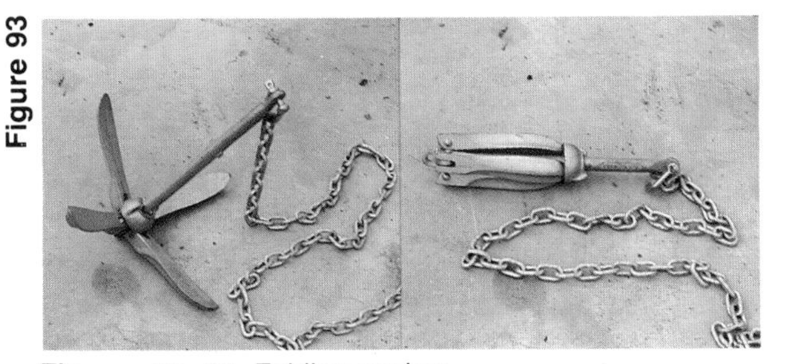

Figures 93–94 Folding anchor

Figure 95

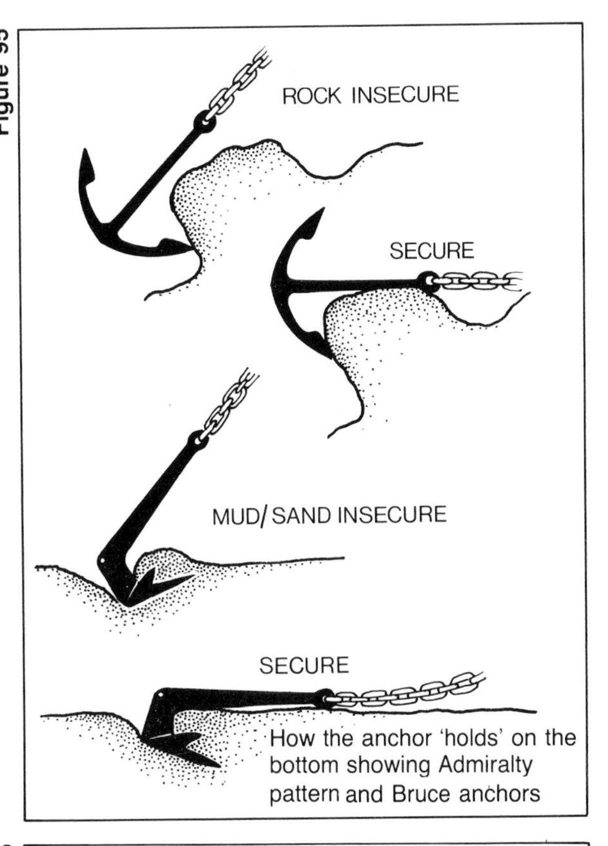

How the anchor 'holds' on the bottom showing Admiralty pattern and Bruce anchors

Figure 96

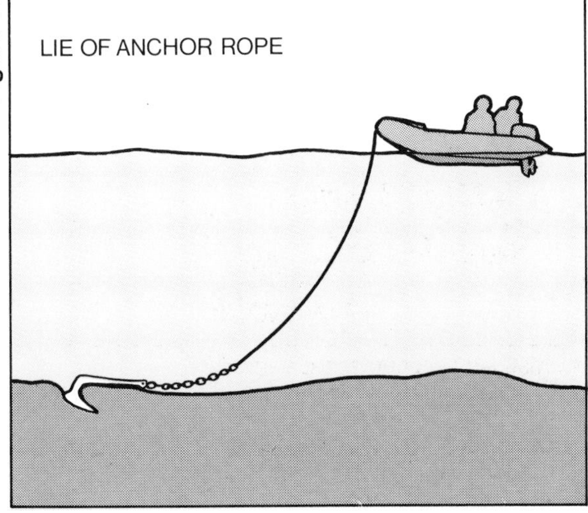

The anchor stock should lie parallel to the bottom for the greatest effect; the chain helps ensure this

Anchoring

Stowage

The anchor needs to be accessible and ready to use at all times, therefore you will need to consider carefully the method of stowage. Space in small diving boats is at a premium, added to which the divers' equipment tends to migrate around the boat in choppy seas.

The logical place to stow the anchor is at the front of the boat, so that when the anchor is deployed and holding, the boat's head points into the on-coming waves or tidal stream.

A hundred metres of rope, chain and anchor take up a considerable amount of room and could foul other equipment unless stowed in either a basket or mounted on a reel.

The inboard end of the anchor rope will need to be secured to a fixed board with a quick-release shackle. In addition, a large buoy (50 cm) should be attached to the rope so that it can be relocated following an emergency.

Figure 97

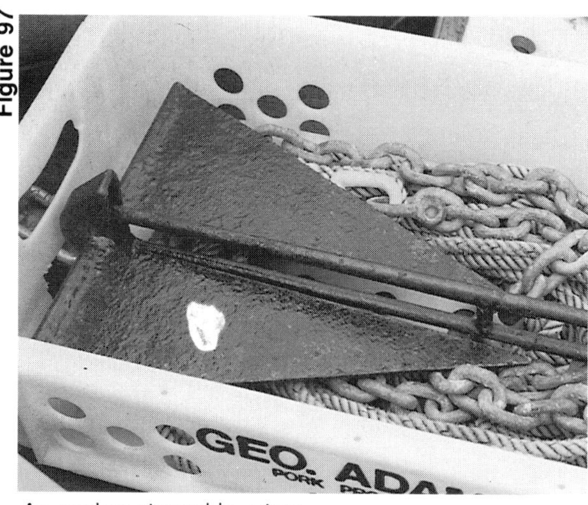

An anchor stowed in a tray

Figure 98

Inboard securing point for the anchor

Figure 99

An anchor buoy

Deploying the Anchor

When anchoring, wait until you are just beyond your selected dive site. Head into the wind or tide (whichever is having the greater influence on the boat), put the engine into neutral and, just as the boat begins to drop back relative to the dive site, deploy the anchor over the side. This will ensure that the rope and chain do not fall on top of the anchor and snag. Allow the rope to move freely and quickly while keeping it under control until you feel the anchor touch the bottom. As the boat drifts backwards, allow more rope to pay out while keeping a slight strain on it. Remember, decreasing the angle between the boat and the seabed will increase the chances of the anchor holding.

Once resistance is detected, give the rope a sharp pull. This will help the anchor to dig in. Using a transit (see page 119) will confirm that the boat has indeed stopped; however, check again to make sure.

Secure the rope to either the painter or the anchor yoke with a snap hook or suitable hitch. Only when you are satisfied that the boat is anchored securely should you stop the engine.

The first pair of divers to reach the bottom should check the anchor to make sure it is held securely and that it can be retrieved cleanly following the dive. They should also check the direction of the rope in relation to the boat, so that any changes in the movement of wind or tide will not encourage the anchor to pull free.

Retrieving the Anchor

Start the engine before attempting to retrieve the anchor; then disconnect the anchor rope from its fixing. Pull steadily in the direction of the lie. If the engine is powering the boat slowly in the same direction, this will help to relieve the strain. The boat should not attempt to exceed the rate at which the rope is being retrieved as this could result in the boat running over the rope and the propeller being fouled.

As you retrieve the rope, 'flake' it into the basket rather than trying to coil it. When the anchor rope is vertical, the anchor should break free. That is the theory. However, in practice it is not always the case. If it fails to break free, try jerking the anchor rope while it is vertical. Failing this, try motoring the boat over the rope in the opposite direction to its original lie.

If, despite all attempts, the anchor still remains fast, buoy it and leave it. It is inadvisable to send divers down to free it, as after a dive not only is there a shortage of air, but divers are generally tired and cold. Added to which, the tide may have turned and conditions may well have become less favourable.

Figure 100 'Flaking-in' the anchor line
Figure 101 A tripping line aids recovery

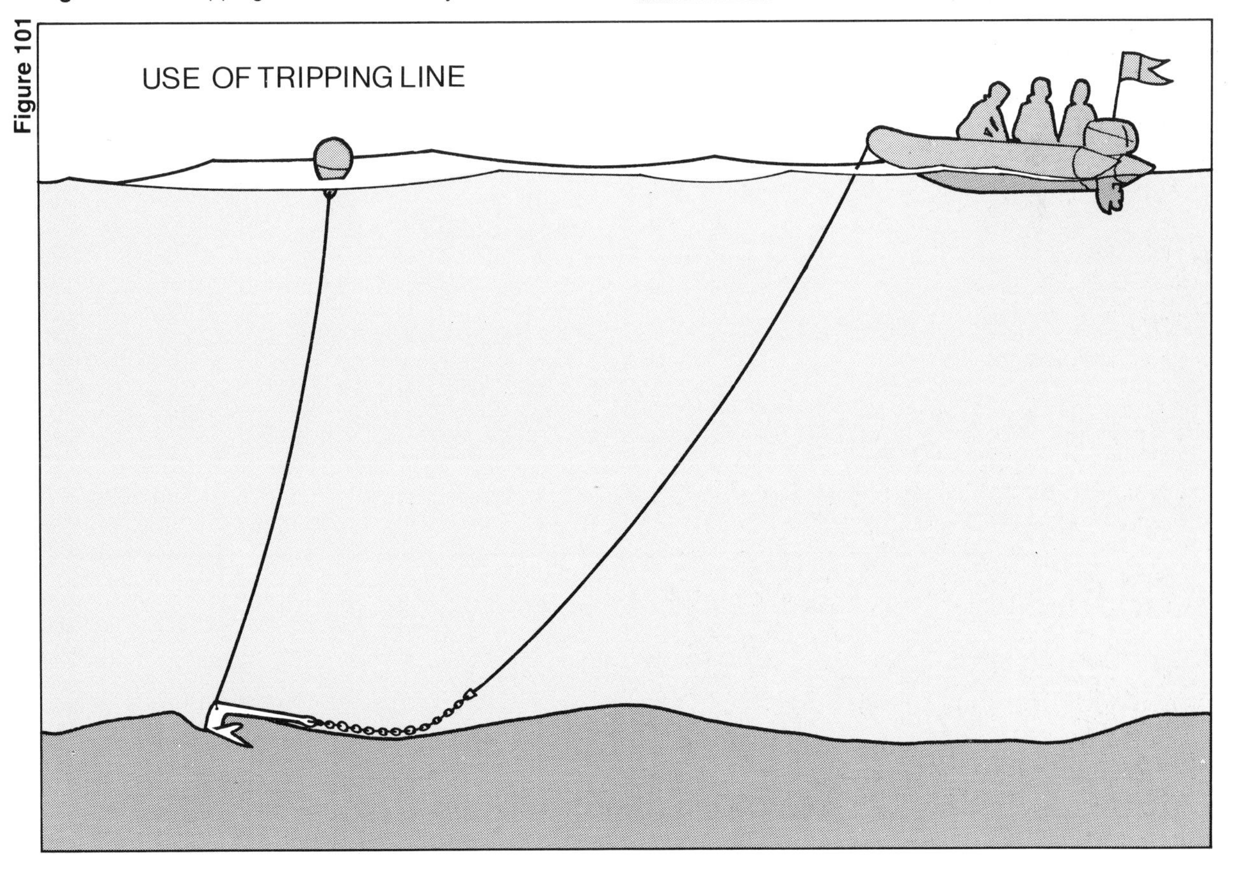

Stowage

The stowage of the boat's safety and emergency equipment is the next important consideration. Pushing everything under the spray canopy may seem the best solution. However, when it is needed in a hurry, this can prove to be one of the most inaccessible positions.

1. The basket containing the anchor chain, buoy and rope should be placed so that they can be used instantly (not under the spray canopy). In rough water the basket will migrate unless it is secured to the floorboards.
2. The emergency watertight box containing flares, engine spares and first-aid equipment should be attached with a length of line to the boat. The length of line is important: should the boat capsize you will want the box to float away, but not too far.
3. Paddles or oars should be placed and secured along the inside of the tubes. Spare line, ropes and other non-essential equipment can be stowed under the spray canopy.
4. If you are going to use a shot line instead of an anchor, this will probably require a separate container.
5. Secure the petrol tank, and any spare fuel, with a line to the boat.

Figure 102

The boat equipment is carefully and securely stowed in allocated positions, leaving room for divers and diving equipment

The diving equipment and the divers themselves will require careful positioning if the boat is to maintain trim. Avoid stacking cylinders and weightbelts in one place at the front or rear – spread them evenly. To avoid damage in rough weather, secure the equipment with a line.

Basic equipment scattered around the boat can become lost or damaged. A small bag or plastic container for each diver's equipment is the neat answer to this problem. This can be placed where the owner is going to sit so that it is easily accessible when the diving site is reached.

Finally, place the divers evenly throughout the boat, not all on one side, making sure that the coxswain retains a reasonable field of vision. When everybody is comfortable, make a final check to make sure that nothing has been overlooked, either boat equipment or diving equipment.

Before the last diver enters the boat, he should point the bow to seaward and check for obstructions. Only when he is safely in the boat should you put the engine into gear.

Figure 103

The divers are positioned and their equipment stowed to allow easy fitting

Launching

Launching an Inflatable

An inflatable boat can be launched either directly from a trailer or carried to the water's edge. If the inflatable has to be assembled on site, or if the beach is unsuitable for the trailer and towing vehicle, then the inflatable will have to be carried to the water's edge. Depending on whether it is high or low water, the distances involved can differ greatly.

The number of divers required to transport the inflatable will depend, to a large extent, on its size. Small inflatables 3–4 m can be handled comfortably by four. However, anything larger will require more people, at least six.

A little advanced planning and man-management will make this process less of an ordeal. The first job on arrival at the dive site should be for the whole diving party to concentrate on getting the boat, and all its equipment, into the water. The best way of achieving this is with the divers dressed in their wetsuits or drysuits only. Try to avoid getting too hot and uncomfortable. In very warm weather it may be prudent to carry the equipment to the water's edge wearing ordinary clothing and change into diving suits later.

The largest piece of equipment to be carried will be the inflatable (without the engine attached). This will require the assistance of the complete team. Most inflatables have moulded carrying handles, located at the four corners, but larger boats may have more. Position divers at each of the carrying handles, and lift the boat clear of the ground. It is useful to have an extra person at the front to keep a lookout for obstructions. If a long distance is involved and a rest is necessary, avoid putting the boat down on a sharp rock or broken glass.

Depending on sea conditions, you may be able to put the boat straight into the water, leaving just one person behind to hold the painter. However, if there are breaking waves, you will need to keep the front of the boat pointing to seaward with more than one person holding it.

Figure 104

Carrying the outboard, with braced arm

The outboard engine will need at least two people to carry it. Engines are best carried as illustrated in Figure 104. If conditions permit, put the engine directly onto the centre of the transom protection plate, tighten the bracket screws, and secure the engine with a wire or rope to the transom. In a swell it is advisable to tilt the engine, to avoid damage to the propeller.

The rest of the boat equipment – fuel tank, boat box, anchor, etc., can be assembled at the water's edge prior to being stowed by the coxswain.

Figure 105

Carrying the inflatable a short distance with engine attached

Launching from a Trailer

Inflatable boats that have the outboard engine permanently bolted to the transom, together with dories and rigid-hull inflatables, will need a trailer as they are far too heavy to carry. The main consideration when launching from a trailer is finding suitable access. The most suitable access points are slipways down which you can reverse your vehicle and trailer until the boat is almost floating. You will then be able to remove the fixing straps and slide the boat into the water. Since the engine is already attached and the boat equipment and diving gear stowed, the vehicle and trailer can then be driven away.

Slipways are simple, until you find there is no water at the end of them. Soft sand or pebbly beaches can prove a nightmare for trailers and cars, so always check the area carefully or, better still, ask the locals.

Provided you have firm sand, it is possible to drive close to the water's edge. However, backing the trailer into the sea should be approached with care, as the sand below the waterline will be less firm. If in doubt, disconnect the trailer and push it into the sea (using the jockey wheel if fitted or, better, a custom-built 2-wheel 'dolly').

If you leave your trailer on the beach, make sure it will not cause an obstruction and ensure that it is parked above the high-water mark.

Submerging the wheels of the trailer in salt water can, unless they have been specially protected, damage the wheel bearings. After submersion the wheel bearings should be stripped down, cleaned and greased. Better still, replace the bearings after a season's use; the cost is often outweighed by the convenience of being able to submerge the trailer.

Figure 106

Back trailer to the water and free fastenings

Figure 107

Release the boat from the trailer . . .

Figure 108

. . . and allow it to float clear

Figure 109

Recover the trailer

Getting Underway

Before the diving party enters the boat, the coxswain should first check that the outboard engine will start and that it is running correctly; secondly, that the tubes are at the correct pressure; and, finally, that the boat's safety and ancillary equipment is present and stowed correctly.

Engine Checks

1. Make sure you have sufficent depth between the propeller and the sea bottom.
2. Check the contents of the fuel tank to make sure there is sufficient fuel to get you to and from the dive site. Remember, more fuel will be consumed if the sea conditions are choppy or if you will be going against the tide. It is better to have a good reserve of ready-mixed fuel available for unforeseen circumstances.
3. Connect the fuel line to the engine and prime the soft rubber ball until it is hard.
4. Check that the engine is out of gear. On most engines, whether changing gear is manual or from a console, the lever should normally be in a vertical position. On some outboard engines the gear-changing control is incorporated into the throttle arm.
5. Only experience will tell how much choke to give the engine. Normally close the choke when the engine is being started cold and open it again when the engine fires. If an electric start is fitted, use it for no longer than 20 seconds at the most. The tendency is to over-choke, so be careful.
6. Make sure that nobody is standing around the propeller before you start the engine. If your engine is fitted with a pull cord, pull the starter cord slowly until the follower catches, and only then pull the cord firmly and in a continuous movement. Then let the cord re-coil itself automatically. Make sure that when you start the engine there is nobody standing directly behind you when you pull the cord as you may hit them with your elbow.
7. When the engine fires, check the 'telltale' (see Figure 114) to see whether water is coming out. Allow the engine to run for a minute or two before pushing in the choke. It should then idle evenly.
8. A wise precaution is to motor the boat around for a few minutes before loading the divers and their equipment. But first make sure you are not alone in the boat, and that you have loaded all the boat's safety equipment.

Figure 110

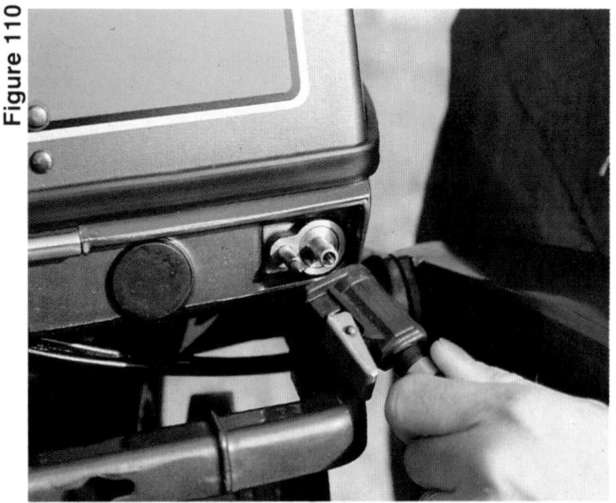

Figure 112

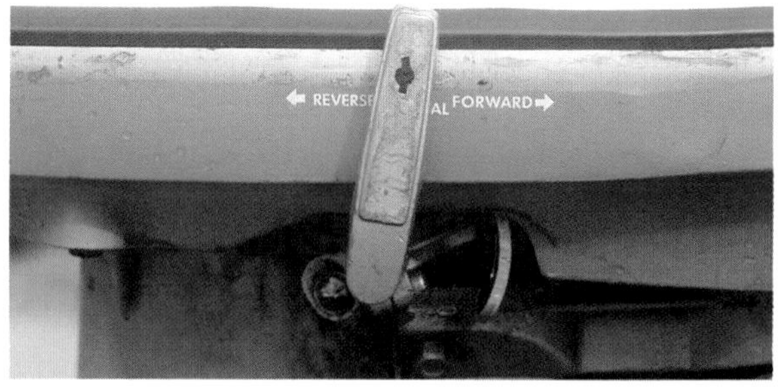

Figure 111

Figure 110
Connecting the fuel line

Figure 111
Priming the fuel

Figure 112
Ensure gear lever is in neutral

Figure 113
Tightening the engine bracket screws onto the transom

Figure 114
The cooling water 'telltale'

Figure 113

Figure 114

Boat-Handling Skills

Picking up a Mooring

This manoeuvre is not too difficult provided you remember to use the tide or wind, whichever is having the greater effect on the boat. This will give you maximum control as the tide or wind will act as a brake.

When picking up a mooring give yourself as much sea room as possible. Try to approach the mooring in a straight line and, as the distance closes, reduce speed so that you are almost stopped. With an inflatable boat it is easier to increase speed than to reduce it quickly.

Decide beforehand on which side of the boat you will take the mooring. With practice it should be possible to lean over and pick up the mooring without having to move position. Have a line ready so that you can secure the mooring. Remember to put the engine into neutral just before you reach the mooring.

Figure 116

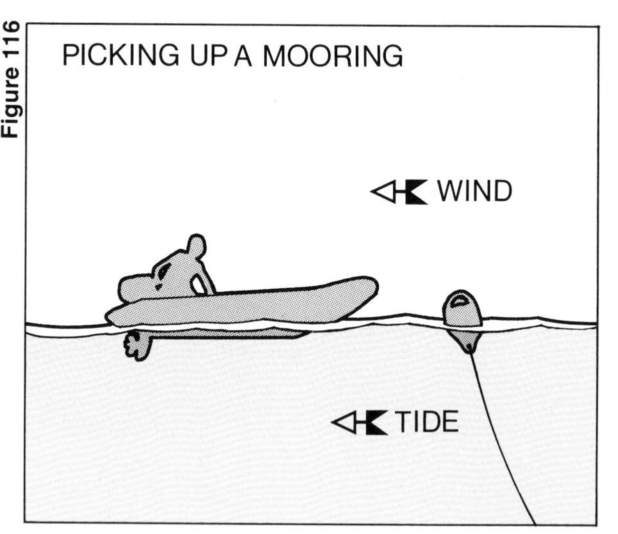

Figure 115

Picking up Divers

Unlike moorings, divers are not stationary in the water. However, the same principles of using tide and wind apply. Since both boat and diver are similarly affected by the tide, come up into the wind. As you approach the divers, put the engine into neutral as soon as they are alongside the bow.

When a boat (especially an inflatable) loses power, even in light winds, it is surprising how quickly divers can become separated from it if it stops downwind. However, in normal conditions it is probably better to manoeuvre the boat at right angles to the wind, and slightly downwind of the divers in the water. In this way the divers will drift down towards the boat. In strong winds or tidal streams care should be taken not to allow the boat to overrun the divers.

Remember that in an emergency situation, when a diver has surfaced in distress, your boat's power must be used effectively. The boat should head directly towards the diver at speed from whichever direction is the shortest and safest, only putting the engine into neutral at the last possible moment.

Divers surfacing near rocks can cause a problem for the coxswain, especially if there is the added problem of a swell. Unless the divers are in distress, it is better to encourage them to swim away from the rocks into open water. This should give you enough sea room and time to get them into the boat.

If the divers are in distress, manoeuvre the boat carefully towards them (check for submerged rocks). Once you are close enough, throw a line, secure it and gently reverse the boat, towing the divers into safer water. Depending on sea conditions, it may also be possible to anchor the boat and to drift backwards toward the divers, paying out the anchor rope until a line can be thrown.

Figure 117

Divers already aboard help the coxswain pick up divers

Figure 118

Inflatables can operate close inshore when conditions allow

Coming Alongside

The principles discussed earlier apply to coming alongside, and to some extent it is much easier than picking up a mooring. The main difference is that you are putting the boat against a jetty or quay, which is often bigger and harder than your boat. Another problem is that around quays there can be strong wave reflections and eddies.

With the wind blowing off an unsheltered berth, make your approach from downwind, at an angle of about 30°, or against the tidal stream, whichever is the dominant factor. A tidal stream is quite useful as it enables you to steer the boat parallel to the berth until the last possible moment. It should be possible with practice to hold the bow against the berth while a line is taken ashore and secured. A line can then be secured at the stern and the boat pulled close alongside.

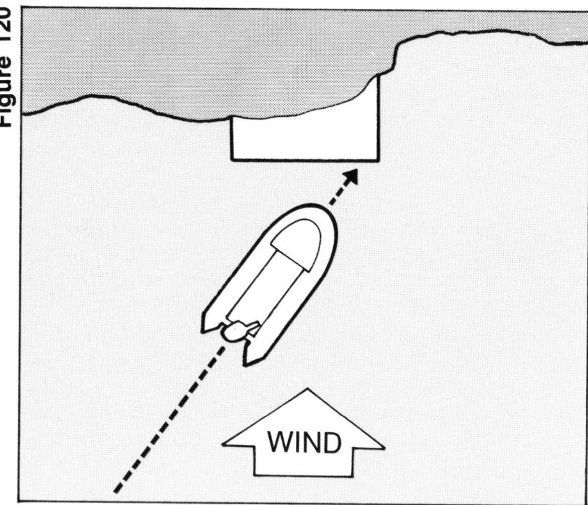

Figure 120
An onshore wind demands a careful final approach

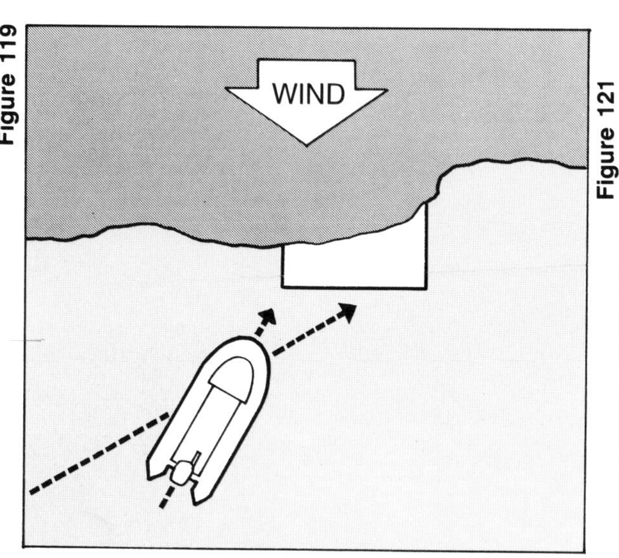

Figure 119
Approach at 30° into wind direction; note the boat's head and the direction of travel may be different

Figure 121
Unberthing using the painter

Unberthing

Obviously an offshore wind will make the process of unberthing a fairly simple manoeuvre. An onshore wind can be more troublesome. It may be better to leave stern first, allowing the boat to pivot at the bow to avoid scraping the boat along the side of the berth by going forward. As soon as there is sufficient sea room you can turn into the wind.

Alternatively, release the stern line and put the tiller over as if to drive the boat at the berth, then go ahead slowly. Watch the bow carefully as the stern moves out. When you are at right angles to the berth, put the tiller over in the opposite direction, let go the bowline and engage the engine in reverse. The boat should then be clear of the berth.

Figure 122
Coming alongside with caution

Turning in a Confined Area

Turning an inflatable in the open sea with power on is a fairly easy manoeuvre, but at slow speeds in restricted areas this can be one of the most testing of all boat-handling skills. Turning the boat around in a confined area requires a combination of good engine control and a knowledge of what effect the propeller has on the boat when reversing and going ahead at slow speeds.

To make a three-point turn, pull the tiller hard over, at the same time giving the throttle a short burst; quickly throttle back and put the engine into neutral. As the bow begins to swing, engage reverse and put the tiller hard over in the opposite direction, again giving the throttle a short burst. As the bow begins to swing in the direction of your exit, engage neutral again, engage forward gear and increase power. When reverse gear is engaged, make sure that the engine tilt lock is locked in position.

Figure 123

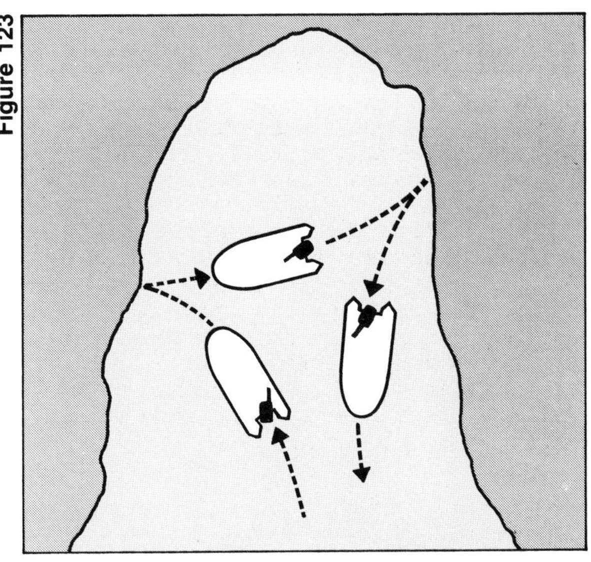

When turning in a confined area remember that the engine will move the stern of the boat with the bow acting as a pivot

Handling at Speed

Most inflatables and dories are capable of high speeds. To achieve these speeds the boat must plane.

To achieve this the throttle should be opened firmly – not suddenly – to full power. As the speed through the water increases the bow will begin to rise as a wall of water builds up beneath the bows. This is partly due to the change in trim, but it is also due to the hull beginning its transition from a displacement to a planing hull. As the boat climbs over the hump the boat begins to level off.

As you increase the speed further the bows will settle down into a level position with only the deepest parts of the hull in the water. Power can be reduced at this stage without any apparent loss of speed as the boat is now planing. Powering back will reduce fuel consumption without affecting the speed significantly. Boats which have barely enough power to get on the plane may require a slight redistribution of weight in the boat or an adjustment to the 'rake' (see Outboards, page 139) of the engine.

If the boat is lightly laden, you should be careful when planing, as any head wind will increase the angle of the bows to a point at which there is a risk of the boat being flipped over backwards.

Avoid decreasing speed suddenly. If the throttle is suddenly closed, the boat will come off the plane in a very short distance and the following wave will catch you up. This is generally not a problem with inflatables as the extended stern tubes lift the boat before the wave breaks. However, with dories the following wave can wash right over the transom and into the boat.

Always decrease speed slowly. Remember that within headlands and harbours there are often local byelaws governing the speed of craft. Excessive speed in all but calm conditions subjects your boat to wear and tear, and possible damage. Keep a lookout when nearing the beach for people in the water.

Figure 124

An inflatable will not achieve planing speed, even if reasonably powered, unless the load is evenly distributed

Power Turns
Rigid-hull boats generally hold power turns better than their inflatable counterparts. This is because, with more of the hull actually in the water, they can resist the centrifugal force. The important thing to remember is to allow plenty of sea room to make the turn. When making a power turn from a stationary position, use the throttle rather than the tiller or wheel to pivot the boat on its axis.

Figure 125

A rigid-hull inflatable making a power turn

Towing
As water users, we will be called on from time to time to render assistance to other craft. Typically engine failure is the commonest cause, and trying to repair an engine in open water is not easy. Provided the boat in difficulties is not too large for the rescuer's boat, towing to a more sheltered site or harbour is often the best solution.

Figure 126

Towing an inflatable

Towing an Inflatable
Approach the disabled boat on its leeward side. Secure a rope to a point as far forward as possible on the boat to be towed, usually the painter. Secure the other end of the rope to your transom, ideally with a snap hook through a ring bolt for quick release. Do not attach the rope to your engine.

Figure 127

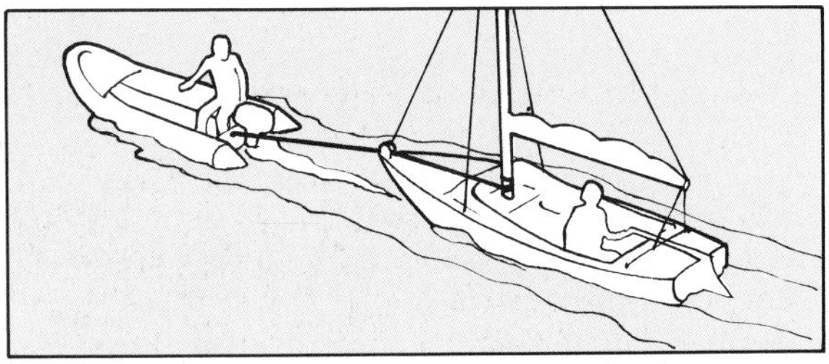

Towing a sailing vessel from a secure point

The length of the rope is important. It should be long enough to allow both towing and towed boat to be in the trough of successive waves or on their crests at the same time. However, if the boat is full of water, you may need to shorten the rope to keep the bows up. As you get underway take the slack up slowly. Avoid snatching.

In the towed boat the crew should sit as far back as possible to keep the bows from digging in. Tilting the engine will also reduce drag. If the disabled boat is near to rocks, use your anchor to drift backwards to a point where you can throw a rope. You can then pull yourself towards the anchor before engaging drive.

Towing a Sailing Vessel
On a sailing vessel it may be better to secure the towing rope by passing it through the fairlead and securing it to the mast. If the boat has sails, they should be lowered to prevent wind resistance. It is better not to use your anchor for towing as you may need it yourself. If you do not have a suitable rope, use the disabled boat's anchor rope.

Handling in Rough Weather

For small boats you should consider carefully whether to launch your boat in wind conditions greater than Force 4–5 on the Beaufort scale (see page 147). However, sea conditions can change quickly due to opposing wind and tide or changes in tidal flow. No matter how careful you are in checking the weather forecast, sooner or later you will find yourself having to cope with rough sea conditions.

If the wind begins to freshen and the waves become more pronounced, reduce speed. High speed can damage both the boat and its occupants. In rough water everyone should hold on firmly and not allow themselves to be pitched around the boat. It may be safer for the divers to sit inside the inflatable to avoid the risk of falling overboard – this will also improve the coxswain's field of vision.

When heading against the sea try to keep the boat's head into the waves. Apply enough power to climb the wave and push through the crest; do not attempt to increase speed, otherwise you will become airborne and drop into the trough in front of the next wave, which is uncomfortable for the passengers and could damage the boat. Avoid turning the boat broadside on to breaking waves (broaching) as this could lead to swamping or capsizing.

If you need to alter course and head across the direction of the waves, choose your moment carefully. It may be better to run the boat along a trough until a suitable wave pattern develops to allow you to safely turn at an angle and slide down the back of the wave. Zigzagging in this fashion is often the safest way to approach your destination. Even though you will travel farther, you will be able to make greater progress and use less fuel.

The problem with a following sea is the illusion of not moving fast enough when in fact you are! To some extent running in a following sea is more dangerous than heading into one, because you have less control over the boat. The effect on the boat is just like with a surfboard and you will need to adjust your speed so that you are going faster or slower than the wave you are on. If you begin to surf down a wave and the boat is going too slowly, the bow will dig in, so you will need to increase speed to encourage the bows to lift over the wave's back. If you are going too fast, then reduce speed; this will lift the bows as the boat comes off the plane. When the boat settles in the water, increase speed again over the wave's back.

Figure 128
Climbing over a wave

Figure 129
Following a crest

Figure 130
Turning at speed

Sea Anchor

When running with the sea a sea anchor will act like a parachute and prevent the boat from being broached. With an immobilized boat it will slow down its rate of drift. A sea anchor can be improvised by using the boat's anchor basket with a rope bridle.

A boat running with the sea should tow the sea anchor astern; a boat not under power should trail it from the bow, which will help to keep the bows into the sea.

Figure 131

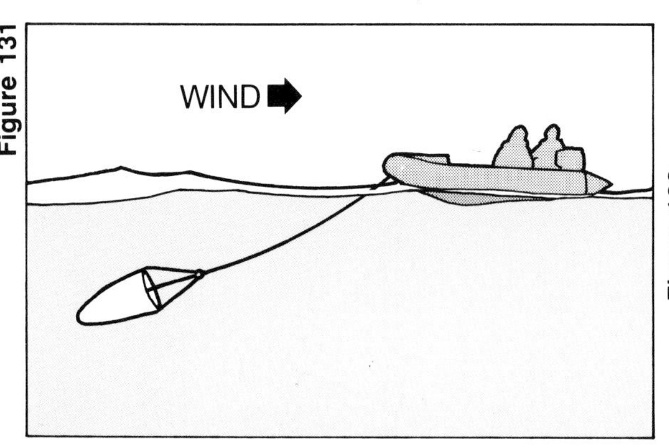

Deploying a sea anchor from the bows

Turning

Turns can be speeded up or tightened by increasing power. This is particularly noticeable with outboard engines. Tight turns at high speed should be avoided – small craft can be swamped and occupants pitched overboard by the unexpected movement.

The boat will lose way quickly when the throttle is closed, but will drift on for quite a distance. Slow down in plenty of time. Reverse gear may be used as a brake, but steering control will be drastically altered. Outboard engines should be locked down before engaging reverse. In reverse, point the tiller away from the desired direction of travel.

Figure 132

Turning at slow speed

Handling at Slow Speed

If the boat is steered by a wheel, the wheel should be turned in the direction you wish to go, as in the case of a car. If tiller-steered, as are most outboards under 40 hp, the tiller is pushed/pulled *away* from the direction in which you wish to turn. The effect is to direct the thrust of the propeller so that the bow of the boat is turned towards the desired direction. When a boat turns, the stern moves out, not the bow. Imagine driving with rear-wheel steering – that is how a boat behaves. Acquaint yourself right from the start with the sensitivity of the steering and throttle response of the boat and engine. Gain confidence at this before driving the boat at speed or attempting other manoeuvres explained below.

Figure 133

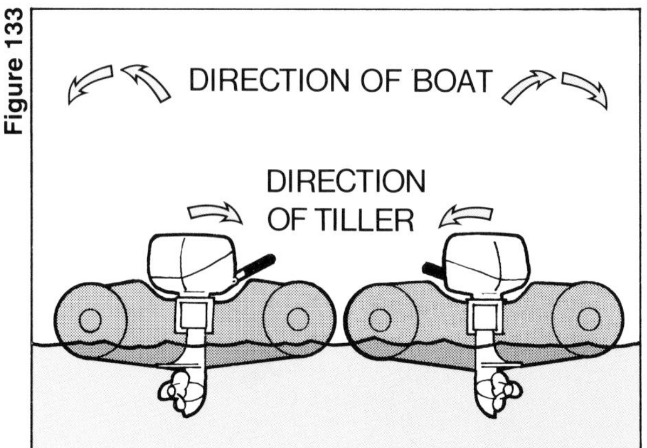

Figure 134

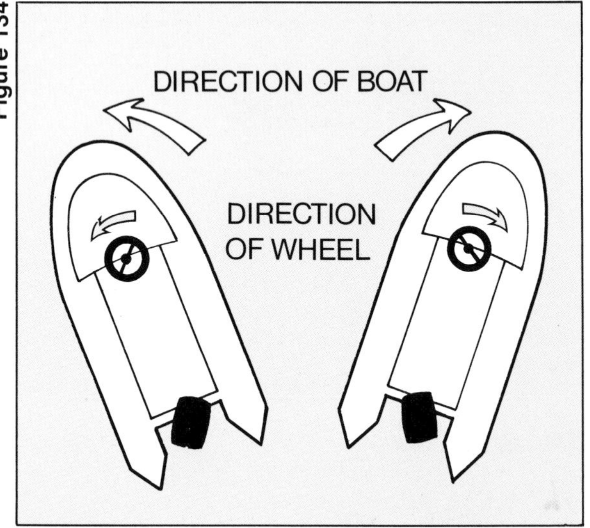

Figure 133
Direction of turn is away from direction of tiller

Figure 134
Direction of turn is same as direction of wheel

Beaching

Calm Conditions

Drive the boat slowly toward the beach with the engine tilt lock off. Keep an alert watch for other craft and particularly for swimmers. Two crew members sitting forward should be ready to go over the side to hold the boat as it beaches. Stop and tilt the engine as the boat runs aground or as the crew go over the side. On soft sand and shingle beaches boats can be pulled up the beach or floated onto the trailer. If landing on a rocky beach, keep the boat afloat until the diving gear and outboard have been removed

Landing in Surf or Rough Water

Study the landing beach carefully before going for the most sheltered and safest spot. Go in on the back of a wave with the crew ready to bale out as you hit the beach and carry the boat clear of the breakers. Alternatively lay out your anchor several metres offshore and go in backwards, paying out the anchor rope. Do not use the engine in this manoeuvre – keep it in neutral. Keep the boat's bows into the waves and hold the anchor rope as each wave passes beneath the boat.

Once the majority of divers and all the equipment have been landed, the anchor can be retrieved and the boat brought back and beached more easily, with help from those already ashore.

Landing in rough conditions is hazardous, so try to find the most sheltered site possible and, remember, always have the engine tilt lock off.

Figure 135

Figure 137

Figure 136

Figure 138

Figure 135
Crew prepare to disembark

Figure 136
Cut the engine then tilt it to avoid damaging the propeller on the seabed in shallow water

Figure 137
Approaching with caution through surf

Figure 138
Crew disembark quickly and hold boat secure before turning the bows into the waves

Emergency Actions

Man Overboard

If someone falls overboard in a heavy sea, it is important to keep them in sight while the boat is being turned. Before you swing the boat around at speed, warn the crew, otherwise you may have more than one person in the water! When you make your turn, ensure that the propeller does not strike the person in the water by pushing the tiller hard over in the opposite direction to which the person fell, or, with a wheel, by turning it in the same direction. Both methods will ensure that the propeller will not hit the victim.

Adopting the same procedure for picking up a diver as described earlier, turn the boat into the wind or tide. If the casualty is in distress or unconscious, you will need to have another diver ready with basic equipment to go over the side to give assistance. With a conscious casualty, getting him or her back in the boat quickly is fairly easy. However, with an unconscious casualty this task can be difficult, especially if the boat has a high freeboard. With assistance from others in the water, a rope sling can be employed to 'parbuckle' the casualty into the boat.

Usually if a diver falls into the water he or she will be dressed in a wetsuit or a drysuit and will generally have sufficient buoyancy to float (unless the drysuit zip has been accidentally left open). In rough sea conditions divers should wear partially inflated lifejackets to give them additional buoyancy. Anyone not wearing a wetsuit or a drysuit must wear a lifejacket, including the coxswain.

Most small boats should be crewed by two people, so that if one should fall overboard the other can recover him. If you are alone in the boat, there should be a system of stopping the engine should you accidentally fall in while the boat is moving under power. Some outboard engines are equipped with a short-circuit switch which can be connected by a line to the driver. If it is pulled the engine will stop, thus preventing the unattended boat disappearing over the horizon or, worse, circling the stranded coxswain in the water!

Figure 140

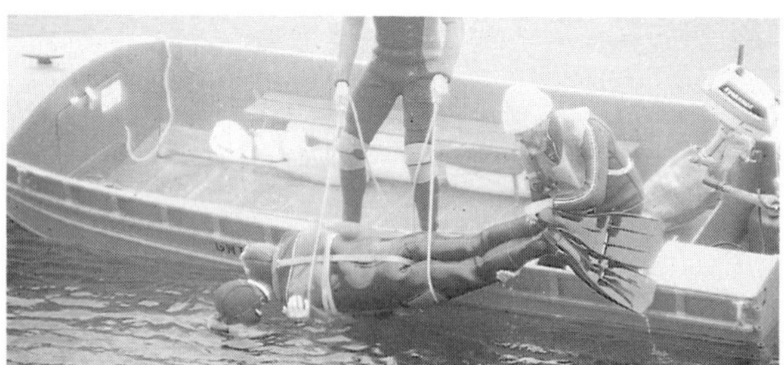

Parbuckling a casualty aboard with assistance from a diver in the water

Figure 139

A passenger can be easily lost overboard in rough weather

Capsized Boat

Any small craft can be capsized by careless handling, or swamped and rolled over by heavy seas. The immediate action is to count heads and make sure that no one is still underneath the boat. All persons should stay with the boat (except perhaps if the boat is capsized in surf when being launched or landed). There is a risk of an overturned inflatable craft being blown away from swimmers in the water while they could also be carried in the opposite direction by the tide.

As soon as possible attempt to right the boat. This is relatively easy with inflatables. Manoeuvre the overturned boat across the wind with the crew on the downwind side tube. Secure the free end of the boat's bowline to the handlines on the windward side, and by pulling on the bowline, roll the boat over towards you. The wind will get under it as it comes up and help it over.

Before righting a rigid boat, first consider whether it has sufficient reserves of buoyancy to stay afloat when righted. If in doubt, leave it inverted. Trapped air may be all that is keeping it afloat. If you feel that it is safe to right it, use the same procedure as for an inflatable. You will find it much harder, as it will be a heavier boat. Seek assistance from another craft to pull on the 'rolling line' if such help is to hand.

Once upright, take care that the boat does not roll over again. If the buoyancy is all under the floor, the boat will be very unstable until most of the water is cleared. Bale the water out and then bring the divers aboard.

If it is not possible to right and board the boat, you will have to summon help quickly by giving some form of distress signal. Make sure that your distress flares can be reached, even in an overturned boat.

Figure 143

Figure 144

Figure 142

Figure 145

Figure 142 Turn the boat broadside to the wind

Figure 143 Assemble crew on same side

Figure 144 Use rope to lift windward side

Figure 145 Over she comes!

Boat Adrift

At this point we are in the same situation as occupants of a boat which has suffered engine failure or some other mishap which has left it at the mercy of the elements. Every effort should be made to stop the vessel drifting away from the shore or towards a more hazardous situation. Unless the boat is being blown or carried by the tide to a safer position, the first action is to anchor. Attempts should be made to get the engine working; if this fails, alternative means of propulsion should be used – oars or paddles.

In such a situation you should make every effort to help yourself to get out of your predicament. Assessment of the situation and efforts at self-help will take little more than a few minutes, but if, through loss of equipment, onset of darkness, or deteriorating weather, you are unable to help yourself any further, you must summon help (see page 150).

Stay with the Boat

All handbooks and instructions to mariners in distress emphasize the need to stay with the disabled craft while it remains afloat. An inverted boat is much more conspicuous than a person in the water. The survival time for an unprotected swimmer in temperate regions is a matter of hours. For the wetsuited diver, survival time is measured in days.

It may be reasonably argued that a snorkel swimmer should be able to swim ashore from a distressed boat to summon help. It is quite likely he would make it, but, on the other hand, if the accident occurs some distance from the shore or in an area of strong tidal streams, he might not. While the diver is the most likely of all distressed mariners to be able to swim to safety, unless tides are favourable and the distance involved is in the order of a few hundred metres with an obvious and safe point of landing, do not swim ashore. *Stay with the boat.*

Figure 146

A drifting boat will be influenced mainly by the wind

Figure 147

Two crew members and four divers make a good combination

DUNEDIN

Figure 148

Diving from Charter Boats

Hard Boat Types

Dayboats Typically, these are 6–15 m long, fitted with a small wheelhouse and with a reasonably sized working area from which the divers operate. Many of them have little diving back-up and the divers may well have to provide their own equipment, compressor and tender.

Converted MFVs These are the norm for charter vessels which offer a catering and accommodation package for periods of several days to two weeks. Typically they will be 18–22 m long and will be fitted with a reasonably sized wheelhouse, an aft deckhouse and a galley; they will have several cabins and toilet facilities. These vessels are usually equipped with a compressor, one or two tenders and sometimes carry diving cylinders.

Sophisticated custom-built charter vessels are rare in British waters. They will usually have the accommodation and galley built and equipped to a higher standard than those of converted fishing boats. They may have a bigger wheelhouse and a larger superstructure with more daytime accommodation. They will be organized and built to offer more convenience and comfort.

Sailing vessels These are sometimes offered for diving charter work. On many of them the space allocated to sailing equipment and the time spent sailing impinge on the diving requirements. This may suit a group who want to enjoy both types of activity, but not every diving party does. The skipper's main aims in running the vessel may even be to the possible detriment of the diving.

Design Features

There are a number of points that can indicate the suitability of a vessel for a particular charter. Slimness of beam and well-flared bows will generally suggest that a boat is designed for speed. Conversely chunkiness in a boat's design suggests that there will be relatively spacious accommodation. A square stern will also increase the space available for a given hull length.

The hull shape exerts significant effect on the maximum speed of a vessel, its seaworthiness, the smoothness of the ride, and the space available for fitting out the vessel. The three basic hull shapes are shown in Figure 151.

The engine should be large enough to give a top speed reasonably close to (say to within 10–20 per cent of) the maximum displacement speed for the hull length (see pp. 66–67).

Fuel and water tanks of adequate size should be fitted. A 20-m vessel will typically be fitted with a 200–250 hp engine. This will use about 5–6 gallons of fuel an hour at normal speed. Based on 60 hours of running per week, about 600–720 gallons will be used a fortnight; therefore fuel tanks of about 800–1000 gallons capacity would be reasonable. Water consumption (allowing for drinking, cooking, washing and reasonable showering) is about 3 tons (about 675 gallons) a week for twelve passengers and three crew; thus about 1500-gallon capacity tanks

Figure 149

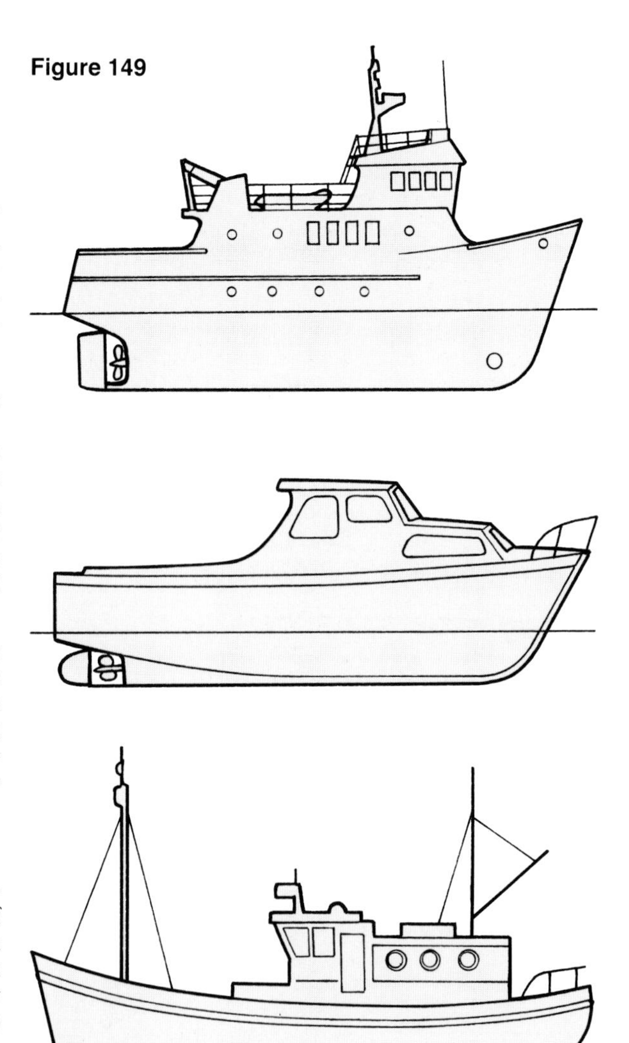

Figure 149
Top: A custom built diving charter vessel
Centre: A dayboat with limited or no accommodation
Above: A converted Motor Fishing Vessel (MFV), common around the British coasts

would be adequate for two-week charters. This figure can be substantially reduced if the vessel is equipped with a desalinator. These figures for water and fuel consumption assume that no additional supplies are available in the destination area.

The vessel should be equipped with good electronic aids for navigation and dive site location. These should include a navigator, radar, an echo sounder and, ideally, a sonar. A radio is essential. A proton magnetometer is a useful addition.

The accommodation for the charterers should be aft for comfort. The movement of a vessel in heavier seas is such that bunks near the bows may become almost untenable. Beware the vessel that has the master's and crew's accommodation at the stern with the charterers' accommodation near the bows. The principle of one *dry* bunk per person should be expected.

It is important that the vessel is equipped with a heavy-duty, effective diving ladder. It should also have an uncluttered and accessible water-entry position.

Charter Vessels around the World

The vessels previously described are those which operate in British waters. Other types are used in different parts of the world. In warmer climates, with more settled seas, covered, flat-bottomed, barge-type vessels are used as dayboats. For longer trips, vessels tend to be faster and sleeker, and ventilation and air conditioning become quite important. Some vessels with very sophisticated passenger facilities operate in the Caribbean and other areas.

Figure 150

A 'flat-top' dive boat popular in the Caribbean

Figure 151

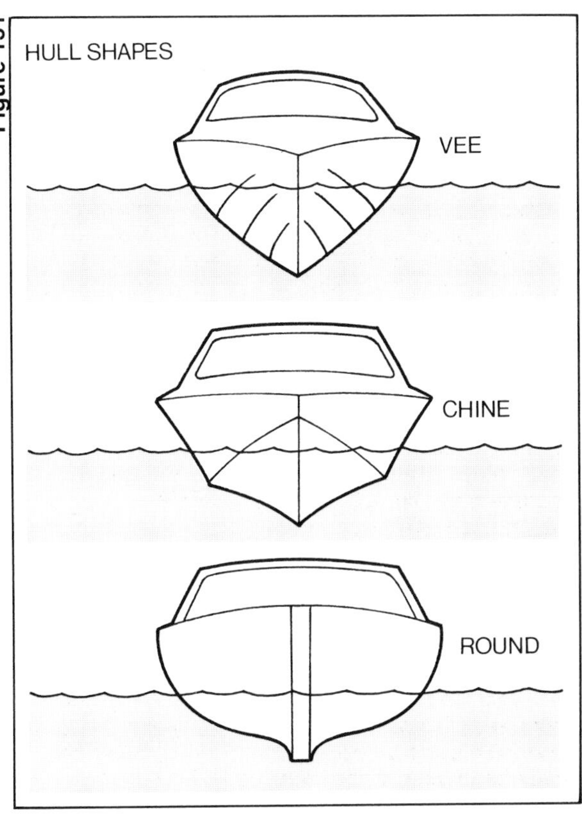

A vee-shaped hull usually gives the fastest and easiest ride at speed in rough weather, but is not very roomy inside.

Double chine with compound curves – provides more internal space. It is designed to reduce the 'wetted' area in higher-speed craft but can be expensive to fabricate.

Round – of the type used on fishing vessels is most efficient for speed from a given engine power. It will roll badly in heavy weather, but is very seaworthy. It gives considerable internal space, especially if the stern is squared off.

Hard Boat Theory

Displacement and Tonnage

The displacement of a boat is the weight of water displaced by the boat when loaded ready for sea. An approximate formula for calculating displacement (in tons) is:

$$\textbf{displacement} = \frac{L \times B \times D \times C_b}{35}$$

where L = waterline length (in feet)
B = waterline beam (in feet)
D = draught amidships (in feet)
C_b = the block coefficient

The block coefficent is the ratio of the immersed volume of the hull to the volume derived by multiplying the length of the waterline by that of the beam and that of the draught. It is typically 0·45 for a boat of moderate displacement.

Centres of Buoyancy and Gravity

The centre of buoyancy is the theoretical point in the immersed volume about which that shape would pivot. The longitudinal centre of buoyancy (LCB) is the pivot point on the horizontal axis of the immersed volume, while the vertical centre of buoyancy (VCB) is the corresponding pivot point in the vertical axis of the immersed volume. The equipment and fittings mounted on and within the hull are arranged so that the longitudinal centre of gravity (LCG) of the vessel falls over the longitudinal centre of buoyancy.

Stability

As a boat rolls her underwater shape changes as different parts of the hull are immersed. The centre of buoyancy (CB) moves across to the centre of this new immersed volume. The weight of the boat still acts vertically downward through the centre of gravity (CG), and this force, coupled with the upward force of the buoyancy, provides a twisting movement which rights the boat (Figure 152). If the roll of the boat is so great that the centre of gravity moves outside the centre of buoyancy, the vessel will capsize.

The lower the centre of gravity the greater the stability of the vessel. The centre of gravity is usually lowered by installing ballast just above the keel of the boat. The higher the freeboard the greater the buoyancy striving to push the boat back on an even keel. Increasing the beam increases the stability but usually reduces the angular range of that stability. If the hull takes in water (through fittings, etc.) when it heels, or if it has a significant quantity of water in the bilges, the restoring movement, and hence the stability, will be reduced.

Speed:Length Ratio

Both speed and length must be considered when comparing boats. The significant ratio is that of the speed in knots (V) to the square root of the waterline length in feet (L).

Resistance to Forward Movement

As a boat moves through the water energy is expended on producing the waves created by the hull. This is called wave-making resistance.

The friction of the water passing the immersed hull, the propeller shaft, the propeller and the rudder gives rise to further resistance, which is called frictional resistance. The immersed hull will have the smallest surface area if it is hemispherical in shape. Marine life growing on the hull increases the resistance to the smooth passage of water. This fouling can increase frictional resistance by 0·5 per cent per day between July and September in British waters.

The total resistance to forward movement is the sum of these two components: wave-making resistance and frictional resistance. Their relative importance varies with speed:length ratio; as shown in Figure 153.

Most large commercial cargo vessels travel at a speed:length ratio of about 0·8, while smaller powered craft (such as dive charter vessels) operate at about 1 to 1·2. Above 1·2 the power required to drive the vessel rises very quickly. This is due to a rapid rise in wave-making resistance as the vessel attempts to climb up and over its own bow wave. If it succeeds in this, the vessel starts to plane – i.e. to ride over the water rather than through it. With the correct hull shape (to reduce the immersed hull area), the amount of power required to make the boat go faster still is reduced. Ratios of 6 or 7

Figure 152

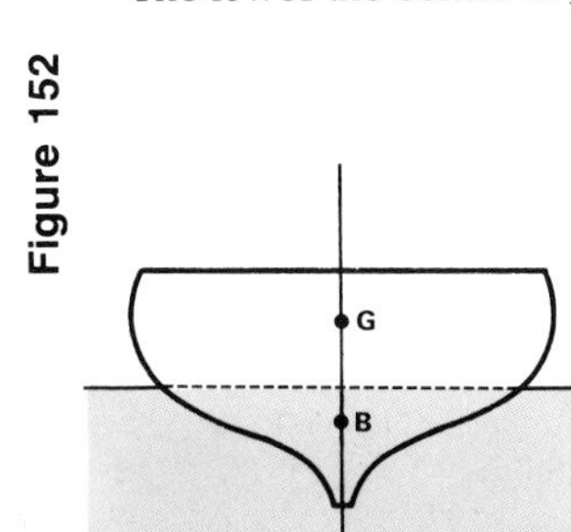

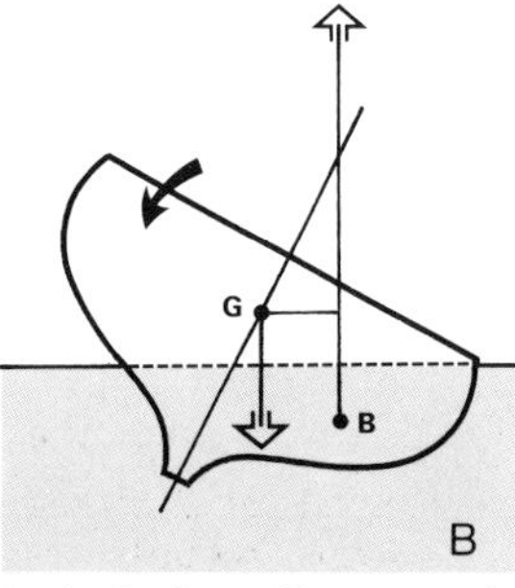

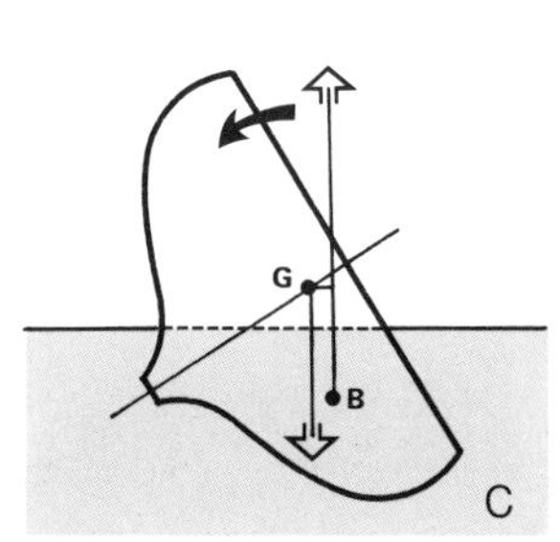

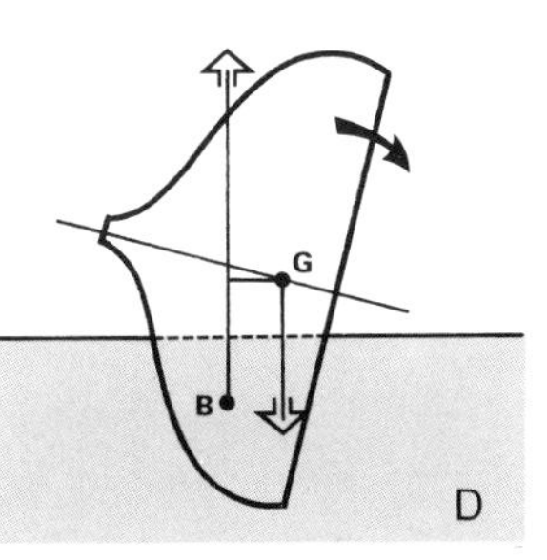

Righting moments acting on the hull of a rolling vessel

Figure 153

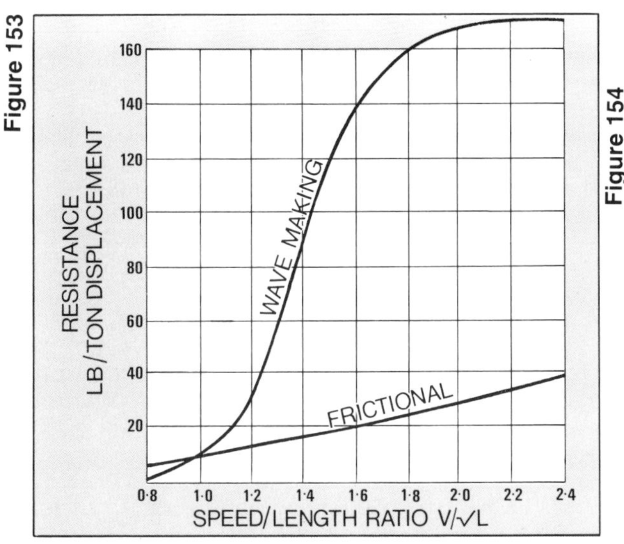

are achieved by planing cruisers, and offshore power racers can reach ratios of 15 or more.

The engine power (in horse power) required to overcome the resistance can be calculated from the expression:

power $= D_i \times R \times V \times 0{\cdot}00582$
where D_i = displacement (in tons)
R = resistance (in pounds per ton)
V = speed (in knots)

For a given engine size and waterline hull length, speed obviously decreases with increasing beam and draught, as both of these will increase the vessel's displacement.

Speed

If the vessel is a planing type then there is little limitation on its upper speed except that of engine power and fuel consumption. However, the costs of building and running a high-speed, large, long-range craft are totally prohibitive, making such vessels generally unsuitable for use in British waters for sports divers.

A displacement vessel is driven through the water rather than along the top of it. Whatever the engine power, there is a theoretical speed which a hull cannot exceed in displacement mode. This is reached when the transverse wave reaches the stern and the vessel then has to attempt to climb up the wave in front of its bows. The normal maximum displacement speed in knots (V max) is related to the waterline length of the hull in feet (L) by the expression:

$$V_{\max} = 1{\cdot}2 \times \sqrt{L}$$

The maximum speed of a vessel is therefore governed by the hull length and shape, the displacement and the engine power as well as the prevailing sea conditions.

For a fishing boat hull the following figures are typical: A speed:length ratio of 1:1 has been used.

Figure 154

MFV's

Hull length	Beam metres	Draught metres	Dis'ment (tons)	Max. speed (knots)	Actual speed knots	engine size (hp)
8.0	2.6	1.2	9.9	6.6	5.4	10
9.0	3.0	1.3	13.9	7.0	5.7	14
10.0	3.3	1.4	18.3	7.4	6.0	20
12.0	4.0	1.6	30.5	8.1	6.6	36
14.0	4.7	1.8	47.0	8.7	7.1	61
16.0	5.3	2.0	67.3	9.3	7.6	93
18.0	6.0	2.2	94.2	9.9	8.1	138
20.0	6.7	2.4	127.5	10.4	8.5	197
22.0	7.3	2.7	171.9	10.9	9.0	278
24.0	8.0	3.0	228.4	11.4	9.4	386
27.0	9.0	3.3	318.0	12.1	9.9	569
30.0	10.0	3.6	428.3	12.7	10.5	808

A huge increase in power is required to approach the maximum displacement speed (see Figure 155). They are for a typical 20-m round-hulled diving charter vessel, with a maximum displacement speed of 10·4 knots.

Figure 155

POWER NEEDED FOR VARIOUS SPEEDS
Hull length: 20 metres
Max. speed: 10.4 knots
Displacement: 127.5 tons

Speed (knots)	Speed/ length ratio	Resistance (friction)	Resistance (wave-make)	Total Resistance	Power (bhp)
1	0.13				
2	0.26				
3	0.39				
4	0.51				
5	0.64				
6	0.77	7	1	8	36
7	0.90	9	6	15	78
8	1.03	11	13	24	142
9	1.16	12	24	36	240
10	1.29	14	53	67	497
10.4	1.34	16	65	81	625
11	1.42	17	94	111	906
12	1.54	19	132	151	1345
13	1.67	21	148	169	1630
14	1.80	23	159	182	1891
15	1.93	26	165	191	2126

There is no point in fitting an engine any more powerful than that required to drive the hull at the maximum theoretical speed. If a larger engine is fitted, then considerable fuel economy can be gained by running the engine so that the vessel's speed is about 10–20 per cent below its theoretical maximum. For this class of vessel, marine diesel engines have a typical maximum speed of about 1000–2000 rpm and they are normally run at about 700–1500 rpm, although older engines run much more slowly. As well as fuel economy, this greatly reduces wear on the engine and thus prolongs its working life.

Hard Boat Systems

The Hull

The material used to make the hull of a hard boat can be wood, steel, aluminium, GRP or ferrocement.

A wood construction is the commonest type for diving charter vessels, as many of these are converted fishing vessels. Wood is subject to attack by a number of marine organisms and needs regular maintenance. All wooden boats leak a little, and regular pumping of the bilges is required.

The strongest material is steel and this is often used for boat hulls. The problem of rusting can be largely overcome by routine painting and by using cathodic protection. Steel is not subject to attack by marine life and is very watertight. It is usually lined with wood.

Aluminium is an expensive hull material, little used in charter boats because it is too liable to corrosion by most other metals used in marine construction.

Glassfibre reinforced plastic (GRP) is used for a vast number of small boats and some large ones. It is used in the construction of many diving dayboats. It is quite strong, easy to repair, highly watertight and free from attack by marine life.

Ferrocement (cement on a framework of steel mesh) is occasionally encountered, but mainly on boats built by amateurs. It is heavy and has the advantage of producing a hard-wearing, watertight hull. The displacement of a ferrocement vessel makes it a good steady platform at sea.

Accommodation

On larger hard boats the deck accommodation usually consists of a deckhouse aft of the bridge. This will normally be fitted with tables and seating. It can double as a lounge and a mess. Normally the galley will be situated at one end of the deckhouse.

On smaller dayboats the deck accommodation may be quite limited and the space is sometimes used for a large, clear working area. This arrangement may well be more suitable for day charters, when the diving activities fill most of the time that the boat is at sea.

The sleeping accommodation on larger vessels normally consists of several cabins to cater for a number of divers. Double bunks are useless in rough weather. The cabins will be fitted with storage lockers and sometimes handbasins. Dayboats do not usually have sleeping accommodation.

Washing and toilet facilities on dayboats is usually fairly rudimentary. On larger vessels there should be adequate arrangements. Typically there will be two showers and two toilets below decks, and usually one toilet on deck.

Heating and Ventilation

Space heating can be achieved with a hot-water radiator system run on waste engine heat, or by diesel or gas space heaters. Electrical heaters are also sometimes used. It is usual for living and accommodation areas to be heated and a heated drying area is often provided. Ventilation and air conditioning should be provided and are virtually essential on vessels operating in hot climates.

Domestic water can be heated by waste engine heat or by an electric immersion heater, although few vessels intended for diving charter work will have enough power to run an immersion heater.

Water Systems

The engine is cooled with sea water, usually indirectly. A pump is normally available to pump large quantities of sea water as a deck wash and for fire fighting.

Boats also contain several fresh water systems for drinking, cooking and washing. A typical layout of tanks, pump, heater and pipework is shown in Figure 158. Note that a manual pump is provided in case of failure of the electrical pump.

Fresh water can be produced by desalination either by boiling sea water and condensing the vapourized fresh water, or by reverse osmosis in which the salt is removed from the salt water by a semi-permeable membrane.

Waste

Food waste is usually thrown overboard. Paper, glass and metal waste from the galley should be collected and disposed of in port rather than at sea.

Waste water from the showers is pumped overboard, as is toilet waste. It is anti-social to do this in restricted waters or harbours. There are often local bye-laws prohibiting raw sewage discharge.

Safety Systems

There are a number of safety systems on vessels; some are specially built-in while others are incorporated in the design of other equipment.

One or more bilge pumps will be fitted to pump overboard any water from the bilges. They may be driven electrically or mechanically from the engine. They must also be capable of being operated manually in the event of an emergency.

Most larger vessels are divided into a number of compartments by watertight bulkheads, sometimes fitted with watertight doors. In the unlikely event of the vessel's being badly holed, these should keep the vessel afloat until assistance arrives.

In the event of fires or flooding of a watertight compartment, at least two escape routes must be available from every boat space. Therefore escape hatches should be fitted; sometimes there will be crash panels (thin wooden panels through which a determined person can penetrate in an emergency), especially at the ends of alleyways. Companionways (stairs) must be of adequate dimensions. All passenger vessels must be equipped with life rafts, the number depending on the number of passengers. These should contain emergency food and

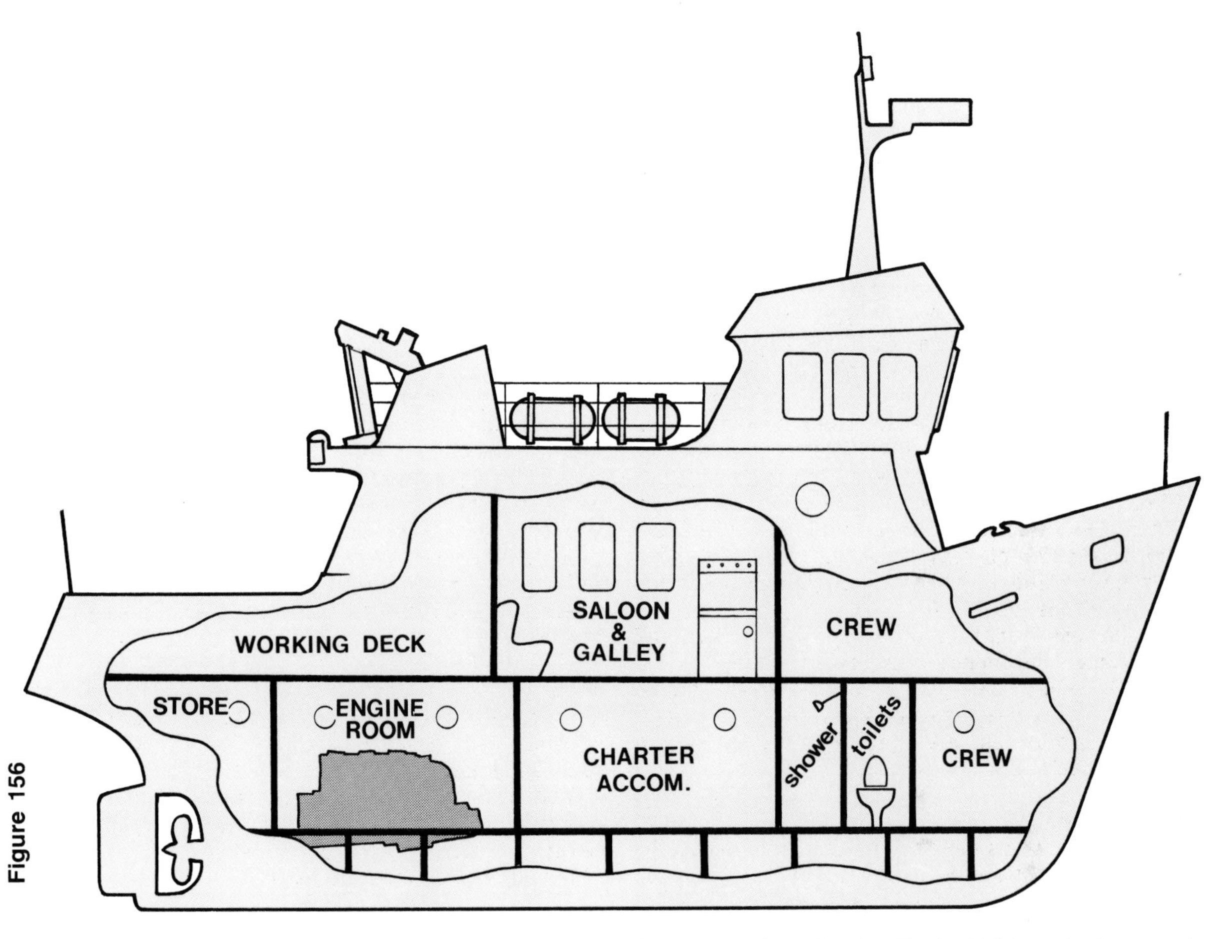

A cutaway view showing the typical layout, above and below decks, of a custom-built diving charter vessel

water supplies, along with other survival aids and equipment.

A vessel should carry a comprehensive first-aid kit which should be checked regularly.

Flares must be carried for emergency. Typically a 20-m vessel going well offshore might carry twelve (four) rocket flares, twelve (four) handflares, six smoke flares and two (two) smoke canisters. The numbers in brackets are those required by regulation.

The vessel will be fitted with appropriate navigation and other lights. It will also carry sound-signalling equipment.

Firefighting Systems

Firefighting systems are most important as fire aboard a vessel is one of the most life-threatening situations that can occur. Fire extinguishers should be situated around the vessel and will use carbon dioxide, halon (a smothering gas, which is becoming more common), dry powder (less popular because of the resulting mess) or water, as appropriate. Some vessels are fitted with automatic firefighting systems so that the boat can be flooded with carbon dioxide if temperatures rise above a certain level. Some engine rooms are fitted with automatic sprinkler systems to cool the machinery.

The Electronics

These are dealt with in detail on p. 120. They normally consist of radio(s), a navigator (and perhaps a satellite navigation system), radar, one or more echo sounders and an autopilot. An underwater sonar may also be fitted. This gives an extremely good impression of the seabed features for up to 1 mile around the vessel.

Engines and Hard Boats

The Engine

The larger vessels used by divers are invariably powered by diesel engines. A typical 260 hp diesel engine will have six or even eight in-line cylinders (each of 2–4 litres capacity); it measures about 3 × 1m × 1m high and weighs between 2 and 4 tonnes.

A diesel engine looks similar to a petrol engine but is different in operation. Most work on a four-stroke cycle. On the induction stroke air is drawn into the cylinder. The compression stroke heats this air so that a very fine spray of diesel fuel, injected just before the piston reaches the top of the stroke, is ignited, thus causing the power stroke. This is followed by the exhaust stroke.

Diesel compression is about twice that of a petrol engine so, for a given power, a diesel engine is more robust and heavier. Usually it is also noisier and smellier, though the fuel is less inflammable.

A diesel engine does not have an electrical ignition system (i.e. spark plugs, etc.); instead a fuel injection pump supplies precisely measured and timed fuel portions at very high pressure to fuel injectors situated at the top of each cylinder.

Of the engine power, about one third is used for propelling the boat, about one third is lost as waste heat and the final third is lost driving ancillaries and by other means. The power is measured in brake horse power (bhp).

Figure 157

A marine diesel engine

The surplus heat produced by the engine demands that the engine is cooled. This is usually achieved by pumping fresh water around the engine; this is then cooled with salt water pumped through a heat exchanger. The salt water is also used to cool the gearbox, engine oil and exhaust. Sometimes the fresh water from the engine is circulated and cooled in pipes running in the keel of the boat.

It is most important that the engine is lubricated with the correct type and grade of oil. The oil level must be checked each day that the boat is being used and the oil filter and oil changed at set intervals.

Figure 158

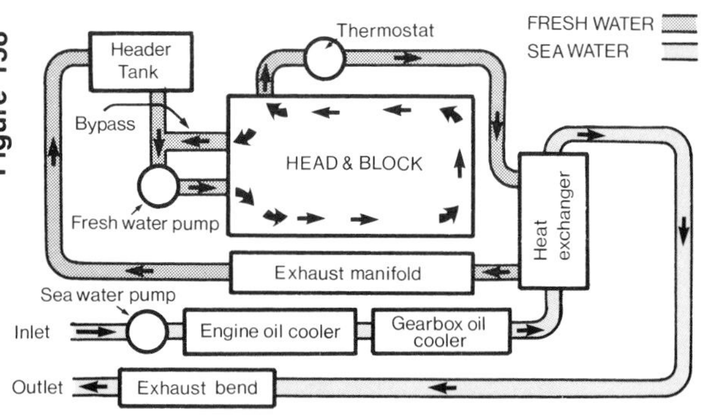

A typical cooling system

A wet exhaust system is frequently used. The cooling water from the engine is injected into the silencer where it quietens and cools the exhaust gases.

Controls for the throttle and the gear change must be situated close to the steering position. The minimum instrumentation will be oil pressure gauge, cooling water temperature gauge, cooling water pressure gauge, tachometer (for engine r.p.m.), ammeter and fuel tank contents gauge (or manometer). Other instruments can also be fitted.

The Fuel

Diesel oil is not as inflammable as petrol, although it is smellier and more persistent. It is usually stored in mild steel tanks, pumped into a header tank and then fed through mild steel pipes to the injector pump by gravity (although a lift pump is sometimes used). The fuel tanks are fitted with anti-surge baffles and with drain cocks to remove any water contaminent. Before reaching the injector pump and injectors the fuel is filtered very carefully through two filters (because the pump and injectors have very fine internal clearances).

The filters must be purged of water frequently and the filter elements replaced at given intervals. The injector pump is manufactured to high precision and the

Figure 159

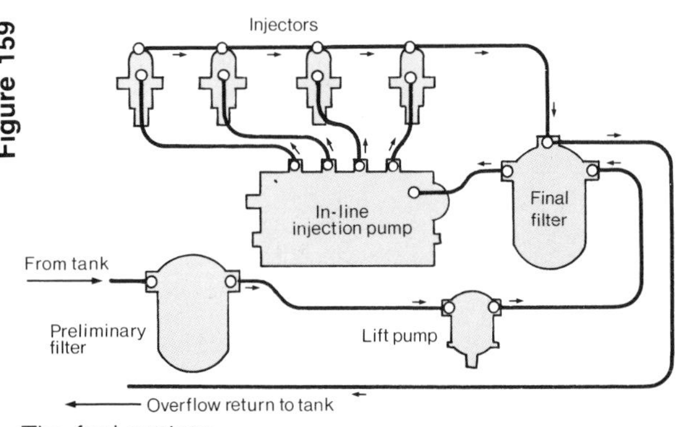

The fuel system

prescribed lubrication and maintenance must be rigidly followed.

Fuel needs air for combustion (in fact, about 15 kg of air for every 1 kg of fuel). This air is filtered to remove particles. It may be necessary to circulate air through the engine compartment to keep it cool.

Transmission of Power

The engine is normally mounted about a third of the distance along the vessel from the stern. It drives a gearbox which turns the propeller shaft and the propeller. The prop shaft runs through a stern tube in the hull. Watertightness is ensured by stern glands fitted to each end of the prop shaft.

The gearbox incorporates reduction gearing which usually halves the engine speed, as propellers are more efficient at around 300–600 r.p.m. It will give forward, reverse and neutral. A variable-pitch propeller may be fitted instead of a gearbox. This varies the pitch of the propeller blades to give ahead/neutral/astern power; it also matches the pitch to the power and speed.

The propeller must be matched to the hull characteristics and should rotate at about 100 r.p.m. for each knot of boat speed. The diameter and pitch (the distance the propeller would move ahead in one revolution) are chosen so that, at full throttle, the engine reaches its maximum r.p.m. and develops full power. Typically, a 20-m vessel will be fitted with a single, three-bladed propeller up to 1½ m in diameter.

Two engines and twin propellers are sometimes used.

Hydraulics

The auxiliary systems of the boat are often driven by hydraulic motors. The engine drives a pump which pumps hydraulic fluid along high-pressure pipes to drive the hydraulic motors. This system is very flexible and versatile and the motors can drive the steering, deck winch, bow thruster, stabilizers, deck crane, etc.

In smaller vessels, instead of the normal gearbox and prop shaft, a hydraulic motor can be used to drive the propeller.

The Electrical System

A hard boat is often fitted with quite extensive electrical systems. Usually a 240V AC circuit is provided for domestic needs (lighting, heating, ventilation, domestic water, cooking, refrigeration, radios, etc.), while the boat requirements and electronics are driven by 24-V dc.

The electricity is produced by a 240-V ac auxiliary generator. Heavy-duty (typically 150 ampere hour capacity) lead/acid batteries supply the 24-V dc circuit; these are charged by the generator. The electrical system must be suppressed to avoid interference with the boat's radio circuits.

Diesel engines are normally started by an electrical starter motor. Because the load on this is so high, electrically driven heater plugs are sometimes fitted in the cylinder head; these are actuated for a short time before starting.

For safety a fuse box will be fitted in either the engine room or the wheelhouse. The modern trend is to fit circuit breakers rather than fuses. The main battery switch should be turned off when the boat is not in use. Two-wire systems should always be used and insulation regularly checked, as leakage currents can rapidly corrode underwater fittings.

Power is transmitted to the propeller via the gear box, flexible coupling, and propshaft

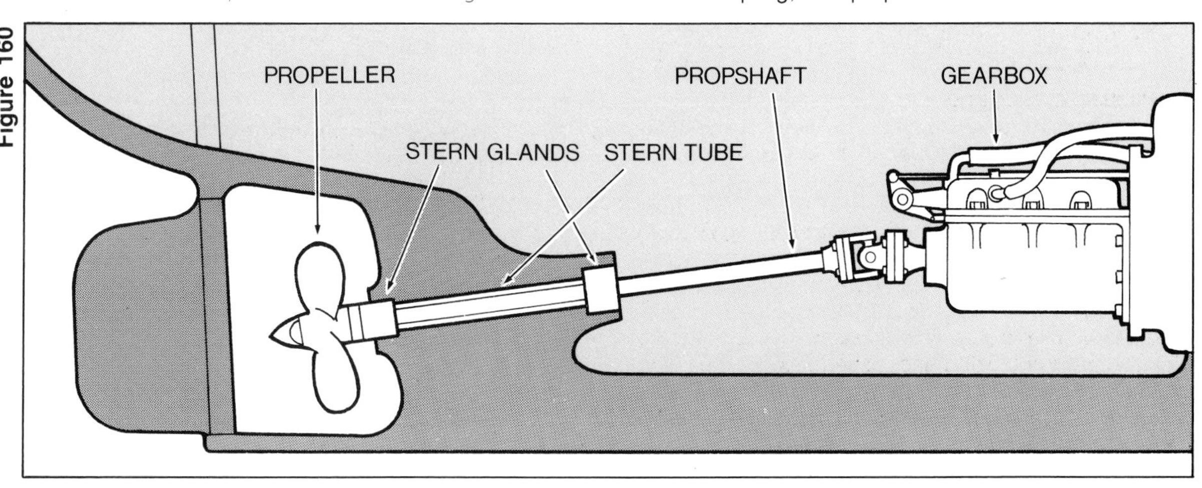

Figure 160

Primary Physical Effects

There are many forces acting on a boat. Those most important to the handling of diving charter vessels are described below.

The Engine

A diesel engine can be stopped and started easily, and it develops its power very quickly. The engine should be handled with as few stops and starts as possible.

Single and Twin Propellers

The rotation of a propeller can be either right-handed or left-handed. The direction of rotation is defined as right-handed for a propeller which, when driving ahead, turns clockwise when viewed from astern (right-handed propellers are most common).

Figure 161

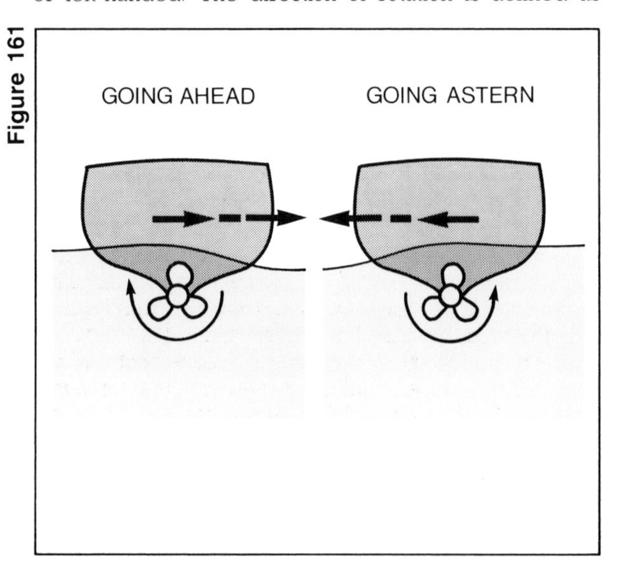

A right-handed propeller showing turning forces

The direction can have a considerable effect on the handling of single-screw vessels. When starting from rest, a right-hand propeller will kick the stern to starboard. When starting off astern or going from ahead to astern, it kicks the stern to port. The effect can be quite marked. A left-handed propeller has the opposite effect.

A vessel fitted with twin propellers can either have them both rotating in the same direction (in which case the propeller effect is still evident) or in opposite directions (in which case the rotation effects of the two propellers are cancelled). When manoeuvring in restricted spaces a twin-screw boat can have one propeller going ahead and one astern, although turning the vessel by this means alone is a very slow process.

Bow Thruster

Some vessels have an auxiliary propeller fitted in the bows of the boat. This is mounted in a small tube running through the bows and the thrust is at right angles to the main axis of the vessel. It is normally driven by a hydraulic motor.

Figure 162

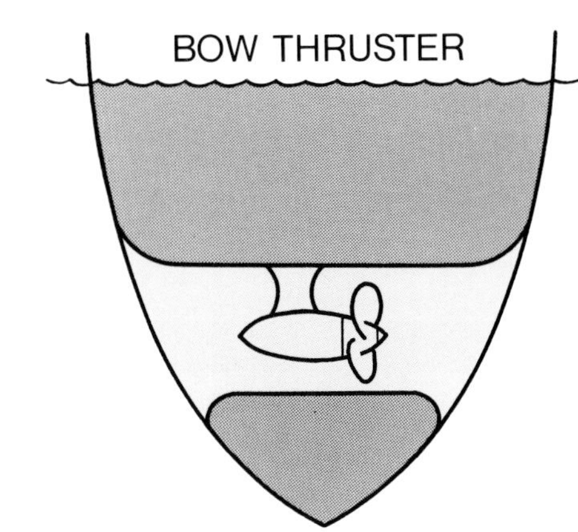

A bow thruster

This bow thrust propeller is used when manoeuvring in restricted spaces or in windy conditions. It has the effect of quickly moving the bow of the boat in the desired direction. This is most useful when there are conditions of wind and tide that make it difficult to head the boat in a particular direction. When this is coupled with limited room for manoeuvring, a bow thruster can be invaluable. It will allow the boat to be turned in its own length.

On smaller vessels the same effect is sometimes achieved by having a thruster jet mounted near the bows. When this is activated a jet of water is pumped out which pushes the vessel's head in the appropriate direction.

The Rudder

The rudder lies abaft of the propeller and its size and shape largely control the turning properties of the vessel. Note that, when going astern, turbulence can make the rudder almost ineffective.

Way

When a heavy vessel is travelling at speed it has a lot of momentum. A large diving support vessel can weigh up to 150–200 tonnes and when it is travelling at 10–12 knots it possesses a lot of energy. When the engine is put into neutral the vessel will still keep moving until the momentum or way is used up in moving the vessel through the water. This could take up to 200 m.

This way must be allowed for, particularly when manoeuvring in restricted spaces such as harbours. Of course, at low speeds the way is reduced.

Wind

The wind has a substantial effect on larger boats. Deep-draught vessels are affected less than shallow-draught,

Figure 163

Pushing a bow wave

flat-bottomed craft. The effect will be increased by a large superstructure. If this is concentrated at one end of the boat then a strong wind can have a noticeable turning effect. However, the normal effect with most boats is for the wind to blow the whole vessel steadily downwind.

When a vessel is stopped she will adopt a position so that the wind is roughly on her beam.

When going ahead a vessel's movements are very much dependent on the amount of windage forward and abaft of her pivoting point, and the relative direction of the wind.

When going astern the vessel's pivoting point moves aft, and with all her windage forward of this point she rapidly ends up with her stern pointing directly into the wind.

The main importance of the wind to divers is its effect on recovery after the dive. Normally the tender collects the divers and transfers them to the hard boat on its lee side. If, however, the diver is boarding the hard boat directly from the water, more caution is needed. With insensitive boathandling the diver may have to swim hard to reach a boat being blown by the wind; the effort required rapidly exceeds that which can be sustained by the diver. If a diver is in the water in the lee of the vessel at the foot of the diving ladder, there is some danger of the vessel's being blown on top of him while he is removing his fins; a central-spine type of ladder prevents this by allowing the diver to climb out without removing his fins (see p. 86).

Tide

A vessel in a strong tide will normally just move along with the tide and so will not have uneven forces acting upon it. A vessel stemming the tidal stream at slow speed may complete the first part of her turning circle almost within her own length.

When a vessel is operating in a narrow channel with a strong tidal stream running it will be affected by differing strengths of water movement as it moves in and out of stronger areas of tidal flow. Great care will have to be taken when using the water movement when approaching and leaving jetties, and also when poking a nose out into the tidal stream. Steering in these conditions can be extremely hazardous.

Heavy weather can cause overfalls and turbulence where strong tidal streams flow through narrow channels or over very uneven bottoms. At some places these can cause trouble to even quite large vessels. They should be avoided when conditions are very difficult.

Navigating in a strong tideway

Figure 164

Secondary Physical Effects

There are many additional forces acting on a boat and many other effects that should ideally be considered before handling such a vessel.

The Wake Current

When a boat moves through the water, a cavity is created by its stern. The water swirling into this cavity is termed the 'wake current'. The effect increases with the speed and beam of the vessel. The bigger the wake current, the greater will be the adverse effect of turbulent water on the rudder.

Sideslip and Pivot Point

When a vessel turns under helm, her ends skid about her pivoting point. This point differs when going ahead and going astern. When going ahead, the pivot point is well forward, so that the stern swings out when the helm is put over. This demands care when manoeuvring close to an obstruction. When going astern, the pivot point is quite near the stern and, in any significant wind, the stern will tend to come up into the wind due to the effect of the wind on the boat's superstructure farther forward. When stopped, the pivot point is approximately amidships.

The Turning Circle

When a vessel alters course under helm through 360 degrees she moves on a roughly circular path called a turning circle. Throughout the turn her bow will be slightly inside the circle and her stern a little outside it. The circle will be the path traced out by the centre of gravity. However, the circle is not complete due to some sideslip when the helm is first used.

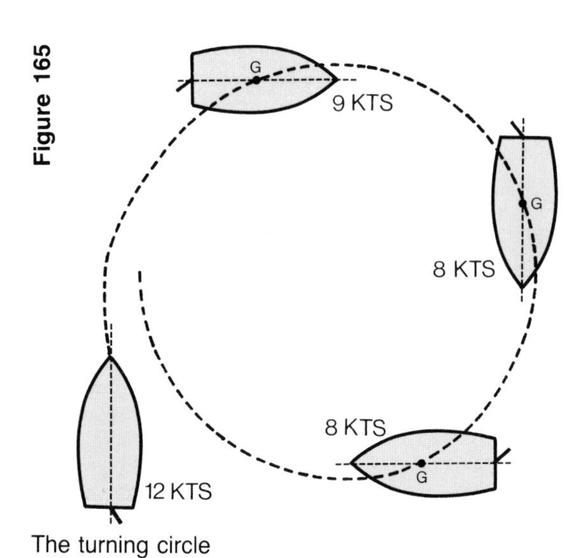

The turning circle

The vessel will lose about a quarter of her original speed after the first 90 degrees; the speed will drop by a third of the original speed after 180 degrees; thereafter the speed falls no farther.

The average advance while completing a turning circle is about four vessel lengths. With a right-handed propeller the circle to port will be slightly smaller, and vice versa.

Loading

When deeply laden a vessel will carry her way longer. She will be sluggish at gathering speed and will have a larger turning circle. Dive charter vessels rarely alter their loading very much, although the difference between a full load of fuel and water at the beginning of a cruise and the same tanks when they are nearly empty can be significant.

Trim

A vessel trimmed by the stern has her pivoting point farther aft than if she were on an even keel. The turning circle will increase, though she will steer well and turn more readily downwind; she will also develop maximum power. All these trends are reversed if she is trimmed by the head. These effects should not normally be experienced on a diving charter vessel.

List

A listing vessel will turn more readily towards her high side. This effect should not normally be experienced on a diving charter vessel.

Shallows

As a vessel moves through shallow water there is more resistance than normal to the inflow of water to replace that displaced by the hull. The propeller and hull are operating in a partial vacuum. The handling of the vessel becomes sluggish; in depths of water of one and a half times the vessel's draft or less, the steering can become erratic. Consequently, in shallow water a vessel should only be operated at slow to moderate speeds.

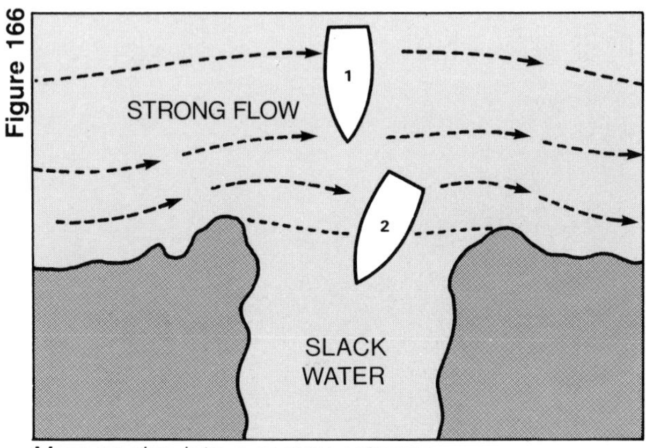

Manoeuvring into a narrow entrance

When a vessel nears extremely shallow water she can rapidly sheer first towards the shoal then away from it; this is called 'smelling the ground'. When moving through shallow water the bow and stern waves become more pronounced and the stern of the vessel can be drawn down towards the bottom; this is called 'squatting'. If the keel strikes the seabed it can cause the vessel to sheer about unpredictably.

Figure 167

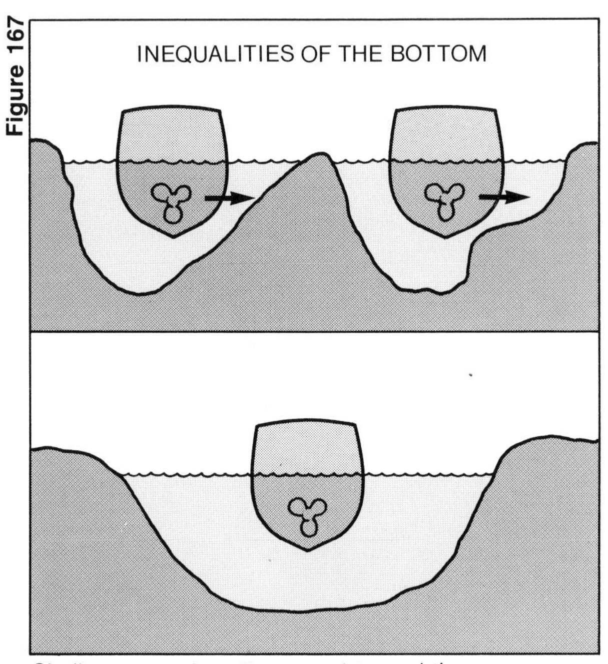

Shallows may draw the vessel toward them

Sternway
Going astern is fairly predictable in calm conditions. In a wind, steering astern becomes quite difficult unless going dead into the wind, otherwise the vessel tends to seek the wind.

Narrows
In a narrow waterway all the shallow water effects described above are present, but there are additional effects. The vessel's bow and stern waves increase in size, demanding slow speeds. If the vessel strays too close to a bank there is a venturi effect that can draw the vessel ever closer to the bank, an effect known as bank suction. The stern is usually more affected than the bows and the effect can be to slew the vessel at an angle to the channel. Note that ships passing each other closely can have the same effect on one another.

Figure 168

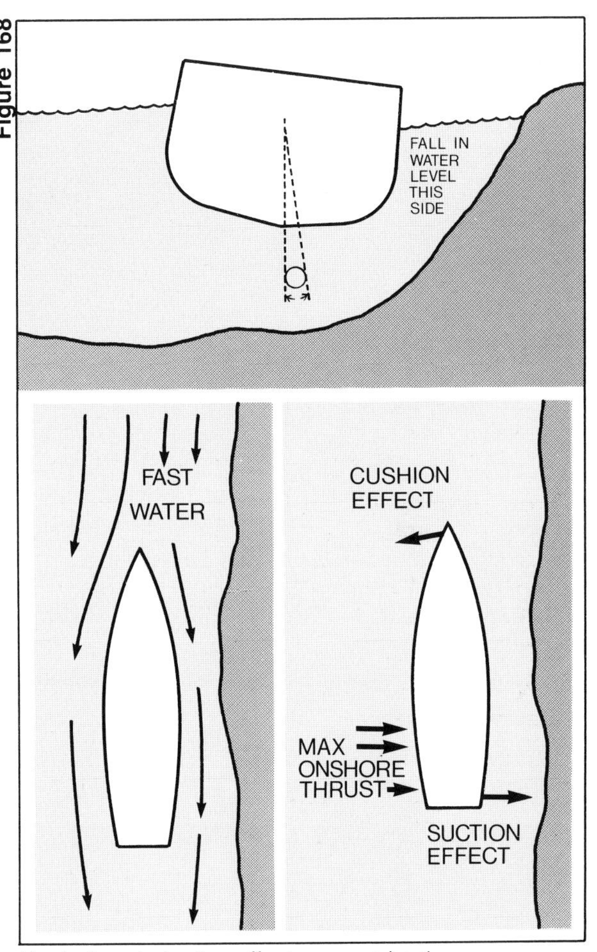

Venturi and slewing effects near a bank

Bends
Negotiating bends in narrow channels with flowing water can be quite awkward. With a following water flow the stern will be sheered towards the outer curve of the bend, whereas when running into the flow the stern will be pushed outwards.

Narrow Openings
When entering a narrow opening from water with a strong flow, such as into a dock or lock, the stern will swing away with the water flow as the bow enters the still water. A bold approach and a readiness for quick correcting action are required (see Figure 166).

Moored Ships
These will surge considerably in the wash of a passing vessel, so speed should be reduced. The bank suction effect can also occur and great care should be taken when manoeuvring near to another vessel.

Running Hard Boats

In this section, which deals with the practical running of larger vessels, we provide the information needed by an experienced diver and small-boat handler to reach port safely if the skipper of his charter vessel is taken seriously ill. If your intention is to own and run your own vessel, then a greater depth of knowledge is required. This can be learned from personal study, Royal Yachting Association night classes and, most importantly, from practical experience.

Vessel Start-up Procedure

Forecasts

Before leaving harbour in a large vessel you should:
Obtain the weather forecast (usually via the coastguard or shipping broadcasts).
Assess its possible effect on your plans.
Decide on your destination and have planned alternatives in the event of worsening weather.
Assess the tidal state and tidal streams and use them to your advantage.

Coastguard Liaison

It is important to maintain good relations with the coastguard so:
Notify the coastguard of your intentions.
Discuss any special difficulties and heed any advice that may be offered.
Report in to the coastguard from time to time, especially when making a long voyage.
Sign off at the end of the voyage.

Figure 169

The engine instruments

Crew

Allocate duties to the crew commensurate with their abilities.
Check that the crew have carried out what was asked of them.
Ensure that the crew are at their positions before proceeding. (Normally this will mean manning the warps to assist with leaving the quay.)

Engine

There are a number of checks that should be carried out before starting the engine and proceeding to sea. These are the main items:
Check that the fuel level is adequate and you have a reserve.
Check that the oil level in engine and gearbox is adequate.
Make sure that the circulating water seacock is open.
Start the engine (usually battery start).

The following routine checks should be made once the engine is running:
That there are no leaks of fuel, oil or water;
That the oil and water temperatures are correct;
That the batteries are charging;
That the controls are operating.
In the event of serious noises or other malfunction, shut down the engine.

Electronics

There are a number of procedures that should be carried out with the electronic equipment before you go to sea.
Switch on the VHF radio and set it to Channel 16 (if dual watch, set to channels 16 and 6).
Follow the start-up procedure for the radar (usually all you need to do is switch on and wait several minutes for it to warm up and settle down).
Switch on the echo sounder if required.

General

There are also a number of general duties that should be carried out before proceeding to sea.
Ensure that you have adequate supplies of food, water and safety equipment on board.
Start the generator.
Check the bilge pumping system.
Check the bilges and pump them out if required.
Check that any tenders are recovered and correctly stowed.
See that all hatches are secured.
Check that everything is shipshape on deck and in the saloon(s).
Check that the radar reflector is in place.
Display any appropriate lights.
Ensure everyone is aboard before leaving.
Check that there are no ropes over the side and that the propeller is clear.

When you are ready, recover the anchor or let go the mooring warps recover and stow the fenders.

Running

Engine

Once the engine is running continuous monitoring should be maintained on:

oil temperature
oil pressure
cooling water temperature
cooling water pressure
engine temperature generally
fuel level.

Figure 170

The steering position

The best fuel economy will be achieved by maintaining the engine revs at about 75 per cent of maximum. Engine life will also be maximized.

Steering

Larger vessels are normally steered by remote control from the wheelhouse by means of a wheel or perhaps a lever (with hydraulic steering).

Holding a course in heavy seas is not easy, as the head of the vessel can swing substantially. Resist the temptation continually to make minor adjustments to the wheel every two or three seconds; only make more major corrections. Watch the heading on the steering compass. The use of an autopilot greatly eases strain on the helmsman; in heavier weather its sensitivity must not be set too high.

You must be familiar with and observe the Rules of the Road (see p. 22 and Appendix 2, p. 148).

Radio Use

It is important that you should be able to use the radio; especially if an emergency situation occurs. Radio procedures are specified in detail on pp. 95–98.

Night Passages

Night passages are often easier than daytime passages because lights are readily visible and there is less traffic. Advantage can be taken of favourable tides. When sailing at night:

Check everything is shipshape aboard the vessel before nightfall.

Improve your night vision by reducing the number of internal lights.

Set the compass illuminator to the dimmest position.

Show the correct lights. These consist of a white masthead light, green (starboard) and red (port) sidelights and a white stern light (see Rules of the Road, p. 24 and Appendix 2).

Have white flares and a signal lamp to hand.

Keep warm, and have snacks and warm drinks available.

Be very careful if you have to work on deck.

The skipper must leave clear, written instructions for the person on watch.

Sharpen your lookout for unlit objects such as buoys and floating debris.

Fog

The main dangers in fog, are the risk of collision or of running aground. In this situation radar is invaluable; a large radar reflector is also very comforting. It may not be wise to proceed to sea if it is very foggy, particularly if the vessel is not fully equipped or manned.

In the event of fog take the following actions:

Slow down.

Get a navigational fix if at all possible.

Sound the fog signal. This is one long blast (two if stopped) every two minutes if making way through the water (see p. 25 and Appendix 2).

Switch on the steaming lights.

Watch the echo sounder very carefully when in shallow water.

Keep a very good lookout, preferably with someone in the bows.

Prepare the anchor if you are near the shore or shoal water.

Check that the liferaft is ready for launching.

Navigation

The position of the vessel must be known at all times. This is ascertained by integrating information from the navigator, the radar, the echo sounder and other instruments. (See p. 104).

Handling Hard Boats

Leaving A Quay or Jetty

Screwing off a quay

Before leaving, consider wind and tide to see in which order the mooring warps should be let go. With the wind or tidal stream on the bows, let go the lines until the vessel is held by just the after-spring, which should have been previously arranged as a slip rope by taking it round a bollard ashore and bringing the end back aboard. Go slow astern on the engine and the wind or tide will push the bows out from the quay. The spring can be recovered and the vessel can proceed ahead away from the quay.

Springing off a Quay

With the wind or tidal stream from astern, or with a wind blowing onto the quay, the quay is best left astern. The fore-spring is arranged as a slip rope and is let go last. Go ahead against a fender near the bow; the stern will swing out from the quay and, when the desired angle is reached, let go the spring and go astern.

Figure 171

Making a hard turn to port

Figure 172

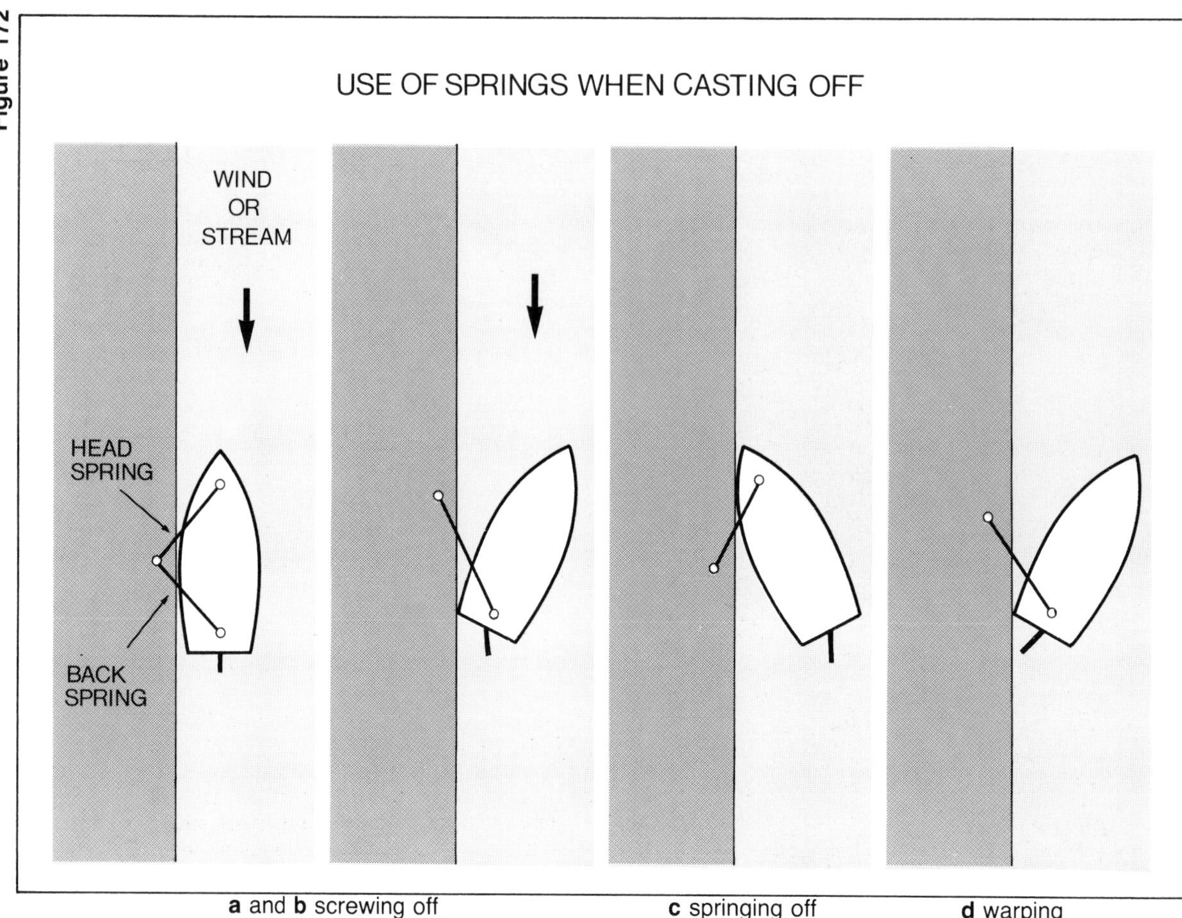

a and **b** screwing off **c** springing off **d** warping

Warping

When space is very limited it is sometimes possible to use a warp led ashore to help manoeuvre. By using this warp as a spring, the vessel can pivot round very quickly to avoid obstructions.

The wind and/or the tidal stream and the propeller effect should also be used intelligently to reduce manoeuvring distance.

Leaving a Mooring

This is usually just a case of casting off and going astern until the buoy is cleared. If a tidal stream is running and the vessel is lying to a buoy, head to tide, moving the warp about one-third of the way aft will turn the boat across the tide, and this can be very helpful if that direction is the one desired.

Steering

Steering is usually effected by means of a wheel, though this is usually amplified by some mechanism. It is very tiring to have to steer a vessel which relies solely on muscle power to turn the rudder for long periods. With hydraulic steering a simple lever is sometimes fitted.

It is important to remember that there is no steerage unless water is flowing past the rudder, and that the rudder has a maximum effect at an angle of 35°. More than this will be counterproductive.

The propeller effect must be allowed for when manoeuvring, especially at low speed. Most single-screw boats have right-handed propellers.

Figure 173

A right-handed propeller with rudder aft

When attempting to steer a particular course it is important to use the compass at all times. An autopilot connected to the steering and the compass can reduce fatigue.

The Rules of the Road must be followed. They are explained on pp. 22–25 and Appendix 2.

Turning

Figure 174

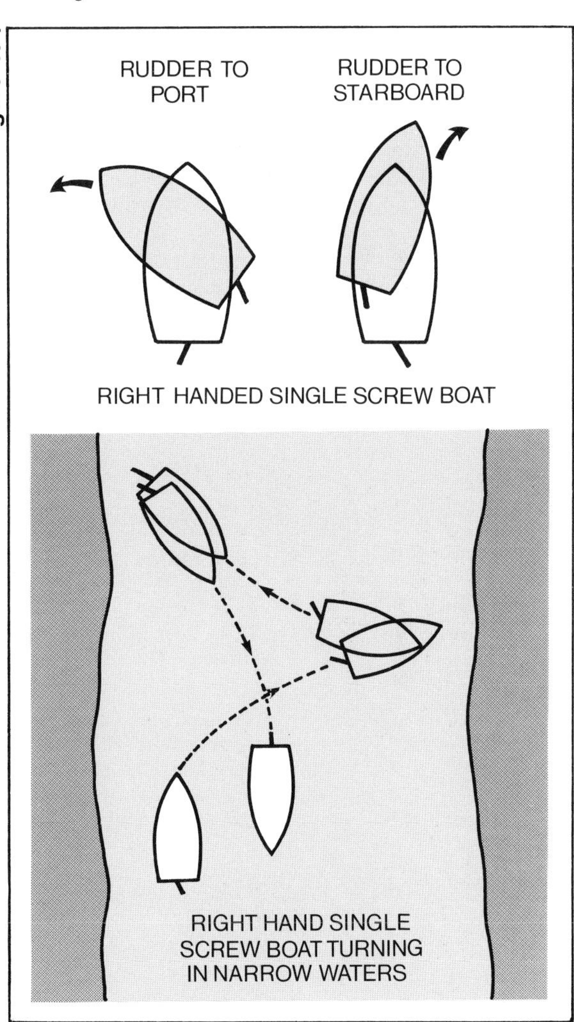

Turns in relation to propeller rotation direction

Use an anchor to turn in a restricted tideway. The anchor is dropped, if necessary by tender, and the vessel can be turned by swinging around the anchor. The anchor may have to be recovered later by tender.

This whole manoeuvre is relatively straightforward in a dayboat or a yacht, but with a 20-m vessel the weight of the anchor and chain will be too great for them to be lifted from a tender.

Anchoring

The same principles of anchoring that were described in the section on small boats apply to larger, hard boats. A few extra points are worthy of inclusion.

The anchor gear on a hard boat will consist of the anchor itself and a warp of chain, while on smaller vessels there will often be an initial short length of chain and then a rope warp.

The anchor chain must be fastened to the boat at an extremely strong point of the vessel. Normally this will be a winch which is firmly bolted through a reinforced area of the deck. The chain is normally stored in a chain locker and can be marked at intervals so that the amount used is known.

When anchoring, the following points should be borne in mind:

Before approaching an anchorage, study the chart to select the best spot for anchoring with regard to depth, holding ground, wind and swell directions, landing position, etc.

Anchor in sufficient depth of water so that the vessel does not take the ground (hit the seabed) at low tide.

Do not anchor in or near moorings – there is a risk of fouling ground chains.

Do not anchor in channels or fairways.

Do not anchor too near other craft.

Allow enough space for the vessel to swing with wind and tide.

When anchoring, note in which direction other vessels are lying relative to their anchors.

The vessel will drop back several lengths after the anchor is dropped.

Come up head to wind or tide, release the anchor as the vessel comes to a stop. Pay out enough chain for the anchor to reach the seabed and then pay out more as the vessel drops back. The anchor should be set (driven into the seabed) by briefly not paying out chain while going astern.

The minimum amount of cable to be veered (paid out) should be not less than three times the depth of water.

Once firmly at anchor, note the bearings on three prominent objects so that it is possible to tell if the anchor drags.

Display the anchor signal. This is a black ball in the forepart of the vessel in daylight, replaced at night by an anchor light.

Ensure that all preparations for sea are made before weighing anchor.

Hauling on a tripping line (a line running from the crown of the anchor to a buoy) may help if the anchor fouls the seabed.

If the anchor fouls the bottom and no tripping line is being used, try freeing the anchor by pulling the chain from different directions.

Divers are obviously very useful in the event of a fouled anchor, but there are certain circumstances in which their use might be contra-indicated.

Figure 175

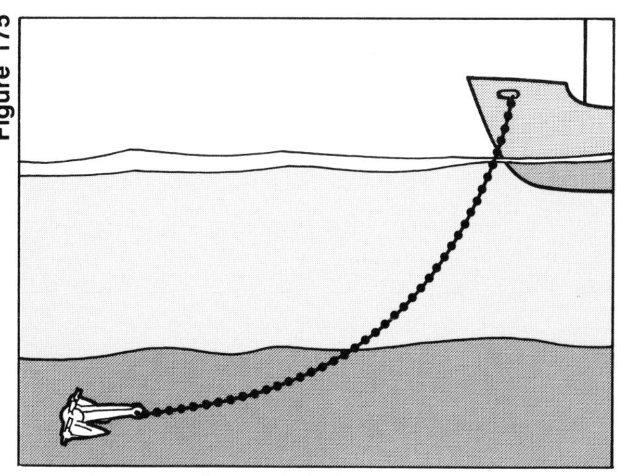

Deploying an anchor and chain

It is sometimes necessary to carry out overnight anchor watches. Although these can be very tedious they are prudent in exposed anchorages and heavy weather. A careful watch on anchor bearings and the radar screen is required.

Mooring with Two Anchors

In restricted waters or in heavy weather it may be helpful to set two anchors. These will reduce the circle through which the boat swings as the wind and the tide change; they will also increase the holding power.

In a tidal stream the two anchors are normally in line with the tidal flow with the vessel lying beween them (Figure 176). In threatening weather anchors should be set ahead of the vessel, one on either bow. The angle between them should be about 30°–40° (Figure 177).

Figure 176

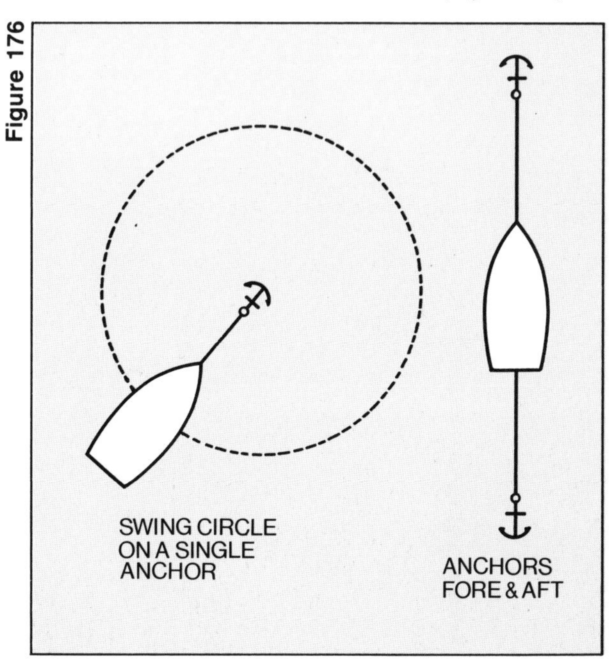

One anchor, or two?

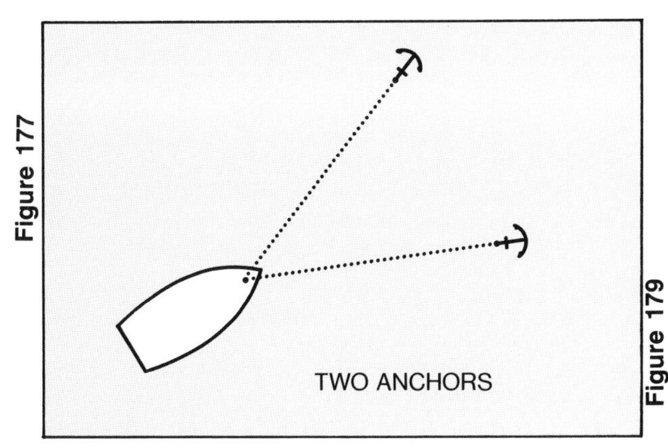

Figure 177

Anchoring for heavier weather

Winching

On larger vessels the anchor and chain will be far too heavy to recover by hand so a winch is always used. This may be powered by hand, by electric drive, by belt drive from the engine or by hydraulic drive. The main engine should be used to drive the vessel to a position directly above the anchor while the winch is recovering the chain. As the chain is retrieved and run through the gypsy (the wheel on the winch designed to mesh with the chain links), it should be fed down into the chain locker and coiled so that it will not jam when it is next run out.

Picking up a Mooring Buoy

Use a crew member to point to the buoy as it will disappear from sight under the bows when viewed from the wheelhouse.

In a single, right-hand-screw boat the propeller effect will throw the bow to starboard if the boat is put astern to check the boat's way at the last moment. Thus the buoy should be approached fine on the starboard bow (Figure 179).

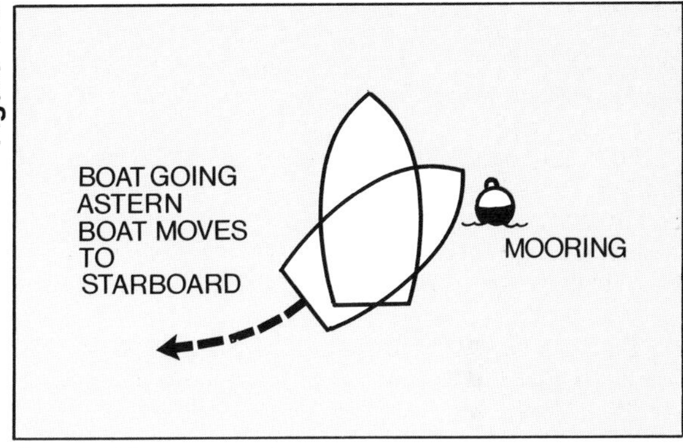

Figure 179

Approaching a mooring

Before leaving a mooring buoy, check the strength and direction of the wind and the tidal stream, motor ahead a little to relieve tension on the mooring line so that the crew can release it, then drop astern until the buoy is well clear ahead and there is little danger of fouling the propeller with the mooring line.

Figure 178

Weighing anchor

Figure 180

Picking up the mooring

Manoeuvring in Harbours
Operate at low speed to avoid disturbing other vessels unduly with your bow wave and wake. Observe one-way systems and any other local regulations and byelaws.

Coming Alongside

Figure 181

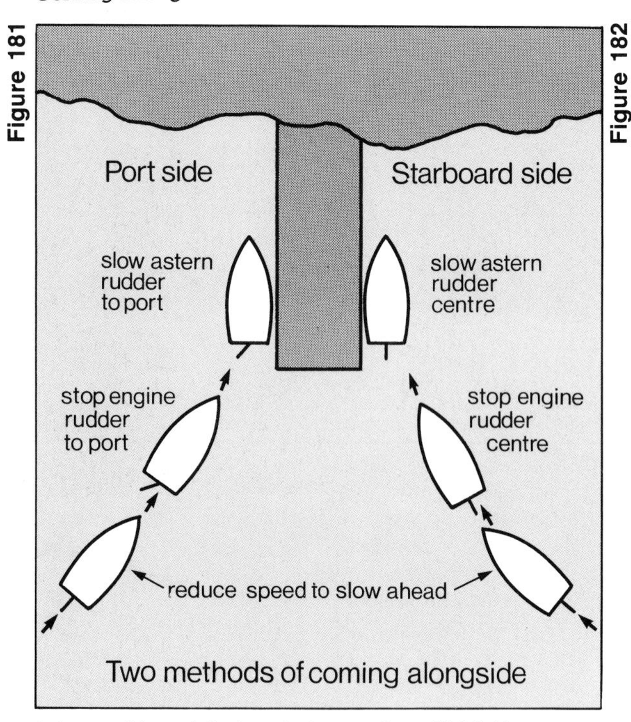

A boat with a right-handed propeller will 'kick' to port when going astern. Use this feature along with an appropriate rudder position to approach either side of a jetty

Tying up
When mooring to a bollard to which a warp is already looped, pass the eye of the fresh warp through the eye of the existing mooring rope.

Four ropes are necessary to secure to a quay. A head rope and a stern rope, both led well along the quay from the vessel, and fore and aft springs. In non-tidal waters or when lying alongside another vessel, breast ropes can be used at right angles to the quay.

Figure 182

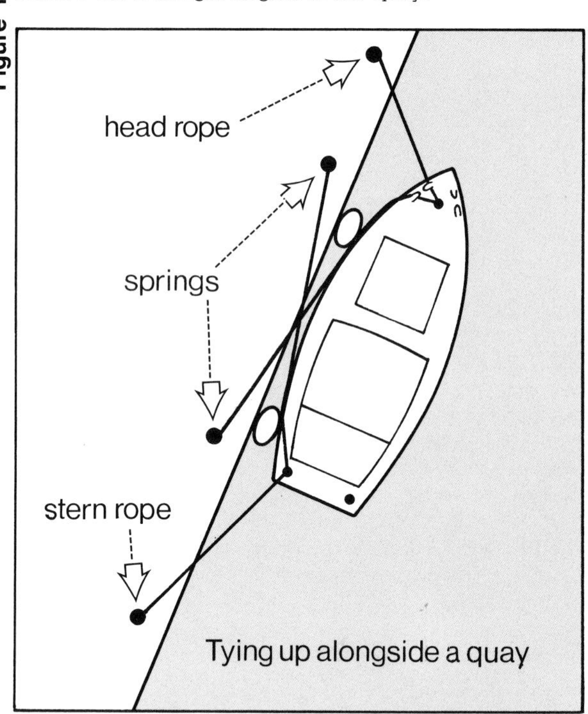

All four lines must be used to make a safe mooring. The combination will keep the boat in position. When moored to a jetty the lines may have to be periodically adjusted to allow for tidal rise and fall

Before coming alongside check the depth of water along the quay, the state of the tide and its rise and fall. Check also that mooring lines are ready and that end loops have been formed from bowlines.

Approach as slowly as possible commensurate with maintaining steerage. Always head into wind or tide, whichever is the stronger.

A boat with a right-handed screw will be easier to berth on the port side because the propeller effect will help bring the boat parallel to the quay by swinging the stern to port when going astern to check the boat's way.

Handling in Rough Weather
It is best to run for shelter before any heavy weather that has been forecast actually arrives. Of course, there is always the risk of running before imaginary weather, especially in the North Atlantic, where there is nearly always threatening weather somewhere. The advantage of using a fast vessel is obvious.

Care is needed in a heavy following sea because of the danger of surfing and broaching on big waves. Heavy seas will slow a vessel down to perhaps 1 or 2 knots. Thus, a long time can be spent covering a relatively short distance. Heavy seas can also cause sediment in the fuel tanks to be stirred up, possibly leading to a fuel blockage in the fuel pumps and consequent engine failure.

Seas can reach such a size that driving into the weather and the waves is the only sensible action. This could last for twenty-four hours or more. It is obviously a good idea not to be caught in such conditions as they are very tiring for the crew, very wearing on passengers and potentially threatening to the vessel.

The Department of Transport regulations define rough weather as that causing the vessel to take green water onto decks, etc. This, of course, will vary with the type and size of vessel. The conditions required to generate this situation will depend on shelter and fetch, plus the effect of the tidal stream.

Seaworthiness is related to the size and design of the vessel – basically the bigger the better. Full-decked dayboats are preferable to open craft. Round-hulled MFV-type boats are better than sleeker, faster craft.

Simply stated, in heavy weather there is little comfort on a hard boat. The best position is one-third of the way from the stern of the vessel at the waterline, in the centre of the vessel.

On deck there is a danger of being thrown overboard or onto sharp projections; inside the vessel the dangers are being thrown around, being hit by flying objects, and suffering burns and scalds in the galley. Minor but unpleasant injuries often occur while recovering divers and tenders and when filling cylinders.

Stability

The factors affecting stability – hull shape, superstructure, centres of buoyancy and gravity, loading, etc. – are discussed on p. 66.

Figure 183

Divers returning to the parent vessel

Figure 184

A charter vessel in moderately heavy seas

Emergencies on Hard Boats

There is *no* set procedure for every emergency at sea. Some situations may well have no solution. The danger of panic cannot be overstressed. Virtually all situations will be improved by a methodical application of common sense and a sound knowledge of damage-limitation procedures. Additionally, some emergencies may be somewhat lessened by having a crew of divers.

Mayday and 'Pan Pan' calls are available if required, but they should only be made if they are totally necessary. Others may need the emergency services more acutely (see p. 98). Medical emergencies such as acute illness or an accident (such as a broken limb) require immediate action from the skipper. He should radio the coastguard and then make as much speed as possible in the appropriate direction. The coastguard will arrange for helicopter evacuation if necessary.

If a diver suffers a barotrauma, the correct boating procedure is to radio the coastguard, again making as much speed as possible in the appropriate direction. In the event of helicopter evacuation the helicopter will keep very low over the water and may well go round the coast. Evacuation under pressure (if and when available) will be beneficial to the victim and may bring better, though more distant, chambers into range.

A person falling overboard is a very serious crisis as he or she is lost from sight very rapidly even in moderate conditions. The recognized procedure is to shout 'Man overboard to port/starboard' and a crewmember should point continuously to the position of the victim. Meanwhile the helmsman should immediately slam the helm hard over towards the side from which the person fell and the engine should be stopped. A lifebuoy should be thrown to the victim if possible. If some distance has been travelled after the person was lost, carry out a Williamson turn: with the helm hard over the vessel is turned approximately 60° from her original heading; with no pause, the helm is swung hard over in the opposite direction until the vessel is on the reciprocal of her original course. The victim should be dead ahead. If the victim is not sighted, then a search pattern must be adopted.

Engine and/or rudder failure can be most serious, particularly in heavy weather. Ascertain the problem and try to correct it. Meanwhile use a sea anchor to reduce downwind drift. It may become necessary to make a distress call if the problem is serious.

When a tow is required it is prudent to remember the law regarding salvage. Only accept a tow if you must, as the person giving the tow is entitled to a substantial salvage claim, though on the basis of 'no cure – no pay'. A heaving line will be used to make initial contact and this will be used to draw the warp across. Use your warp for the tow and use a tyre or heavy weight in the middle of the tow as a buffer spring. A very firm securing point must be used for the warp, possibly by linking several points on the boat. Adjust the length of the warp to permit both vessels to sit in wave troughs.

Figure 185

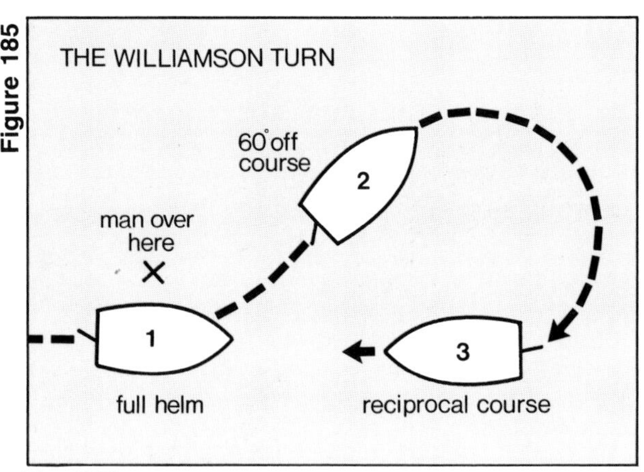

The Williamson turn

Running aground in shallow water can be very serious on an ebbing tide, though somewhat less serious on a rising tide. Attempt to get free by going astern, or by laying out a stern anchor with the tender and attempting to winch off, and/or by lightening the vessel, or by accepting a tow from another vessel. A combination of all four may be needed. A boat with a deep keel can be heeled over with movable ballast to reduce its draught. If the vessel is inevitably going to dry out on a falling tide, make the vessel heel towards the shallower side, as this will facilitate subsequent refloating.

Figure 186

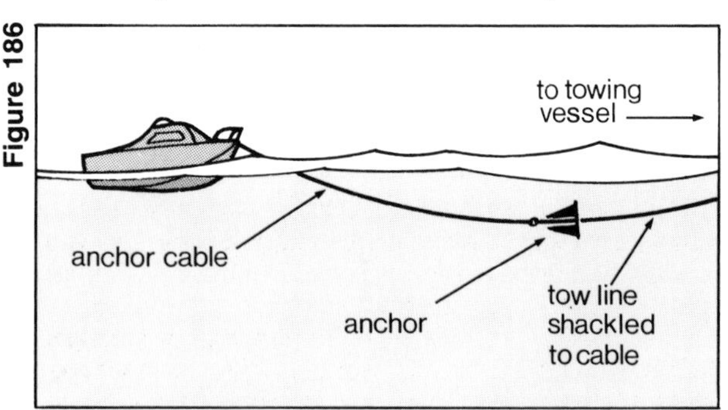

A weighted tow line

Going aground on a lee shore is most serious. Lay out the anchor with the longest warp available and attempt to winch off. Plan for rising water and an onshore wind. In some circumstances there may be no alternative but to abandon the vessel.

There is an ever present risk of explosion aboard boats, especially from gas cookers and petrol for outboards. Take great care, therefore, to operate such equipment safely. It is quite normal to have sniffer systems installed in the bilges and other enclosed areas.

Short of a vessel sinking, a serious fire on board is perhaps the most dangerous situation that can occur. Consequently, any fire, however small, should be

Figure 187

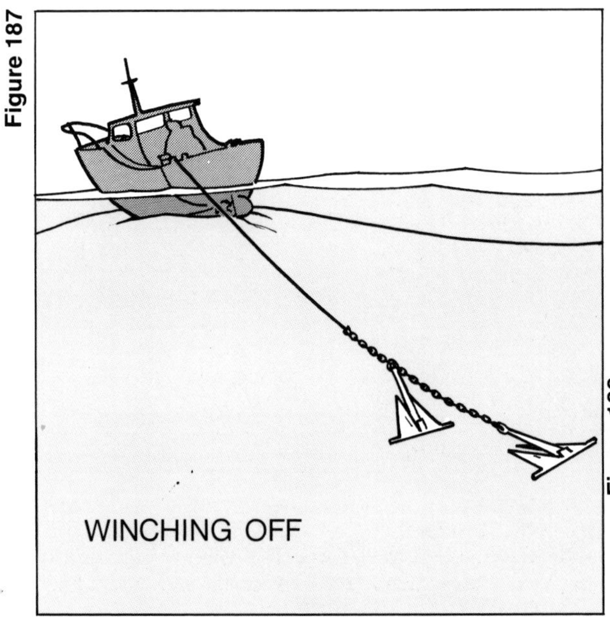

Figure 187
Anchors have been laid by the tender in deeper water and the grounded vessel attempts to pull off with its winch

Figure 188
A bad hole may be filled with a through-hull patch

Figure 188

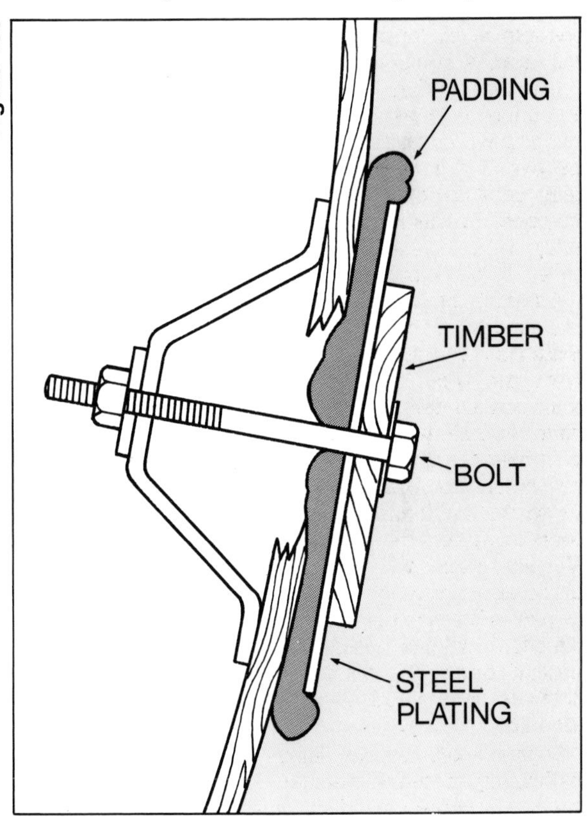

extinguished as fast as possible by using fire blankets and/or extinguishers. Many vessels have automatic firefighting systems installed, especially in the engine room. In the event of a serious fire it may well be necessary to abandon the vessel. Remember that it may be possible to rejoin the vessel later from the liferaft if the fire burns itself out.

The danger of capsize is usually only a significant risk in smaller vessels. Stay with the capsized vessel, as you will be found more easily by rescue craft. Only swim for the shore if it is very close.

In crowded waters there is always a risk of collision. Many collisions are not too serious, but it is possible, though unlikely, for a small vessel to be damaged and sunk. In this event swim away from the propellers of the colliding vessel if you are thrown into the water, then swim back to cling to floating debris. You may be seen and picked up by the colliding vessel, but sometimes large vessels do not even know that a collision has occurred. Should you find your flares container floating in the water or if you can locate it, then you can fire the flares to attract attention.

If the vessel's hull is badly holed in a collision it is important to act swiftly. For example, a 15-cm-square hole less than a metre below the waterline will admit about 2500 litres of water per minute. Stem the water flow with collision mats, through-hull patches, wooden plugs, rags and caulking, etc., as fast as possible. Meanwhile pump out the bilges by every means available. A water-cooled engine can be used as an auxilary bilge pump by connecting the water inlet to the bilges (fit a filter over the intake). The seacock on the normal water intake *must* be shut.

If a vessel is sinking there is no choice but to abandon ship. But remember that many swamped vessels have continued to float for days and they are much easier to locate than a liferaft, so only abandon ship when absolutely necessary. If abandoning ship becomes inevitable, transfer as much emergency food, water and equipment to the liferafts as possible. Before leaving the vessel send Mayday calls giving the sinking condition and the position.

Distress signals and the rescue services are covered on pp. 100–102.

Working with Divers

The comments on these pages may appear to concentrate on the negative aspects of operating under difficult conditions. It is completely wrong to suppose that this is the norm for the operations described herein. However, it is in such conditions that equipment, plans and people's nerves are stretched, and it is then that flaws become apparent. Consequently these areas are explored below.

Stowage of Equipment

Equipment can be stored in bins lashed to the outside of the deckhouse or along the bulwarks of the vessel. The bins should have drainage holes in the bottom.

Figure 189

Equipment stowage on a charter vessel

Lockers under the deck seating can also be used to advantage. If dive bags are used they should be well lashed down to prevent loss. Cylinders must either be stored in specially designed racks or firmly lashed to the vessel. Suits can be hung in a drying locker or spread over lines between the rigging. Be careful to stow suits before heavy weather or before leaving the vessel for a trip ashore. There should be stowage in the deckhouse for cameras, binoculars and identification books. Seaboots and oilskins can usually be stowed by the deckhouse door. If a sensible system is not worked out in advance, a state of chaos rapidly develops.

Diving Ladders and Platforms

The ideal arrangement is for divers to enter the water directly from the hard boat. In this way they will reach their site in a much happier physical condition even if the sea is rough. Direct entry also speeds up a two-wave dive by as much as 60–90 minutes.

Figure 190

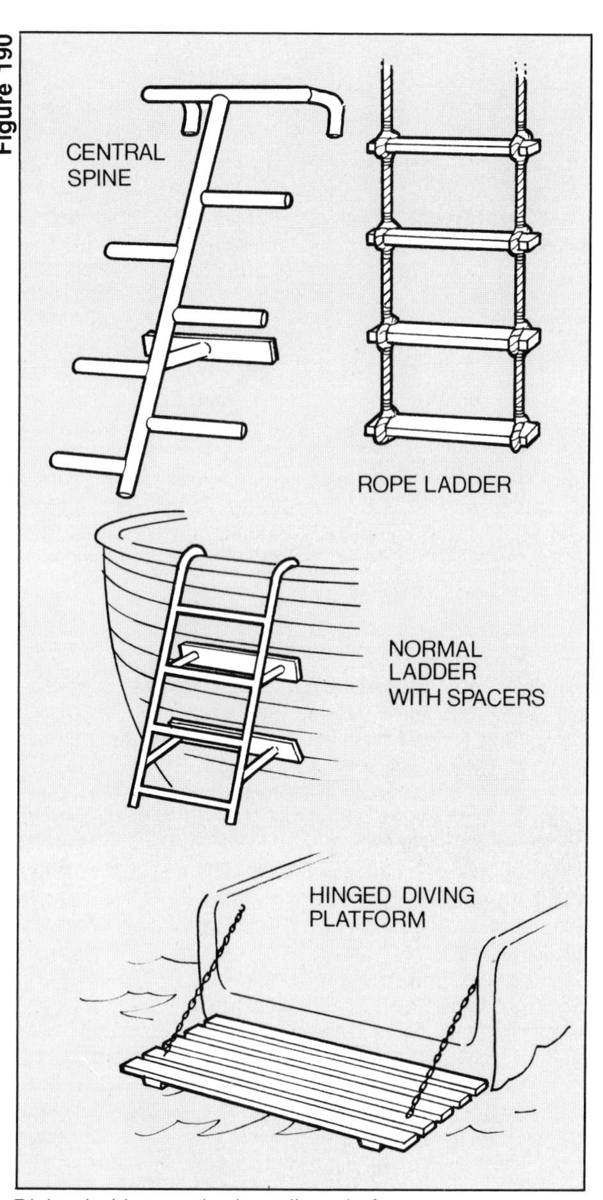

Diving ladders and a boarding platform

To facilitate the divers' entry into the water there should be either a gap or a removable section in the gunwale.

For the return a specially constructed diving ladder is virtually essential, especially on bigger craft. The simplest, consisting of wooden steps linked with chain or rope, is not really suitable, but if no other type is available it is better than nothing. A normal ladder (which must be offset from the side of the vessel with spacers) is preferable. The ideal type has a central spine with rungs projecting on each side. If this is offset from the vessel's side, a diver can climb it while still wearing his fins and all his equipment. All diving ladders should extend for at least 1 metre underwater to enable divers to get a good footing.

A hinged diving platform fitted to the stern of the vessel is convenient in calm conditions, but in rough seas it is virtually useless because of the pitching of the vessel.

The skipper should always bear in mind that the divers can be very tired after a dive, and in such circumstances a sensible diving ladder is a welcome aid.

Working with Tenders

An inflatable makes an ideal tender when working with a hard boat. Its seaworthiness, buoyancy, 'bounceability' and general robustness are welcome features when operating in heavy sea conditions. It should carry the usual safety equipment. The temptation to dispense with safety equipment because of the proximity of the parent craft should be avoided.

The tender should be launched, loaded and recovered in the lee of the parent vessel. Launching and recovery are usually effected by means of a boom and winch; a hydraulic crane is the ideal. Direct manhandling over the side is straightforward enough in calm conditions if you have several helpers, but in heavy weather it can be very difficult indeed. Launching from davits is the simplest operation and the tender can be stored in davits on the deckhouse roof or on deck.

The parent craft should keep fairly close to the diving party in order to reduce commuting distance. This saves time and tempers, facilitates communications and is safer in any event. The skipper and the diving leader should guard against having to cover widely separated groups, either in boats or in the water.

In heavy seas the skipper should allow for considerable difficulties in transferring equipment on the return of the diving group. It may be necessary to tie lines onto heavy items so that they can be recovered if accidentally dropped overboard.

Figure 191

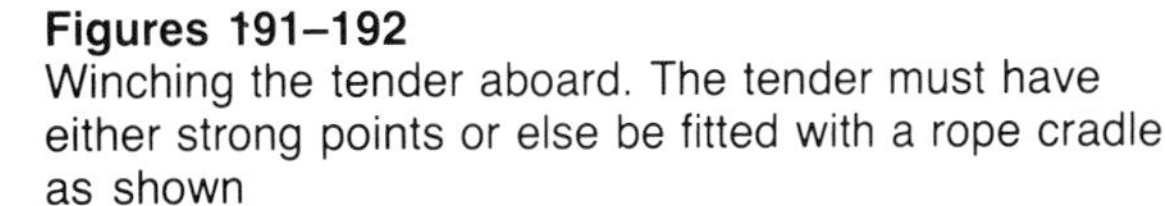

Figures 191–192
Winching the tender aboard. The tender must have either strong points or else be fitted with a rope cradle as shown

Figure 192

Diving from Hard Boats

Operating in Restricted Diving Waters

From the point of view of a boat skipper, divers always seem to want to dive in awkward places. Of course, this is because they are normally interested either in relatively shallow areas close to shore or in wreck sites. Naturally, wrecks frequently occur in restricted waters, near shorelines, on lee shores, near rocks or shoals, or in areas with strong tides. Divers may also want to search shallow wrecks which come uncomfortably close to the surface for the skipper.

Any person who wishes to operate as a charter-boat skipper plying for hire to divers will have to reconcile himself to divers' requirements and attitudes.

Covering Divers

The skipper must liaise closely with the diving leader. Jointly they will need to evolve a plan for the day and then follow it. However, it is important to be sufficiently flexible to meet changing circumstances.

It is quite difficult for divers to kit up if a boat is pitching heavily. To avoid this the skipper should briefly choose a heading which will reduce the pitching. Alternatively he may seek nearby shelter before reaching the chosen site.

Figure 193

Direct entry from the deck of a charter vessel

Entering the Water Direct from the Parent Vessel

Direct entry is to be preferred to having to transfer to an inflatable to reach the dive site. The procedure is:

1. The cover party launches the inflatable, checks it over and starts the engine.
2. The parent vessel proceeds as close to the site as possible.
3. The divers are fully kitted and ready for entry.
4. The engine is put in neutral.
5. The divers exit through door in the gunwale or over gunwale in smart succession.
6. As soon as they hit the water the divers should quickly swim away from the parent vessel.

Entering the Water via an Inflatable

This procedure may have to be used when the site is in very shallow or extremely restricted water. The procedure is:

1. The divers may wear sets or not, depending on the state of the sea, but they do not usually wear fins.
2. The divers descend the ladder into the inflatable.
3. The inflatable proceeds to the dive site and the divers enter the water as usual.

Recovering Divers

It is imperative that the skipper understands very clearly that, compared to the strength of vessels, waves and tidal streams, divers are very weak when in the water. Usually pick-up is by means of a tender, though sometimes direct pick-up by the parent vessel is employed, especially with smaller day boats.

Divers are almost totally at the mercy of wind and tide. They often cannot catch a boat being blown by a relatively gentle wind. They cannot make much headway against even quite weak tidal streams nor reach a boat with any way on at all. Also they find being buffeted by substantial waves most uncomfortable. Consequently when the divers reach the surface in such conditions they need to be picked up quickly. As soon as they are seen on the surface the boat should signal with its whistle or the 'OK' signal.

Recovery by Parent Vessel

This method can only be employed in fairly calm seas. In a very strong wind there is the danger that the boat will be blown over the diver in the water. People should probably not dive in such conditions.

The recovery procedure is:

1. Immediately the divers surface, approach them cautiously yet quickly.
2. Keep the divers in the lee of the vessel.
3. Put the engine in neutral.
4. Allow the divers to swim the last few metres (remember, they may not catch a vessel being blown by the wind).
5. Have help ready to receive gear being passed up the ladder.

6. As the divers climb up the ladder or onto the platform be prepared to assist them, particularly if they are tired or heavily laden. A tired diver should be allowed to climb the ladder at his own pace, provided this does not endanger the diver or the vessel. Too many grabbing hands can be a nuisance!

Recovery by Inflatable

This is normal procedure in most conditions. It also allows the divers to be covered more effectively during the dive. The procedure is:

1. Collect the divers quickly and efficiently after they surface.
2. The divers should remove sets and weightbelts.
3. The divers should be brought to the lee side of the parent vessel.
4. The hard boat should have its engine in neutral and way lost.
5. Take the tender to the boarding ladder.
6. Two divers, situated bow and aft in the tender, should hold grab lines on the parent vessel.
7. The divers in the inflatable smartly transfer themselves and their equipment up the diving ladder.

Figure 194

Recovering divers up the ladder. An assistant takes the fins and then allows the diver clear access

Figure 195

Transferring equipment from the inflatable. This may prove difficult in rolling conditions

Tactics of Wreck Location with Instruments

How we go about locating a position on a stretch of water depends on the surrounding environment. If the position is well out to sea and out of sight of land we have no option but to use some electronic means of position location. If we are off a plain, flat, featureless coastline we will again have problems, and electronic position fixing will once more be important. When operating off mountainous coasts it is usually quite easy to find good transits, although describing these so that another person can use them may be quite difficult. Estuaries usually provide easy conditions for the location of transits, as do small areas of fresh water.

When locating a wreck on the seabed it is best, if possible, to start by using transits; it may be necessary also to use electronic methods. This process can take months. Finally the wreck is usually snagged by dragging before sending down any divers.

Most of the methods described below can be used from small boats. However, it is often much more comfortable and much more successful to use a hard boat or a charter vessel.

Navigators and Radar

Radar can be used to assist position fixing over a wreck which is lying fairly close to recognizable land features or substantial buoys. The Navigator is an excellent system for position fixing and wreck location and is widely used by charter vessels and other larger craft.

Figure 196

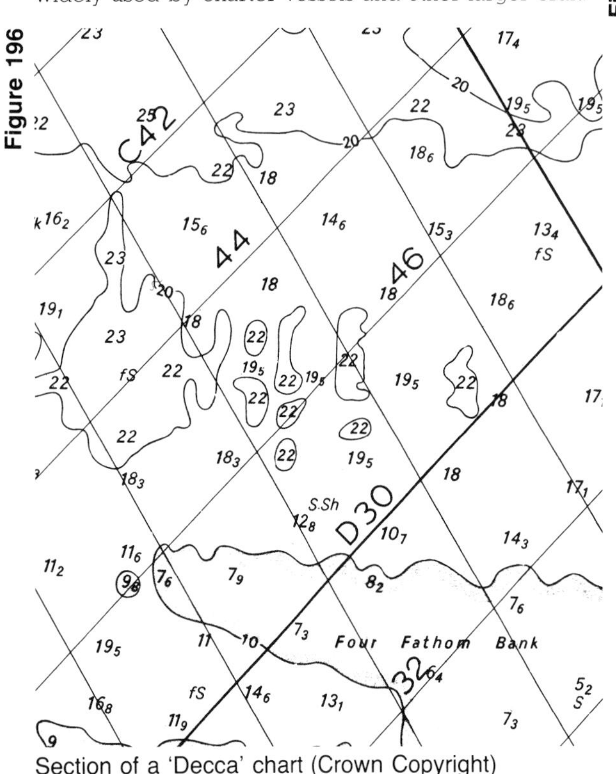

Section of a 'Decca' chart (Crown Copyright)

Echo Sounding

Current high-quality sounders give a very good readout of the seabed and even allow evaluation of the type of bottom. Wrecks and shoals of fish are well displayed. The best plan is to start from the datum position (from transits or other sightings) and then sweep slowly around this, or work at a fixed depth along the slope if the wreck is at a known depth on a steady slope. Once the wreck is located it is easy to gain a better idea of its layout by means of several echo sounder runs before actually diving. (With small boats it is necessary to go slowly to avoid false echoes from turbulence around the transducer.)

A point worth noting is that any sounder will display the nearest echo. On underwater cliffs a neon-type sounder will display multiple echoes, while the paper-readout type will display a continuation of the slope before the cliff, often with a second echo from the base of the cliff becoming confused with the angled echo. (With neon sounders fitted to small boats it is sometimes possible to get just one reading by angling the transducer away from the cliff until the edge of its beam coincides with the cliff base.)

Figure 197

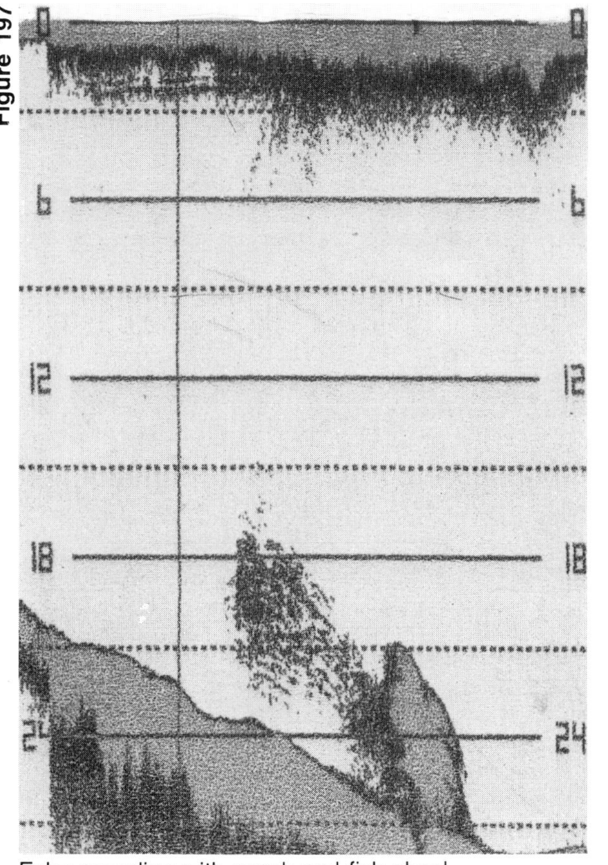

Echo sounding with wreck and fish shoal

Proton Magnetometer

The magnetometer must first be set up according to the manufacturer's instructions. This usually entails tuning it for a particular locality, then adjusting it for a null reading, before beginning the tow. Tow at low speeds or the sensing head will jump out of the water. By towing in an east–west direction maximum sensitivity is achieved because the earth's magnetic lines of force are being crossed at 90 degrees. On nearing the wreck a deflection of the needle is seen and/or an audible signal is emitted. Drop a buoy, then sweep around to maximize the signal.

The sensitivity of the equipment varies, but typically it will detect 1 ton of ferrous metal at 15 m, 10 tons at 30 m, 100 tons at 70 m, 1000 tons at 150 m and 10,000 tons at 300 m. Therefore in theory one can sweep lanes of about double these widths in shallow water. However, at the limits of detection the signals are very weak and can easily be missed or confused with signals from debris on the seabed, so it is probably best to halve these figures.

When using a proton magnetometer in conjunction with an echo sounder, the echo sounder will be sensing below the search vessel while the magnetometer will be sampling some distance behind it. At a distance from the wreck the magnetometer will, it is hoped, detect it and indicate in which direction you should aim your search. When you finally pass over the wreck the sounder will respond first and then the magnetometer will confirm the success.

A word of warning: the proton magnetometer, although extremely useful, is not a great wreck finder. For that you will need a side-scan sonar.

Figure 198

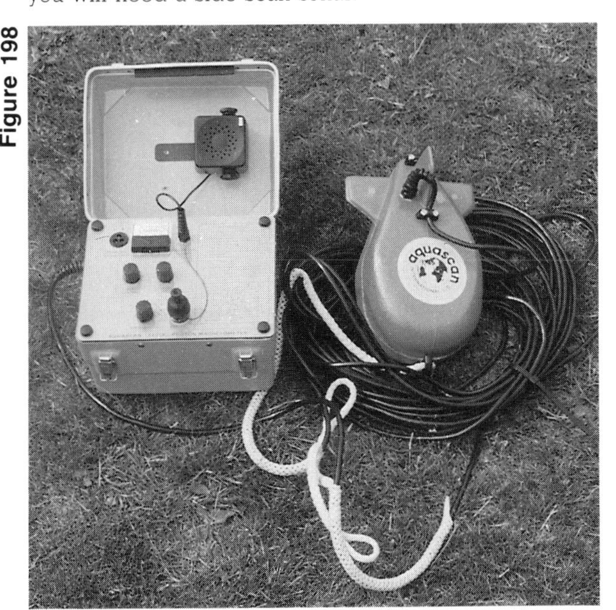

A proton magnetometer

Sonar

The use of sonar radically simplifies the location of wrecks. With a sweep all round the vessel of at least several hundred metres, seabed features can be observed and the distance and direction assessed. It is then a relatively simple matter to move to the wreck and detect it on both the sonar and the echo sounder.

Figure 199

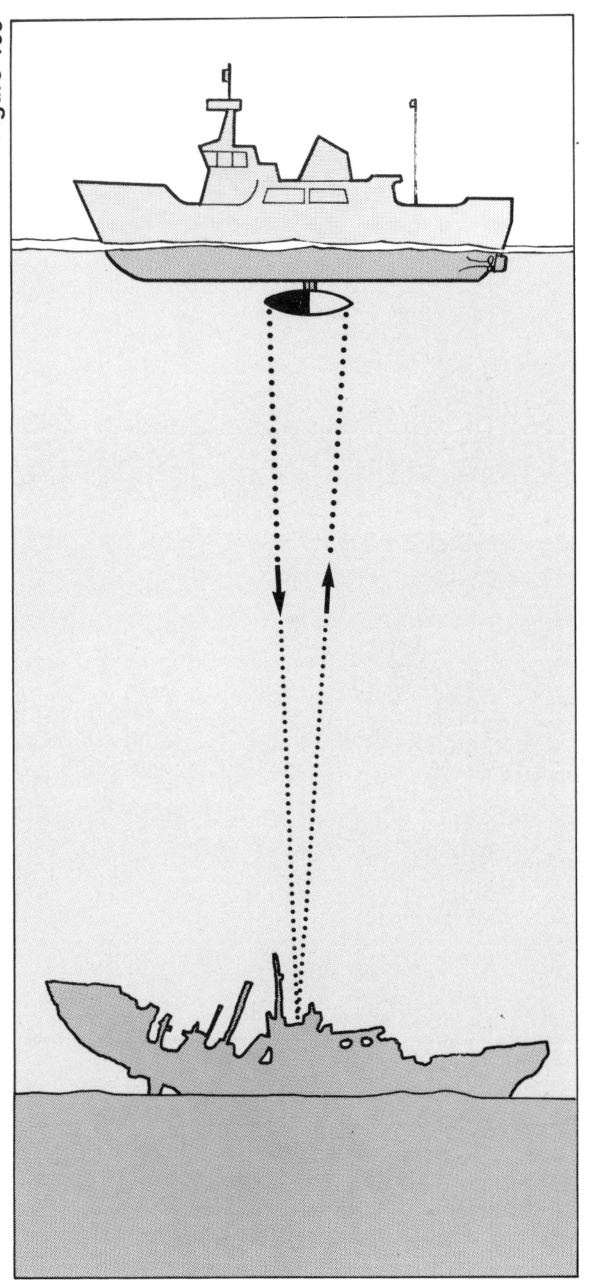

Sonar in use

Search Tactics

The tactics of searching are based on common sense. A reference buoy is dropped as a datum at the best estimate of the wreck's position. Then you can either sweep around this, or backwards and forwards in a grid pattern. Further buoys can be dropped to mark the areas that have been searched or to mark the initial magnetometer contacts. On full contact another buoy is immediately dropped before undertaking extra sweeps to delineate further detail.

When searching from a small boat, use the tide and wind to maximum benefit. Remember that it is unpleasant to motor into a heavy sea in a small boat, so arrange the direction of your runs accordingly. Electronic equipment is somewhat uneasy in a small boat and takes up a lot of space. Several buoys, sinkers and lines are also required. It is best, therefore, to have only the equipment and the surface search team in the boat for the search itself. On contact and after buoying the wreck, the main diving teams can be collected from the shore or the base vessel in order to carry out the dive.

Figure 200

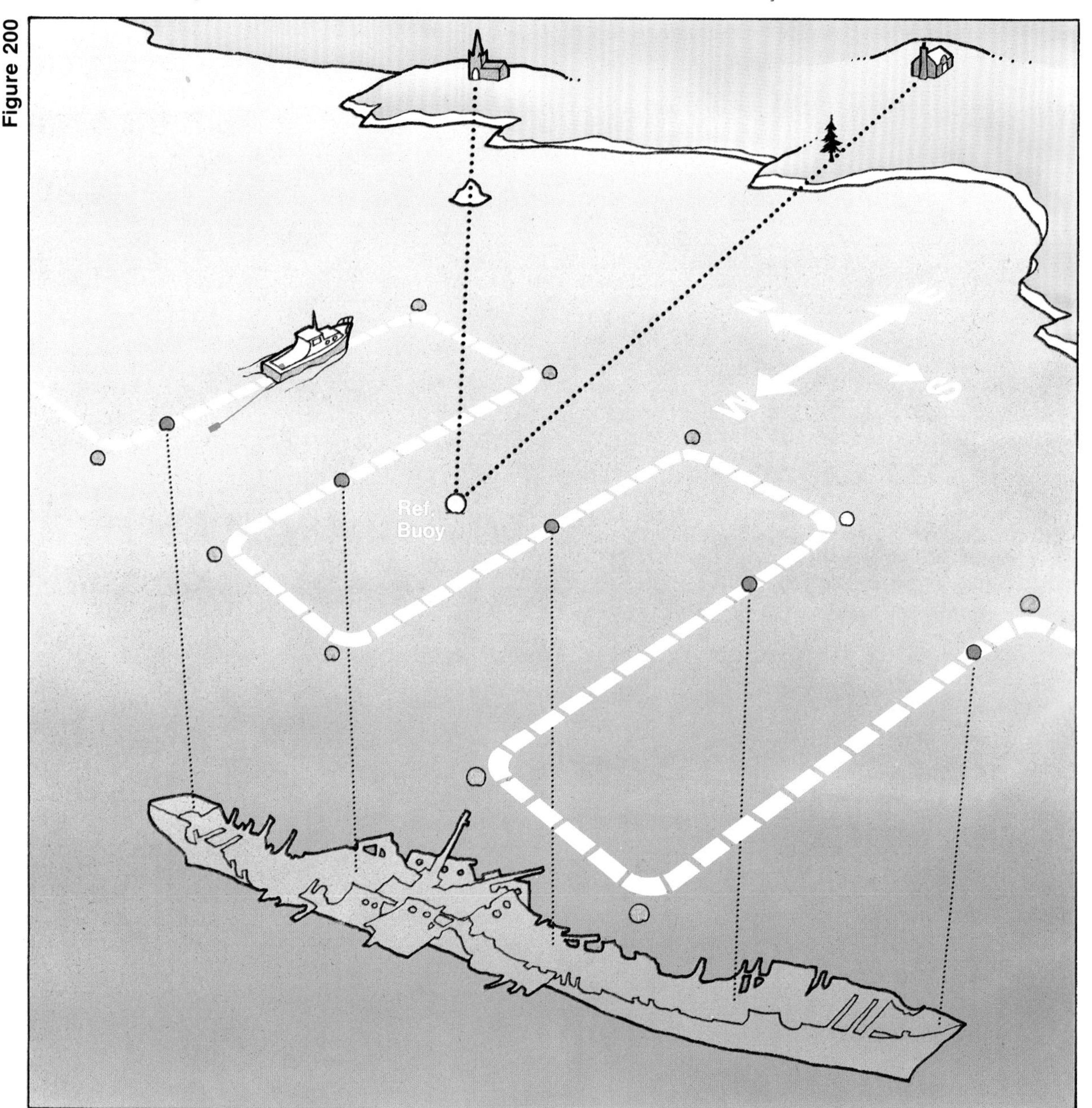

A systematic search using a proton magnetometer to scan a wreck

Grappling

With a large boat the navigation is usually sufficiently precise for a shotline to be dropped straight into the wreck.

When operating from small boats, search techniques and tactics are important if you are not to miss the wreck. A good grapnel, with flukes designed to engage and hold a contact, is much better than an anchor. Aim your snagging run across the broadside of the wreck if this position is known. If possible, drift down with the tide or wind onto the wreck. Pay out enough line to reach the bottom easily, but not so much that you anchor yourself. About one and a half times the depth will be about right. If you are using the engine to make the snagging run, then do so gently – otherwise the grapnel can fly over the wreck and miss it. When turning allow for the length of rope paid out and ensure that the line is running out straight behind the boat before starting your next run. On contact with the wreck, pull the grapnel in firmly, taking care not to drag it off the wreck, and quickly send down a pair of divers to secure the line to the wreck. Beware of snagging hawsers near the wreck rather than the wreck itself; the only certain way of confirming this is to send divers down.

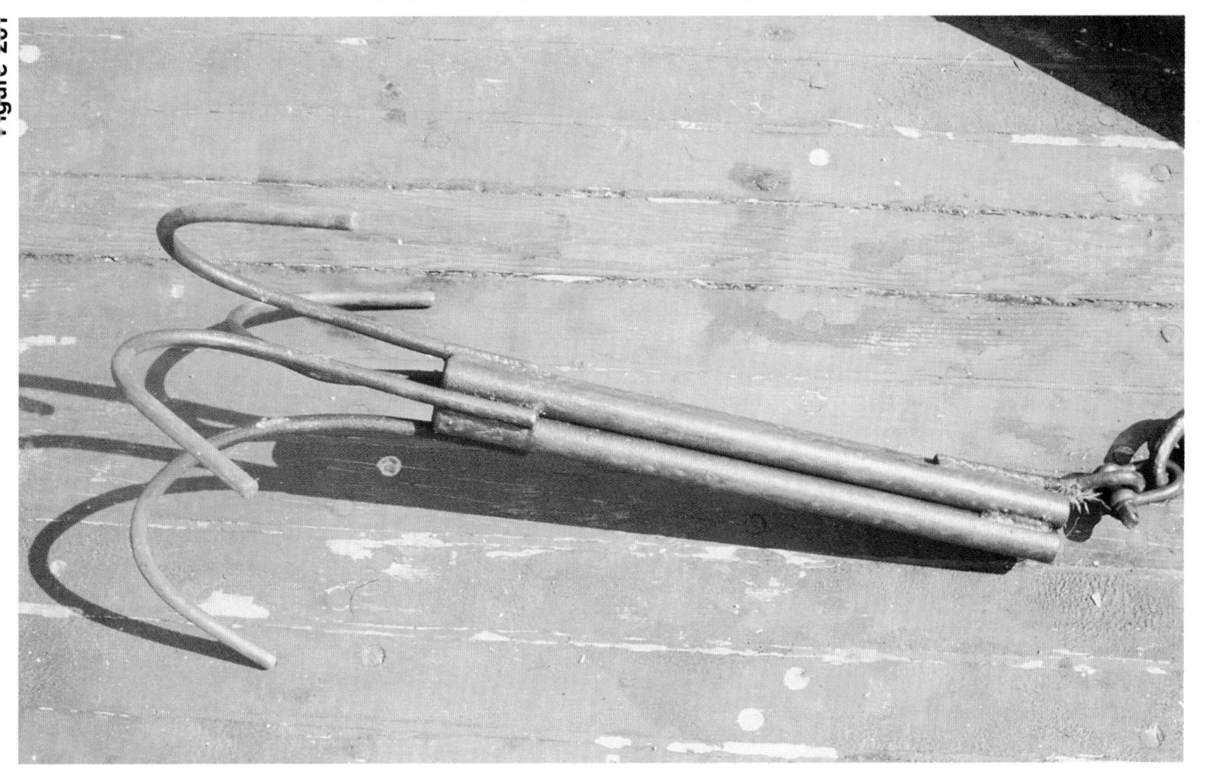

A grapnel

Special Methods

Unusual situations often lend themselves to special approaches. For instance, in an estuary it is possible to take photos from the land that will enable you to locate the wreck from the sea. To do this, the wreck's position must be accurately charted. Two well-separated identifiable points on the shore are chosen and the magnetic bearings to the marked wreck position are determined from the chart. At the first position a stake is knocked into the ground by the shore, a compass is placed on top and set so that it reads the appropriate bearing, and a photograph is taken showing both the pole and the far shore. The best lens to use is a 200-mm on a 35-mm camera. The procedure is repeated at the second shore station. The resulting photographs can then be used as transits from the boat, and should be sufficiently accurate to ensure that location by echo sounder and dragging is reasonably quick.

Visual Signs

A number of visual signs can indicate the presence of a wreck. A surface disturbance, such as very local waves or tidal stream diversion, is indicative of an obstruction of some sort. The vessel's fuel tanks may leak, leaving a telltale oil slick on the surface. There is sometimes a colour change in the water over a large wreck. Finally, visible shallow weed in otherwise deep water indicates a wreck or shoal.

Locating Wrecks Underwater

In essence this should involve divers descending a snag line to find the wreck. However, there are occasions when it becomes necessary to conduct underwater searches.

Radios and Communication

Types of Radio

There are several types of radio and radio telephone of interest to hard boat users. These are:

> **high frequency (HF)**
> **medium frequency (MF)**
> **very high frequency (VHF)**
> **low frequency (LF)**
> **citizens' band (CB)**

HF equipment operates in the range 4–25 MHz and can give worldwide coverage. HF sets are much more expensive than VHF sets and are not normally found in small vessels.

MF equipment operates in the range 1·6–4·2 MHz and has a range of 200 miles or more. The MF distress frequency is 2182 kHz (2·182 MHz) and there is a three-minute silent period every ninety minutes. Unfortunately MF sets are also much more expensive than VHF sets and are not often found in small vessels.

VHF equipment operates in the frequency range 156–174 MHz. The range is line of sight (or slightly better) between the two aerials, which limits it typically to 10–15 miles between vessels and somewhat further (typically 40–60 miles) between vessels and coastal stations. There can be exceptional local conditions which can increase or, more usually, decrease these ranges substantially. The power output is limited to 25 watts and this means that many stations, provided they are well separated, can use the same frequency. Channel 16 (156·80 MHz) is used for distress and safety, and for calling and answering before switching to another appropriate channel.

Simplex operation in radio telephony means that transmission is only possible in one direction at a time. This is the normal arrangement for diving boats. Conversely *duplex* operation allows a simultaneous two-way conversation, but this demands the use of two frequencies and usually two aerials.

Many modern VHF sets are fitted with a *dual-watch* facility. This is most useful as it allows two channels to be monitored by the set at the same time. Typically these will be channels 6 and 16. It is possible to have attachments that scan more channels simultaneously.

Portable radio sets (usually VHF but also MF and CB) are particularly useful in diving situations. They can be used to maintain contact between the parent vessel and the diving tender. The VHF sets are usually fitted with channels 6 and 16. They can be operated as extensions to the licence held by the hard boat.

The use of *Personal Locator Beacons* (PLBs) and *Emergency Position-Indicating Radio Beacons* (EPIRBs) is now quite widespread. EPIRBs use VHF of 121·5 MHz (monitored by civil aircraft but not over European coastal waters) or 243 MHz (monitored by military aircraft). They are, of course, invaluable in an emergency in ocean waters.

Frequency-modulated CB radio operates on two wave bands – normally 27·6–28 MHz (VHF) and occasionally 934 MHz (UHF). Power output is limited to 4 watts. Although some small boats are fitted with it, it is no substitute for VHF. It can be useful for social and domestic conversations. Channel 9 is used for emergency, but there is no official monitoring carried out. Channel 14 is the general calling channel.

Radio waves in the marine environment are usually specified in terms of frequency rather than wavelength. Many small vessels will be equipped to receive 'Long Waves' (150–400 kHz) and Medium Waves (550–1600 kHz). In particular it is useful to be able to receive the shipping forecast on long wave (at 1500 metres); this is better specified as 200 kHz in the LF band. The relationship between wavelength and frequency is:

> **Wavelength (m) × frequency (Hz) = 3×10^8 m/s^{-1}**

Marine communication via the International Maritime Satellite organization (INMARSAT) is now available and ship earth stations (SES) can communicate with one another or with coast earth stations (CES) almost anywhere in the world. A 1⅓ m (4-foot) parabolic antenna is required and obviously the cost is beyond small boat operators.

Regulations

A licence is required for any radio that is used at sea. There are four types:

1. A Ship Licence authorizes the installation of a sending and receiving station.
2. A Ship (Receiving Only) Licence allows the use of a receiving set for messages from coastal and other stations in addition to normal broadcast programmes.
3. A Ship (Emergency Only) Licence authorizes a sending and receiving station in emergency only.
4. A CB Radio Licence authorizes CB use for both sending and receiving.

Sets must comply with certain performance specifications. The Home Office, Licensing Branch, Radio Regulatory Division, Waterloo Bridge House, Waterloo Road, London SE1 8UA, will advise.

Other than for CB, authorized radio installations must be operated by a person holding an appropriate certificate of competence. For most divers this is the Certificate of Competence, Restricted VHF Only. Details can be had from the Examination Duty Officer, Maritime Radio Services, British Telecom International, 43 Bartholomew Close, London EC1A 7HP.

A person not qualified to use a radio installation can be subject to stiff penalties if the rules are contravened. In a genuine emergency, however, one would expect this to be overlooked.

The licensing authorities set out the general procedures and the rules of operation. Many of these are based on common sense when examined carefully.

They are contained in the HMSO publication *Handbook for Radio Operators*.

Operation of VHF Tranceiver Sets

For the benefit of newcomers to VHF radio telephony the following channels are the most used:

Channel 16: Mandatory; international distress; safety and calling
Channel 6: Mandatory; primary intership frequency
Channel 8: Alternative intership frequency
Channels 12 and 14: Port operations
Channels 2 and 7: Port operations; public correspondence
Channels 26, 27 and 28: Ship-to-shore; public correspondence

Synthesized multichannel VHF sets with fifty or more channels immediately available can now be bought quite cheaply.

The operation of a typical VHF set likely to be fitted in a small vessel is quite straightforward:

1. Switch on and set the volume control midway.
2. Select the appropriate channel.
3. Adjust the squelch control until the background noise is barely audible.
4. Only use low power if the other station is in sight.
5. Hold the microphone about 5 cm away from your mouth.
6. Press the switch on the microphone to transmit; speak normally.
7. Release the switch immediately after speaking and then await the reply.

The procedures for radio telephones are described below.

VHF Radio Procedure

The procedures laid down for the use of radio telephones are many and complex. These pages can only give a brief introduction. Appropriate reference books should be consulted if you plan to use VHF radio telephones other than unexpectedly or in other unusual circumstances.

Transmission Rules

The following are strictly forbidden:

1. Transmissions that have not been authorized by the skipper or other authorized VHF operator.
2. Operation of a radio telephone by unauthorized persons. Passengers and crew members may only make calls under supervision.
3. The transmission of false or deceptive distress, safety or identification signals.
4. Transmissions made without identification, i.e. without the vessel's name or call sign.
5. The use of Christian names or other unauthorized identification in lieu of the vessel's name or call sign.
6. Closing down a radio telephone before finishing all operations resulting from a distress call, urgency or safety signal.
7. Broadcasting (i.e. transmissions not expecting a reply) messages or programmes.
8. Making unnecessary transmissions or transmitting superfluous signals.
9. Transmission of profane, indecent or obscene language.
10. The use of frequencies or channels other than those covered by the vessel's licence.
11. The broadcasting of music.
12. The broadcasting of messages intended for shore stations other than a coast radio station.

Figure 202

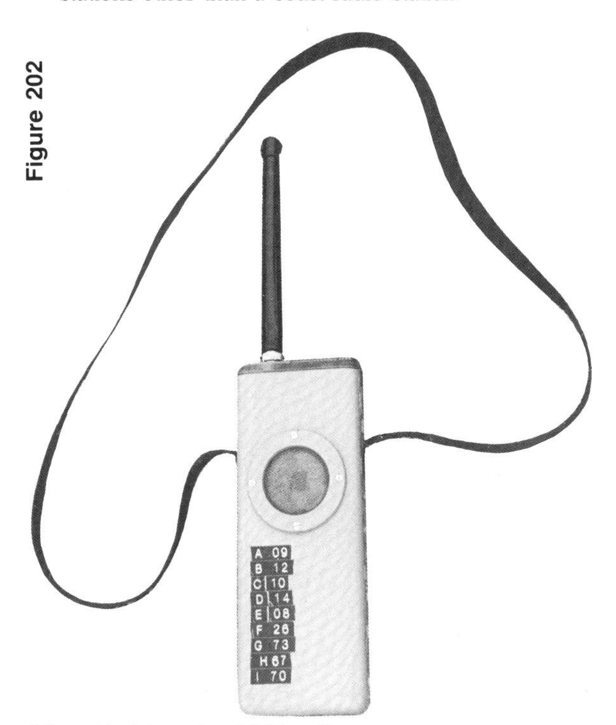

A hand-held marine VHF radio

Figure 203

The Phonetic Alphabet

The phonetic alphabet which is used with the English pronunciation is as follows:

Letter	Word	Pronunciation in English
A	Alfa	*AL* FAH
B	Bravo	*BRAH* VOH
C	Charlie	*CHAR* LEE or *SHAR* LEE
D	Delta	*DELL* TAH
E	Echo	*ECK* OH
F	Foxtrot	*FOKS* TROT
G	Golf	GOLF
H	Hotel	HOH *TELL*
I	India	*IN* DEE AH
J	Juliett	*JEW* LEE *ETT*
K	Kilo	*KEY* LOH
L	Lima	*LEE* MAH
M	Mike	*MIKE*
N	November	NO *VEM* BER
O	Oscar	*OSS* CAH
P	Papa	*PAH PAH*
Q	Quebec	*KEH BECK*
R	Romeo	*ROW* ME OH
S	Sierra	SEE *AIR* RAH
T	Tango	*TANG* GO
U	Uniform	*YOU* NEE FORM or *OO* NEE FORM
V	Victor	*VIK* TAH
W	Whisky	*WISS* KEY
X	X-ray	*ECKS* RAY
Y	Yankee	*YANG* KEY
Z	Zulu	*ZOO* LOO

(The syllables to be emphasized are shown in italics.)

The following pronunciation is used when transmitting numerals:

Numeral or Numeral Element	Pronunciation
0	*ZE-RO*
1	*WUN*
2	*TOO*
3	*TREE*
4	*FOW-ER*
5	*FIFE*
6	*SIX*
7	*SEV-EN*
8	*AIT*
9	*NINE-ER*
Decimal	*DAY-SE-MAL*
Thousand	*TOUSAND*

In radiotelephony all numbers are transmitted by pronouncing each digit separately, except that whole thousands are transmitted by pronouncing each digit in the number of thousands followed by the word 'thousand'. For example,

600 is spoken as 'Six zero zero'
1580 is spoken as 'One five eight zero'
12,000 is spoken as 'One two thousand'

Voice Technique

Pitch the voice slightly higher than normal for added clarity. Hold the microphone a few centimetres away from your mouth and speak at normal volume. Speak clearly, slowly and with appropriate pauses, and emphasize weak syllables in words that could be misconstrued. Use plain language. Use prowords and the phonetic alphabet whenever possible (see above).

Standard Marine Navigational Vocabulary

Repetition: It is worthwhile repeating important parts of the message.
Position: This is given in degrees, minutes and tenths of minutes, latitude first then longitude. If the position is given as a distance and a bearing, then the bearing shall be from true north and shall be that of the position from the mark.
Course: This is always expressed in degrees notation from true north.
Bearing: The bearing of a vessel or mark is expressed in degrees from true north. They may be given from either the mark or the vessel.
Relative bearing: This may well be expressed in degrees relative to the vessel's bow.
Distance: This is given in nautical miles (or cables), not kilometres.
Speed: Speed is given in knots through the water, unless the ground speed is specified.
Numbers: These are spoken as individual digits.
Geographical names: Use those on the chart or in the sailing direction.
Time: This should be expressed in twenty-four-hour notation.

Prowords

There are procedure words used by operators to minimize the number of words that need to be spoken in order to communicate the speaker's meaning.

All after: Used after 'say again' to request repetition of part of a message.
All before: Used after 'say again' to request repetition of part of a message.
Acknowledge: Asks a station if it has received and

understood a message.
Confirm: Asks for confirmation of understanding of a message.
Correct: Reply to a message repetition that has been preceded by 'read back for check' when it has been correctly repeated.
Correction: Cancels the last word or group when an error has been made during transmission.
In figures: The following numerals are to be written as figures.
In letters: The following numerals are to be written as letters.
I read back: Used before repeating back a message of doubtful accuracy.
I say again: Used before repeating a transmission or portion thereof.
I spell: The next word or group of letters will be spelt phonetically.
Out: The end of a transmission.
Over: An invitation to reply after a transmission (do not use the contradictory 'over and out').
Radio check: A request for the strength and clarity of a station's transmission.
Received: Acknowledges receipt of message.
Say again: Asks for a message or portion thereof to be repeated.
Station calling: Used when a station receives a call from a calling station of uncertain identification.
Text: Used to indicate that the next portion of the transmission is the text of a radiotelegram.
This is: Used to prefix the station's call sign when transmitting.
Wait: Asks a station to wait (usually the delay is specified).
Word after or *word before*: Used after 'say again' to identify misunderstood portion of message.
Wrong: Used in reply to an incorrectly repeated radiotelegram.

Normal Procedures

Call signs

Coast radio stations normally identify themselves by using their geographical name followed by the word 'radio'. Ship stations should identify themselves by the name of the ship. The international call sign assigned to the ship can also be used when two vessels of the same name exist.

Priorities of Radio-Telephone Calls

Internationally these are set down as

1. Distress
2. Urgency
3. Safety
4. Radio direction-finding
5. Aircraft navigation and movements
6. Shipping navigation and movements
7. Government radiotelegrams bearing prefix Etatprioritenations'
8. Government radiotelegrams bearing prefix 'Etatpriorite' or 'Etat'
9. Telecommunications service communications

Figure 204

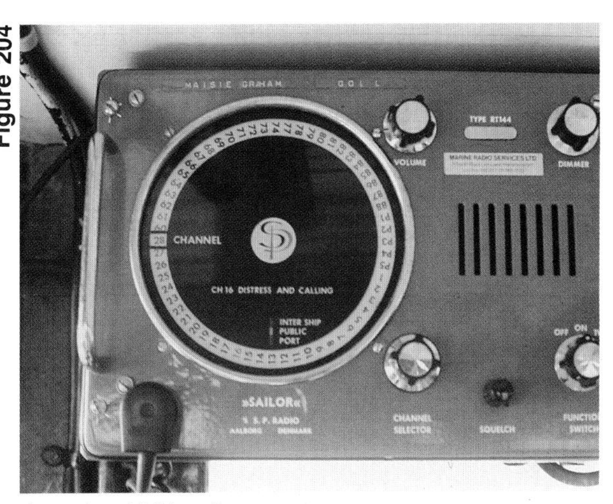

A marine VHF radio

Figure 205

A C.B. radio

Figure 206

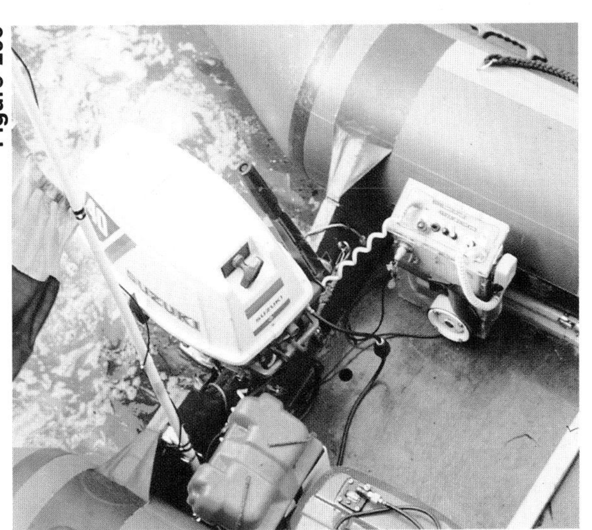

VHF radio mounted in an inflatable

10. All other, i.e. radio-telephone calls, radiotelegrams, etc.

Calling Another Vessel
On Channel 16 call the vessel by name, giving your own call sign, and offer an inter ship working frequency (in crowded waters it is best to avoid the busy Channel 6).

Calling the Coastguard
On Channel 16 call the coastguard by the name of the station followed by Coastguard, giving your own call sign. When they reply you should state the channels fitted to your set so they can offer an appropriate channel.

Calling Harbour Authorities
These authorities listen on dual-watch on both Channel 16 and their own allocated frequency as defined in the *Port Operations Service*. It is in order to call them on their own frequency, but you should identify the channel you are using to avoid ambiguity.

Garbled Calls
When a station receives a call without being certain it is intended for it, it *must not reply* until the call has been repeated and understood. If a call is received but the call sign of the calling station is garbled, it should be asked to 'say again' its message.

Unanswered Calls
Check that the controls on the radio are set correctly. You *must* wait a minimum three minutes before repeating a call, except when sending a distress call.

Link Call via UK Coast Radio Stations
You must first determine the calling and answering arrangements for the coast radio station from a nautical almanac or similar publication. Then call this station on Channel 16 before switching to their suggested channel. Book the call by stating the exchange or routing code and the telephone number. The call booking remains valid until it has been satisfied, refused by the person called or cancelled by the caller.

Contacting a Vessel at Sea
Telephone the appropriate coast radio station (or dial 100 and ask for Ships' Telephone Service) and ask for a call to the vessel by name and, if possible, its international call sign.

Distress and Related Procedures

Silent Periods
There are three-minute silent periods following every hour and a half on the MF distress frequency of 2182 kHz. There are also silent periods of three minutes following every half hour on 156·80 MHz (Channel 16) on VHF.

Distress
This consists of the word 'Mayday' spoken three times. It *must only* be used when the vessel, or another vessel with a disabled radio, is in serious and imminent danger and requires immediate assistance. It may be preceded by a warbling alarm signal. The procedure is:

1. Check that main battery switch is on.
2. Switch the set on and turn the power selector to high.
3. Tune to VHF Channel 16 (or MF 2182 kHZ).
4. If an alarm signal generator is fitted, operate it for at least thirty seconds.
5. Press the transmit button and say slowly and distinctly:
   (a) *Mayday Mayday Mayday.*
   (b) *This is* (vessel's name, spoken three times).
   (c) *Mayday* (vessel's name, spoken once).
   (d) *My position is* (latitude and longitude, or the true bearing and distance from a known point; repeat if possible).
   (e) Nature of the distress (sinking, fire, etc.).
   (f) Aid required.
   (g) Number of persons on board.
   (h) Any other important, helpful information (e.g. whether drifting, distress rockets fired, etc.).
   (i) *Over.*
6. Release transmit button and listen. In coastal waters there will usually be an immediate reply in the form:
   (a) *Mayday* (name of distressed station, spoken three times).
   (b) *This is* (name of acknowledging station, spoken three times).
   (c) *Received Mayday.*
7. If no acknowledgement is received, check the set and repeat the distress call.

A vessel hearing a distress message which is not acknowledged must try to pass on the message in the form:
   (a) *Mayday relay, Mayday relay, Mayday relay.*
   (b) *This is* (name of retransmitting vessel, spoken three times).
   (c) Followed by the intercepted message.

A distress call imposes general radio silence until the vessel concerned or some other authority cancels the distress.

The station controlling the distress may impose radio silence by saying 'Seelonce Mayday', followed by its identification, on the distress frequency. Radio silence may be relaxed by the controlling station with the word 'Pru-donce'. When the distress traffic has ceased the controlling station will authorize normal working with the words 'Seelonce feenee'.

Urgency
This consists of the words 'Pan pan' spoken three times. It indicates that the station has a very urgent message concerning the safety of a ship or person.

Safety
This consists of the words 'Securite' (pronounced 'say-cure-e-tay') spoken three times. It indicates that the station is about to transmit an important navigational or meteorological warning. Such messages usually originate from a coast station.

First-Aid Kits

First-aid kits must be carried aboard all craft, whatever their size.

The best first-aid kit in the world is virtually useless unless people have had training in its use. Consequently all intending offshore divers (and everyone else, for that matter) should attend a first-aid course.

First-aid reference books should also be available on board. One of the most useful is *First Aid* by the St John Ambulance Association.

For an inflatable, a small kit such as that used in a car is suitable; for example:

> 2 triangular bandages
> 2 large sterile dressings
> Rescue blanket or large (2 × 1 m) polythene bag
> Several safety pins
> Aspirin tablets (300 mg)
> Morphine syringes (15 mg)
> Instructions

For hard boats intended for day-long diving trips a more comprehensive kit is appropriate; for example:

> 4 triangular bandages
> 1 crêpe bandage (50 mm)
> 3 gauze bandages (50 mm)
> 1 roll zinc oxide plaster (25 mm)
> Large pack of adhesive dressings
> 6 large, 6 medium, 6 small wound dressings BPC
> Sterile cotton wool
> Scissors and forceps (stainless steel)
> 10 assorted safety pins
> 2 rescue blankets or large (2 × 1 m) polythene bags
> Inflatable splints kit
> Antiseptic solution (Savlon)
> Ultraviolet filter cream (Uvistat)
> Anti-seasickness tablets (e.g. Stugeron)
> Aspirin tablets (300 mg)
> Paracetamol tablets (500 mg) (for pain or fever)
> Codeine tablets (30 mg) (for more serious pain)
> Fortral (pentazocine) tablets (25 mg) (for severe pain)
> Morphine syringes (15 mg) (for very severe pain)
> Instructions
> Oxygen

For vessels carrying up to six people away from facilities for several days, a much more comprehensive outfit should be available; for example:

> 10 triangular bandages
> 10 crêpe bandages (75 mm)
> 10 gauze bandages (50 mm)
> 3 rolls of zinc oxide plaster (25 mm)
> 6 boxes of Elastoplast (75 mm)
> Several large packs of adhesive dressings
> 20 large, 20 medium, 20 small wound dressings BPC
> 20 sterile non-adhesive dressings (Melolin)
> 20 packs of paraffin gauze sterile dressings
> 20 packs of Steristrips
> Sterile cotton wool
> Scissors and forceps (stainless steel)
> 100 safety pins
> 5 rescue blankets or large (2 × 1 m) polythene bags
> 3 inflatable splints kits
> Thermometer
> Antiseptic solution (Savlon)
> Ultraviolet filter cream (Uvistat)
> Cicatrin antibiotic powder
> Tinaderm powder (for athlete's foot)
> Calamine lotion (for bites, stings and sunburn)
> Anti-seasickness tablets (Stugeron is the best; then any of Dramamine, Marzine, Kwells, Avomine, etc.)
> Aspirin tablets (300 mg)
> Paracetamol tablets (500 mg) (for pain and fever)
> Codeine tablets (30 mg) (for more serious pain)
> Fortral (pentazocine) tablets (25 mg) (for severe pain)
> Morphine syringes (15 mg) (for very severe pain)
> Clove oil (for toothache)
> Actifed tablets (nasal decongestant)
> Nasal spray (nasal decongestant)
> Aludrox (for indigestion)
> Lomotil tablets (for diarrhoea)
> Senokot tablets (for constipation)
> Tetracycline capsules (250 mg) (antibiotic)
> Stenetil suppositories (for severe seasickness)
> Chloramphenicol eye ointment (antibiotic)
> Instructions
> Oxygen

Finally, for expeditions lasting several weeks a full marine first-aid kit is required. The medical stores and medicines listed (a list twelve pages long) in the *Ship Captain's Medical Guide* (HMSO) may well be appropriate. This book, though a little dated, still gives a vast amount of excellent advice about almost any marine medical eventuality.
amount of excellent advice about almost any marine medical eventuality. It is intended for use on ships where no doctor is carried.

Of course, on vessels carrying divers it is highly desirable that the means of treating diving ailments are available. Medical oxygen and equipment for administering it are recommended by the BSAC. Attendance at a BSAC oxygen administration course is a sensible precaution for all divers and especially the leaders of diving expeditions.

The use of portable one-man recompression chambers is somewhat controversial. However, transporting a pressure-damaged diver under pressure in such a chamber to a full recompression facility is welcomed by almost all authorities. Major diving charter vessels intended for remote-area operation might well consider such a piece of equipment and its ancillaries. Training in its use would also be required.

Distress at Sea

Distress at Sea

The tremendous increase over the last few years in the use of small boats by divers has inevitably led to an increase in the number of incidents in which rescue at sea has been necessary. This section is designed to give practical tips in order to help to avoid incidents and also to set out some guidelines on what to do if a serious incident occurs.

In order to do this it is necessary to outline the type of diving being carried out and the location. In the British Isles the majority of sea diving is carried out from small boats, usually inflatables or semi-rigid inflatables, which are launched from harbours and beaches. The increasing number of charter vessels around the British Isles has widened the opportunity for diving in remote places and many thousands of dives are carried out from such vessels. In some parts of the world all diving is carried out from charter vessels and dive barges.

It is important to distinguish between the types of boat since a large vessel is more likely to carry rescue aids and equipment than is a smaller boat. These might include accurate navigational equipment, such as 'Decca' or satellite position-fixing equipment and liferafts capable of carrying everyone on board. Small boats will probably carry flares and some will be equipped with marine-band VHF radios, which obviously helps their aid-calling capability. When distress occurs at sea, how well equipped the boat is and how well the crew react will affect just how serious the situation may become.

Most diving takes place around the coastal areas of the world; it is rare for diving parties to operate outside areas where there is good emergency back-up, such as the coastguard services. Diving in places where such help is not available requires extra equipment, expertise and personnel.

Distress at sea can be divided into two categories: incidents involving accident, illness or injury to people and incidents involving equipment only, particularly boats and engines. Some incidents involve both. In the former, one usually has to evacuate the casualty or call for help using a radio.

Perhaps the most common form of distress at sea involving divers is decompression sickness in its many forms. You may be faced with a diver suffering from an air embolism who collapses in the boat with extreme breathing difficulties or more minor symptoms. The reaction to these incidents will obviously be different. In the latter case the diver may be safely taken back to base, with a close watch being kept for developing symptoms and help sought once there.

In the former case the diver will require fast, efficient transportation to a recompression chamber. Possibly, with a serious case, the very worst thing that you can do is to attempt to transport the casualty back to shore in a small boat on a bumpy sea. If he has severe problems with bubbles in his circulation, then to shake him up on a boat journey is the last thing needed. Around the British Isles there are excellent emergency services coordinated by HM Coastguard. The coastguard service can organize helicopter transfer, access to a recompression chamber, ambulance, lifeboat, police escort, etc., and are trained to deal with all manner of emergencies at sea.

If you find that a diver is suffering from life-threatening symptoms, it is imperative that help is called, probably via a VHF radio. The coastguard can be contacted on Channel 16 on which they keep a twenty-four-hour watch. Channel 16 is used for initial calling and for emergency traffic. If you do not have a radio there may be another boat in the area which may well possess one. Fishing boats usually have VHF and their skippers will radio for help on your behalf. It costs many thousands of pounds to initiate a rescue, especially when a helicopter is used, so it is important that you are convinced of the seriousness of the incident before you press the 'red button'. If someone is radioing on your behalf, make sure that he says exactly what you want him to say. If you are faced with a situation in which loss of life is a likely possibility, a Mayday call is justifiable. All other traffic on Channel 16 will cease and any vessel within easy reach of your position is required by international maritime law to come to your aid. Mayday calls are normally broadcast only when a vessel is in danger of sinking and are not normally used in a situation in which individuals have suffered a diving accident.

Assuming that contact is made with the coastguard, it is important that the position of the boat is stated as accurately as can be established; once having given your position, you must maintain it. The coastguard will direct lifeboat or helicopter, etc., to the stated position and the last thing he wants is for you to move. If the rescue is by helicopter, the casualty will probably be winched up from your boat. If this is the case, ensure that the boat is clear of obstacles and that any radio antenna or diving flag has been lowered – helicopter winchmen do not wish to be impaled.

In some circumstances it may be advisable to put the casualty back into the water so that he may more easily be winched to safety. In a decompression incident it is wise to send the casualty's buddy in the helicopter as he or she may develop delayed symptoms. Helicopter crews are aware of the nature of decompression sickness and will evacuate the casualty by low-level flight to reduce further problems.

Distress at sea involving an accident to the boat poses its own set of problems for those who are in charge of the dive party. Probably the most common form of distress involves the breakdown of an outboard motor. Apart from correcting simple faults, there is a limit to what can be achieved in a small boat at sea. A situation in which the outboard motor fails while the boat is going to, or returning from, the dive site requires decisions based on common sense. If the boat is drifting away from land and it is not too deep for anchoring, then this is a good

Figure 207

An RAF rescue helicopter showing the winch just above the door with the winchman in position

course of action. In the past many boats have drifted away from positions in sight of their base while the people aboard tried to start the motor. Anchoring will also point the bows into any seas that are running. If it is too deep for anchoring the use of a sea anchor should be considered.

Flares

Diving boats operating close to the shore (within 3 miles) should be equipped with two hand-held orange flares for daytime and two red flares for use at night. When operating up to 7 miles offshore, four red parachute rocket flares or two red hand flares should be added to the safety box. The shelf life of flares is usually three years so when buying them you should check the expiry dates, which should be clearly marked.

A word of warning at this point. Many divers carry a personal flare which is designed for immersion in water. On occasions these have been used as signal flares by divers, who have deployed them in a non-emergency situation just to signal the boat to come and fetch them. Any flare, regardless of colour, will be taken to mean distress by the coastguard who will initiate the emergency services.

Figure 208 shows two flares which should be found in the emergency box of any diving boat. It is important that all crew members know how to fire the flares. Figures 209 and 210 show the firing of a red parachute and smoke flare. These are extremely powerful and must always be pointed, with an outstretched arm, downwind as well away from the boat and those in it as possible.

Flares must always be carried in a stout waterproof container. A suitable container will have an o-ring seal to the lid. It is a good idea to have two such containers on board, one with flares and other items required only in an emergency; the other, containing personal effects, spectacles, keys, cameras, etc., might be opened several times during a normal dive. This method ensures that the flares do not become wet accidentally.

Out-of-date flares should never be fired at sea or on land. They deteriorate with age and can be unpredictable. Do not use them as fireworks. To dispose of them, you should *weight* them, remove their protective packing and then *dump them in deep water well away from land.* Misfired flares should be handled as little as possible and disposed of immediately.

The firing of flares needs to be considered carefully. There is no point in firing flares if there is no one around to see them. Divers in the past have had a sudden firework display and wished they had kept some for later. If the outboard motor cannot be restarted after the usual faultfinding checks (see pp. 142–143), it is obvious that outside help is necessary. Assuming you are not diving with another boat (it is recommended that the buddy system be applied to boats), you should fire flares to attract any passing vessel or observers on land. Never fire all your flares at once unless you are sure you will be seen. Waving any object is also a sign of distress at sea and this can be a useful method of attracting attention.

Emergency Services

The use of radio in an emergency situation has been mentioned above. In a non-life-threatening situation the coastguard can be contacted on Channel 16. In a non-emergency situation he will usually refer you to Channel 67, which is the small-boat safety channel. Information about local weather and safety information is available via this channel. It is sometimes possible to contact the coastguard direct on Channel 67, but a twenty-four-hour watch is not kept on it and you cannot rely on making contact. Coastal radio stations also have safety and weather information. If a boat has a radio, at least one person aboard should have been trained in its use and have passed the appropriate practical exam on radio procedure. If, for any reason, you get no response using the normal call-sign procedure, it is possible to relay a 'Pan Pan' message. This is one category down from a Mayday signal and means that although life is not being threatened there is a serious enough situation to require immediate assistance. For example, if you were adrift without power and daylight was failing, a 'Pan Pan' message could be the answer in some circumstances.

Once you have established contact with the coastguard, it is important that he is told your position (as accurately as you can estimate it), the number of people involved, the colour, size and type of boat and the exact predicament. Always follow his advice unless something else develops which he is not aware of.

If you do not have a radio, one of your safety procedures should be to phone the coastguard before leaving for the dive, with the promise to confirm your safe return. The alternative is to have a reliable shore party ready to raise the alarm once *you are well overdue*. In this situation it is essential to remain as close as possible to the place where you planned to dive, in order to reduce the possible search area, provided your troubles began in that area.

In most cases it will be a lifeboat or helicopter which finds you. A lifeboat will usually tow your vessel back to port but a helicopter picks up personnel and not equipment – so do not expect your favourite twin set to be winched aboard. In all situations it is important to stay calm and take all reasonable precautions to avoid hypothermia and seasickness. As most diving takes place around the coastal fringes, help is never far away and, provided you are in no danger of sinking or being ...ped, there is no need to panic.

Figure 208

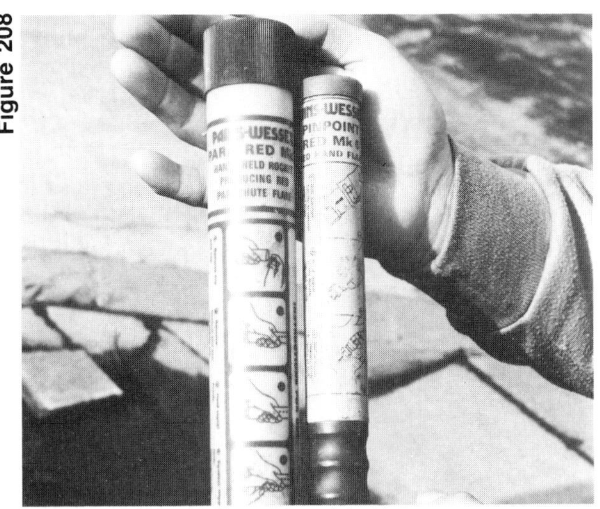

Parachute flare (*left*) and hand-held flare

Figure 209

Operating a parachute flare firing mechanism

Figure 210

Holding a smoke flare clear and down wind

An RNLI Atlantic 21 lifeboat in action

An RAF Rescue Helicopter winching-up a survivor

Figure 213

Navigation

Charts

Latitude and Longitude

The Earth can be thought of as a sphere which pivots about an axis. The top end of the axis is the North Pole and the bottom of the axis is the South Pole. The Earth rotates towards the East and away from the West (Figure 214).

Figure 214

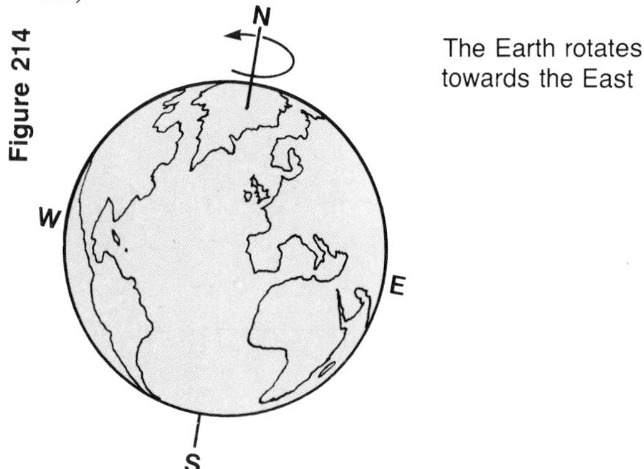

The Earth rotates towards the East

Any position on the Earth's surface can be defined by measuring its distance from a vertical reference point and from a horizontal reference point. These are known as the coordinates of that position; they are similar to the grid reference system on a land map.

The vertical reference point is the Equator. Lines of latitude are horizontal lines drawn parallel to the Equator. These lines are designated in degrees (0° to 90°) north or south of the Equator according to the angle that the line of latitude makes with the Equator at the centre of the Earth (Figure 215).

Figure 215

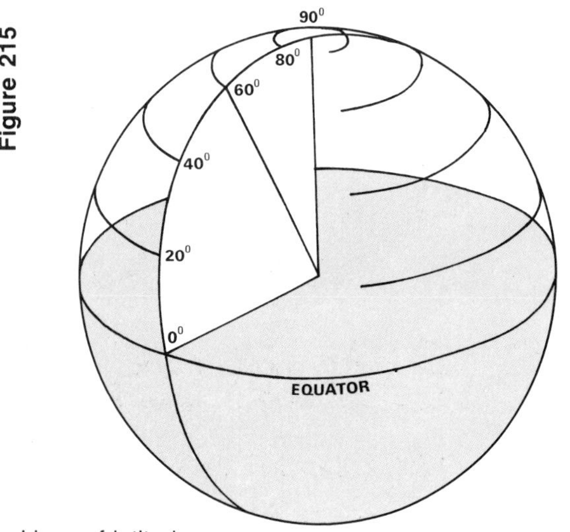

Lines of latitude

The horizontal reference point is Greenwich meridian, near London. Lines of longitude (meridians) are drawn vertically. They are all circumferences of the Earth and they all pass through, and intersect at, the North and South Poles. These lines are designated in degrees (0° to 180°) east or west of the Greenwich meridian (0°). As with the lines of latitude, the designated angle is the angle that the meridian makes with the Greenwich meridian at the centre of the Earth (Figure 216).

Figure 216

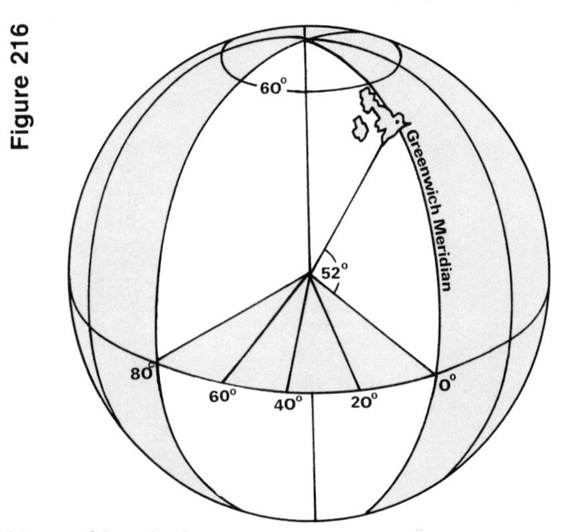

Lines of longitude

Any position is identified by giving its latitude followed by its longitude (its coordinates). Thus Dover is 51° 07′ N, 01° 19′ E.

Charts

A chart is a map of a coastal area and gives as much, or more, detail about the sea as it does about the land. Information about depth, type of sea bottom, tides and tidal streams, etc., is included on the chart. In the United Kingdom the largest and most important publisher of marine charts is the Hydrographic Office of the Admiralty. Charts for all marine areas of the world are produced and constantly updated. Charts of interest to yachtsmen are also produced by other publishers.

Charts of most interest to the diver are those depicting coastal areas and those giving details of harbours, estuaries and other small, localized areas. They will usually be large scale and will contain more detail than the smaller-scale ocean navigation charts.

Since the Earth is almost a sphere, its surface is curved. Maps and charts are flat. Translating the curved surface of the Earth onto flat paper results in some distortion of the areas under consideration, but the chart makers correct this mathematically as far as is possible.

The most useful chart, the Mercator Chart, allows the

navigator to join his start point and his destination with a straight line from which he can then determine the direction in which to travel and distance between the two points. On this type of chart the lines of latitude are shown as straight, parallel, horizontal lines. The meridians of longitude are also straight lines at right angles (vertical) to the lines of latitude and equally spaced from each other (Figure 217).

Figure 217

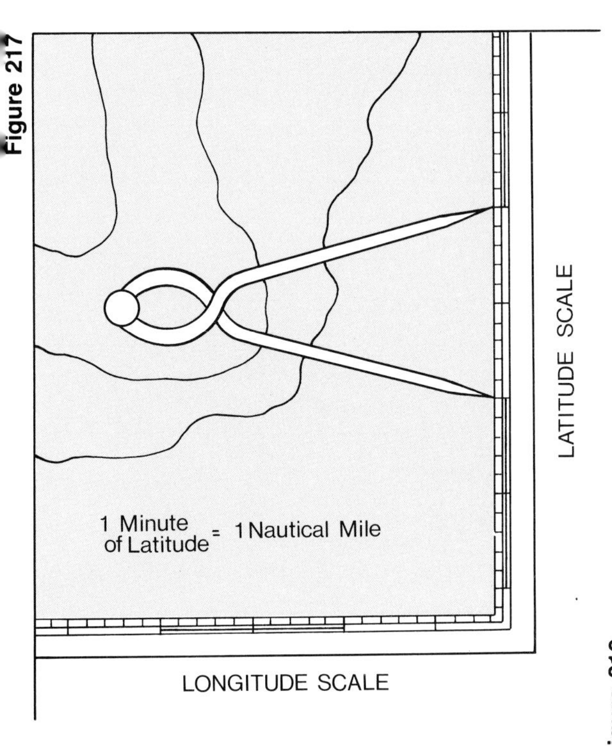

Distance on the chart is measured against the latitude scale at the side of the chart, directly opposite the working position

Any position on the chart can be defined by giving its coordinates, as described above. First of all the position of the point on the vertical (latitude) scale can be measured using parallel rules or dividers. Then its position on the horizontal (longitude) scale can be measured in a similar way (Figure 218). Thus the latitude and longitude of any point on the chart can be quoted.

The scale of any chart is given under its title. It is the ratio of the length of any line measured on the chart to the corresponding distance on the Earth's surface (e.g. 1:500,000 or 1:36,500).

For measurement of distances at sea the nautical mile is used. This is defined as the distance, measured along a meridian, separating two places whose latitude varies by exactly 1 minute of arc (i.e. one sixtieth of a degree). This is usually taken to be equal to 6080 feet or 1852 m. This definition of the nautical mile in terms of angle of latitude enables distances to be measured without the complicated use of scales. Use dividers to span the two points whose distance apart is to be measured. Then lay them against the latitude scale (i.e. the vertical scale, NOT the horizontal one!) nearest to the positions. By reading off the number of minutes, the number of nautical miles can be found directly.

Figure 218

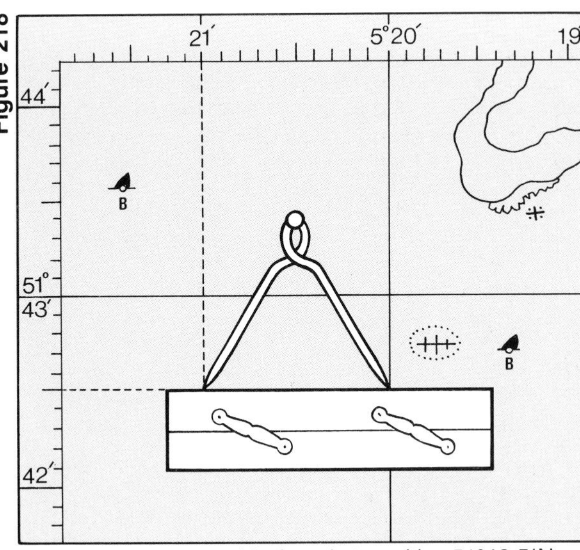

The position indicated is found at position 51°42·5′N 5°21′W

Figure 219

The chart title shows scale and depth units (Crown Copyright)

Charts also show the depth of water that can be expected in the area covered by the chart. This is shown both as individual soundings and as depth contours. Depth contours are lines joining places of equal depth, similar to the height contours of a land map. Depth is measured in metres above chart datum. This is the level below which the tide will rarely, if ever, fall, and is given for every place and port. In other words, the depths shown on the chart are the shallowest that can ever be expected.

Besides indications of depth, the chart also gives abbreviations to indicate the type of sea bottom to be found in any particular area. This information can be very useful to the diver who probably wants to miss the mud (M) and ooze (Oz), preferring to find places that have rock (R), stones (St) or boulders (Bo) (Figure 221).

Figure 220

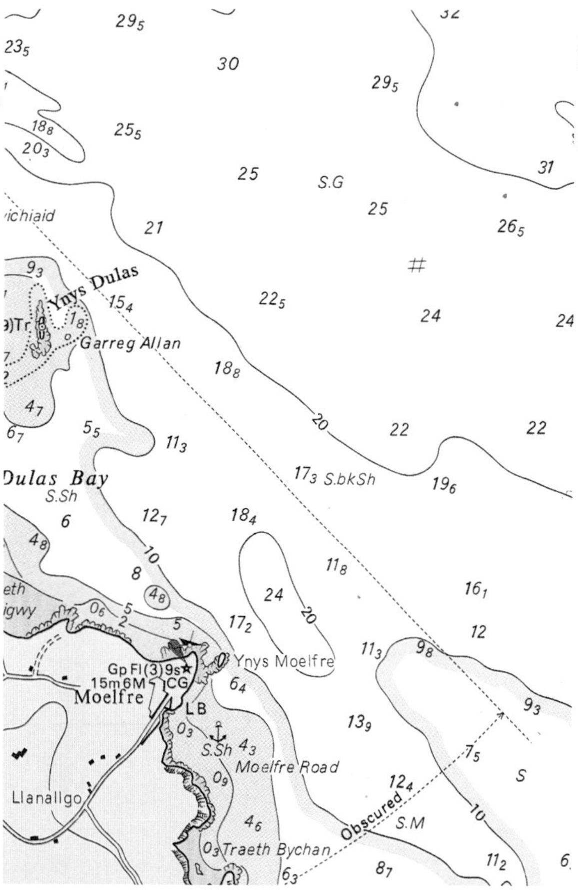

The chart indicates depth in metres, bottom quality, bottom contours, coastal features, light descriptions (Crown Copyright)

The chart also gives information that is intended to help the navigator to fix his position and to navigate safely. Dangers to navigation are shown. These can be difficult tides, eddies or currents – places that the diver might also like to miss. Other dangers to navigation, such as rocks, wrecks and reefs, though avoided by navigators, may be attractive to divers, provided that adequate care and knowledge is used. These are the sorts of area that provide interesting diving.

Surface topography or natural land features may help the navigator to recognize places and fix position or navigate safely. This chart information can also help divers to select launch or landing sites, as coves, beaches, harbours, etc., are clearly marked.

Conspicuous buildings, church towers, steeples, castles and prominent masts are all marked on the chart using appropriate abbreviations. Coastguard stations are also shown. All of these features are potential landmarks that can be helpful to the navigator (Figure 222).

Figure 221

Wk	WRECK	M	MUD
PA	POSITION approx.	Sn	SHINGLE
Bk	BANK	St	STONES
Sh	SHOAL	Wd	WEED
Rf	REEF	f	FINE
Le	LEDGE	c	COARSE
S	SAND	so	SOFT

Abbreviations used to describe the quality of the bottom and bottom features

Other conspicuous objects that can be used for navigation are fixed lights or beacons. These may be lighthouses, lightships or lighted beacons and all have the advantage of being visible in the dark. The chart uses appropriate abbreviations to tell the navigator the colour and type of any navigational light. The chart also indicates the height of any light. This is measured in metres above mean high-water spring tides (MHWS – see p. 123). The chart also tells the navigator over what distance the light can be seen (Figure 223).

Figure 222

USEFUL CHART SYMBOLS AND ABBREVIATIONS	
(4) • (4) ROCK WHICH DOES NOT COVER (Elevation above MHWS)	CHURCH
(1_2) ROCK WHICH COVERS AND UNCOVERS (Elevation above chart datum)	⊙ Tr TOWER
ROCK AWASH AT LEVEL OF CHART DATUM	OIL/GAS PRODUCTION PLATFORM
SUNKEN ROCK 2 METRES OR LESS AT CHART DATUM	PILOT STATION
6_4 SUNKEN DANGER. DEPTH CLEARED BY DRAG WIRE	⊙ ⊙ FS FLAGSTAFF
WRECK SHOWING AT LEVEL OF CHART DATUM	35 *Well* SUBMERGED WELL HEAD (With least depth where known)
(Masts) WRECK, MASTS ONLY VISIBLE	RC RADIOBEACON
POSITION OF LIGHT OR BEACON	Racon RADAR TRANSPONDER BEACON
Lt V LIGHT VESSEL	*Obstn* OBSTRUCTION RADAR REFLECTOR
OVERFALLS AND TIDE RIP	EDDIES

Selected chart symbols

Figure 223

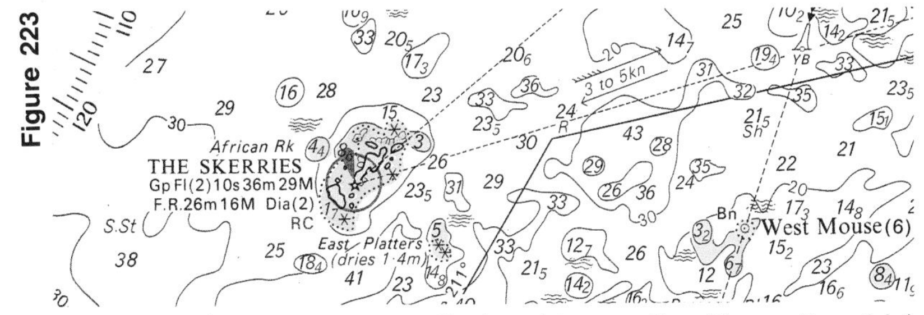

Lights are comprehensively described to aid recognition (Crown Copyright)

The charts also show the position of any navigational buoys. These are shown with abbreviations to indicate the markings and the type of warning (light or sound) they carry.

Buoys are useful for navigating safely to and from a site. However, they are less useful for position fixing (see p. 114) since they are attached to a sinker on the sea bottom by a length of chain which has to allow for the rise and fall of the tide, so the position of any buoy will vary somewhat, depending on the state of the tide and the direction of the current and wind.

Figure 224

The height of a lighthouse will usually be indicated on a chart

On every chart there is at least one compass rose. This usually takes the form of a circle graduated clockwise from 0° to 360°. Bearings and courses are usually quoted using the three-figure notation thus:

> North is 000° (or 360°)
> East is 090°
> South is 180°
> West is 270°

Most compass roses also have a smaller circle inside the big one. This is also graduated from 000° to 360° and automatically allows for the variation in that area; on the diameter of the smaller circle is given the actual variation, the date when it was determined and the correction to be used for later dates (Figure 225).

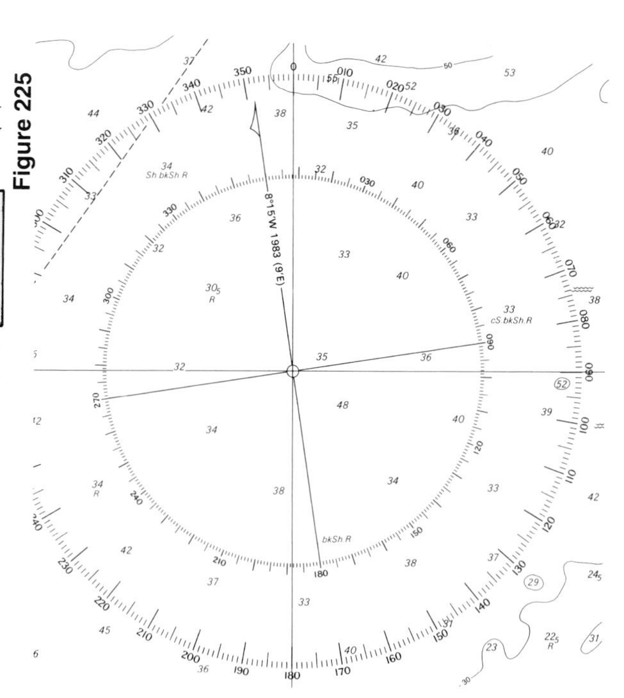

Figure 225
A compass rose (Crown Copyright)

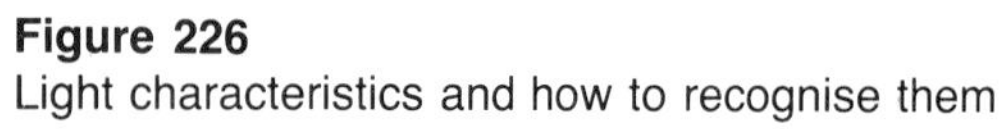

Figure 226
Light characteristics and how to recognise them

LIGHT CHARACTERISTICS

Abbreviation	Description	Symbol
Alt.	ALTERNATING a light which alters in colour in successive flashes or eclipses.	Rd. Wt. Gn. Rd. Wt. Gn.
F.	FIXED a continuous steady light.	
Fl.	FLASHING single flash at regular intervals. Duration of light always less than the period of darkness.	
F.Fl.	FIXED AND FLASHING steady light with one brilliant flash at regular intervals.	
F.Gp.Fl.( )	FIXED AND GROUP FLASHING steady light with two or more brilliant flashes in a group.	
Gp Fl.( )	GROUP FLASHING two or more brilliant flashes in succession at regular intervals.	
Occ.	OCCULTING steady light with total eclipse at regular intervals. Duration of darkness less than that of light.	
Gp.Occ.( )	GROUP OCCULTING two or more eclipses in a group at regular intervals.	
Qk.Fl.	QUICK FLASHING continuous flash at rate of 50 or 60 per minute.	
Int.Qk.Fl.( )	QUICK FLASHING in groups at 50 or 60 times per minute with total eclipse at regular intervals. Group of flashes shown in brackets followed by time e.g. Qk.Fl.(6) 10 secs. means 6 groups of quick flashes within a 10-second period.	
V.Qk.Fl.	VERY QUICK FLASHING continuous flash at rate of 100 or 120 per minute, or in groups as for Qk.Fl.	
Iso.	ISOPHASE a light where duration of light and darkness are equal.	
Mo.( )	MORSE CODE LIGHT the characteristics are shown by the appropriate letters or figures in brackets.	
L.Fl.	LONG FLASHING a flash of 2 or more seconds.	

Pilotage

Compass Card

The compass card can be graduated in a number of different ways, all of which indicate direction.

Point Method

In the point method the circle is divided into thirty-two equal parts or points (Figure 227). Since a full circle is 360°, each point represents 11·25°. It is not unusual to use half points or even quarter points. The advantage claimed for this method is the ease with which the markings can be read.

Figure 227

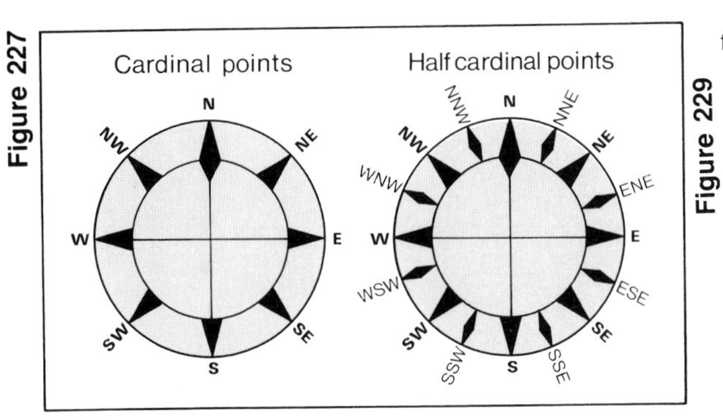

The Cardinal compass card

Quadrantal Method

In this method the four quadrants of the compass card are divided into 90° with 0° at North and South and 90° at East and West (Figure 228). The cardinal directions are simply described as North, South, East and West. Intermediate directions are described from North or South towards East or West – the direction Northwest would be described as N 45° W.

Figure 228

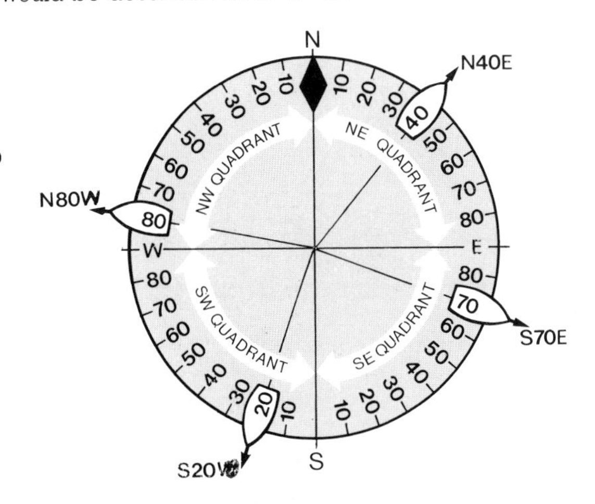

A Quadrantal compass card

Three-figure Method

Here the compass card is divided into 360° and each direction is always described using three figures (Figure 229);

North is 000° (or 360°)
East is 090°
South is 180°
West is 270°
Southeast is 135°

This is the simplest and most accurate method and is the one recommended.

Figure 229

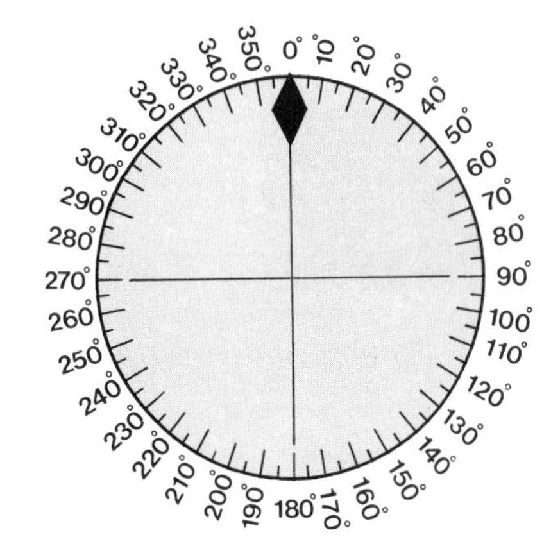

The three-figure compass card

Figure 230

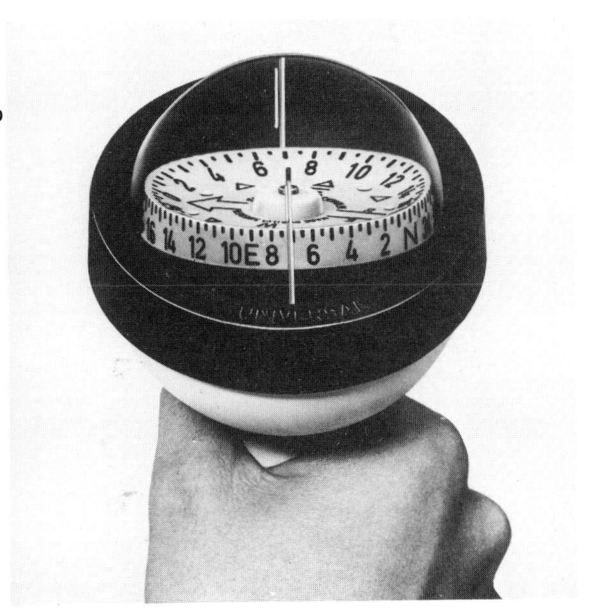

A hand-bearing compass

Compass Error

The Earth rotates about an axis and, as has already been explained, the upper point of that axis is true north. If a magnetic compass is used for navigational purposes, remember that it will point to the magnetic north, provided there are no additional magnetic influences in the vicinity.

The meridians of true north and of magnetic north do not normally coincide, so an allowance should be made when using the compass to indicate direction. The difference in angle between true north and magnetic north is called *variation* and it will be stated on a chart as a number of degrees east or west. It will be found inside the compass rose on the chart.

The value of the variation varies from place to place on the earth's surface and constantly changes over time. The information given inside the compass rose on a chart shows how to allow for this change at dates later than that at which the reading was measured.

If the compass is used in the vicinity of articles with a magnetic influence – steel constructions, electrical gear, etc. – it may not even point to magnetic north but to another position resulting from the combined magnetic fields. This position is termed compass north and the angle between it and magnetic north is called *deviation* (Figure 231). For accurate navigation the boat should have a deviation card which shows the deviation for any particular boat heading (Figure 232).

Figure 231

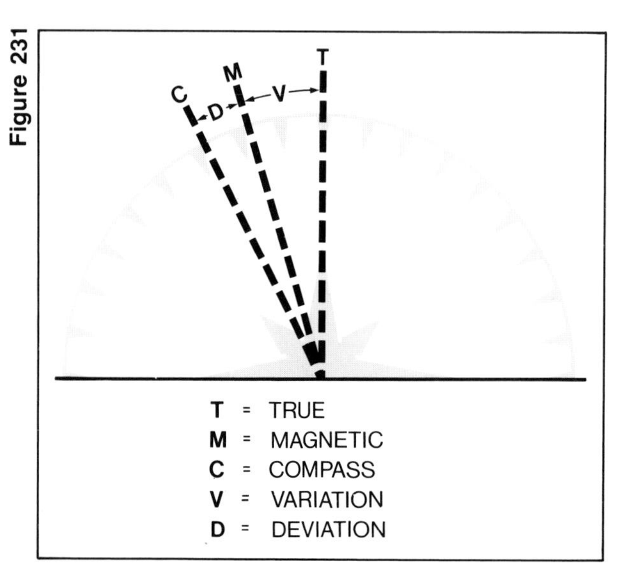

The relationship between True, Magnetic and Compass North, also variation and deviation

Figure 232

Table of Deviations

Ship's Head Compass	Deviation	Ship's Head Magnetic
000°	4E	004°
020°	2E	022°
040°	2W	038°
060°	4W	056°
080°	6W	074°
100°	7W	093°
120°	7W	113°
140°	7W	133°
160°	6W	154°
180°	4W	176°
200°	2W	198°
220°	1E	221°
240°	2E	242°
260°	4E	264°
280°	5E	285°
300°	6E	306°
320°	6E	326°
340°	5E	345°
360°	4E	004°

A deviation card. This should be available aboard any larger boat

If the variation is obtained from the chart and the deviation is read from the deviation card, it is possible to determine the compass error by adding like angles and subtracting unlike angles:

> variation 7° W & deviation 3° W = compass error 10° W (7 + 3)
> variation 7° W & deviation 3° E = compass error 4° W (7 – 3)
> variation 7° E & deviation 3° W = compass error 4° E (7 – 3)
> variation 7° E & deviation 3° E = compass error 10° E (7 + 3)

Once the compass error has been found, any compass reading can be converted into a true reading by either adding or subtracting the compass error to the compass reading. A convenient way of remembering how to do this is:

> Error West – compass best,
> Error East – compass least

In other words, if the compass error is West, the compass reading should be greater than the true reading (i.e. subtract the West error from the compass reading to get the true reading). If the compass error is East, the compass reading should be smaller than the true reading (i.e. add the East error to the compass reading to get the true reading).

When plotting positions and courses on a chart, only true readings should be plotted.

Courses

Any course taken by a boat will probably be maintained by using a magnetic compass (compass course) or by using fixed marks to maintain the course (true course). There are other methods of maintaining a course but these are considered to be outside the scope of navigating a small boat for diving.

When a course is to be plotted on a chart it should first be converted to a true course by making corrections for variation and deviation, as already described. Remember that the amount of deviation will vary according to the boat's heading and therefore a deviation table is needed unless readings can be taken without the risk of deviation (e.g. by using a hand-bearing compass well away from any magnetic influence).

During a voyage the navigator may attempt to fix the boat's position by taking the compass bearings of fixed landmarks. This is a very useful technique, but it must be remembered that, if the boat's compass is being used, the corrections for deviation must be made according to the heading of the boat, *not* the direction of the landmark. After the bearings have been converted into true bearings, they can be plotted on the chart to determine the position of the boat.

The distance travelled by the boat (i.e. the distance between two known fixes) can be calculated from the chart. Larger vessels often have a log. This is equivalent to the speedometer and odometer of a car and is designed to give both the distance travelled and the speed through the water. A speed of 1 nautical mile per hour is 1 knot.

It should be borne in mind that any tidal stream will tend to deflect the boat from its intended heading. When trying to navigate by using the chart, the speed and direction of the tide must be allowed for in order that the boat's course is maintained towards the intended destination.

If the speed and direction of the tide are known, their effects can be allowed for. For example: the boat's speed is 7 knots and the course is 315° true; there is a tidal stream of 2 knots at 026° true. To find the true course to steer.

1. Let the boat's position be A, then draw a line AY at 315° (intended course).
2. Draw a line AX at 026° (tidal stream) and mark off the distance (AB) covered by the tidal stream in a convenient period of time (say, one hour): AB = 2 units (2 miles in one hour).
3. From B, using compasses or dividers, draw an arc of length 7 units (7 miles in the *same period* of time – one hour), to cut line AY at C.
4. Join BC with a straight line. The direction BC is the required course to steer – 299°.
5. AC is a scale length which represents the actual distance that the boat has made towards its destination (distance made good) in one hour – 7·35 miles (Figure 233).

Figure 233

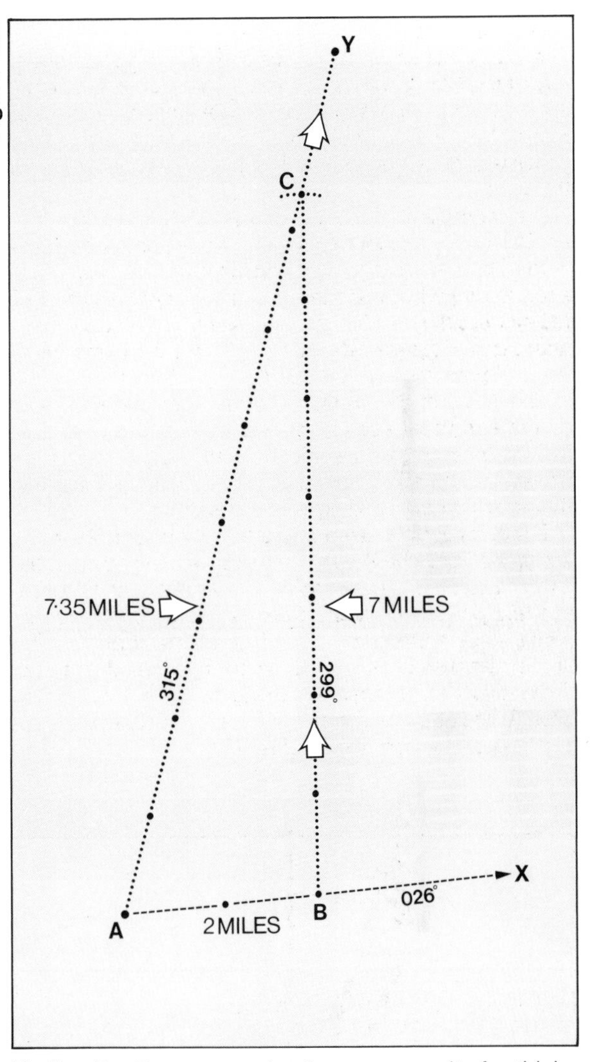

Finding the True course to steer as a result of a tidal stream acting upon the vessel

Position Fixing

Position Fix

A *position line* is a line on the chart on which the boat's position is known to be. A *position fix* is obtained when two, or more, position lines intersect. It is possible to determine a position line in a number of ways and the following are those which make use of fixed marks on the land.

Compass Bearing

A bearing on a visible object which is also shown on the chart can be taken with a hand-bearing compass or with a boat's compass. Remember to allow for compass error before transferring the bearing to the chart.

Figure 236

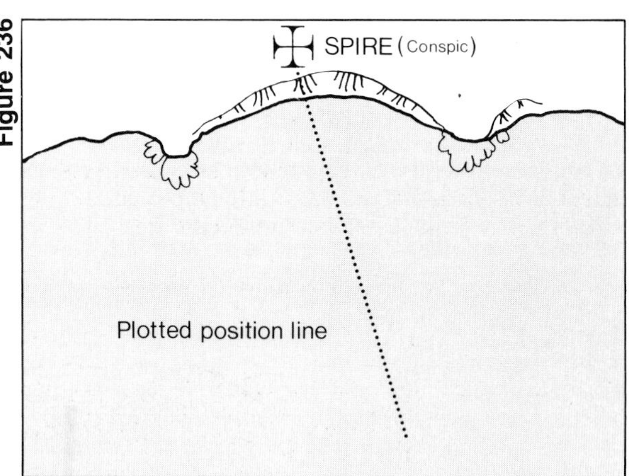

Establish position line

Figure 234

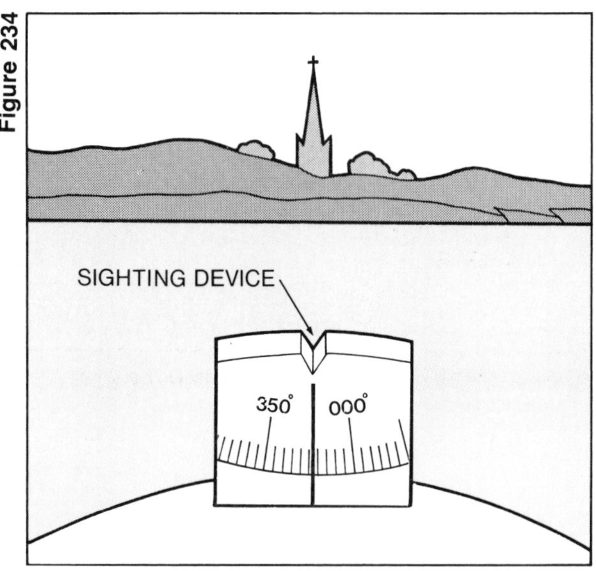

Sighting a hand-bearing compass

Figure 237

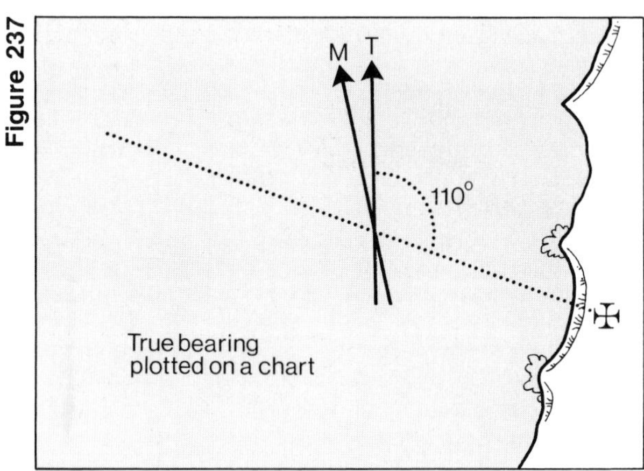

Transfer bearing to chart

Figure 235

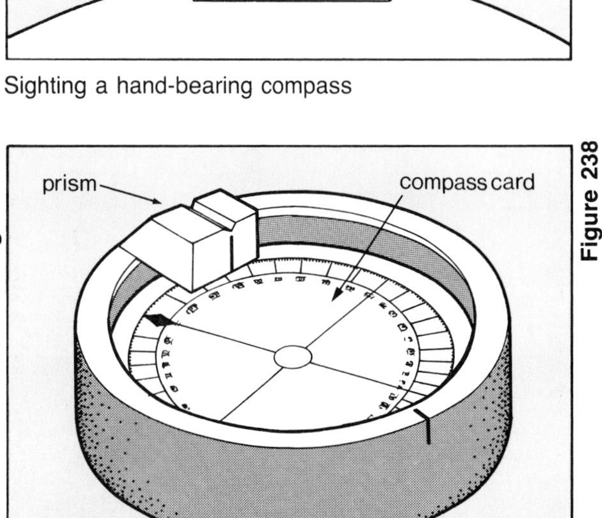

The prism allows the card to be read while sighting the object

Figure 238

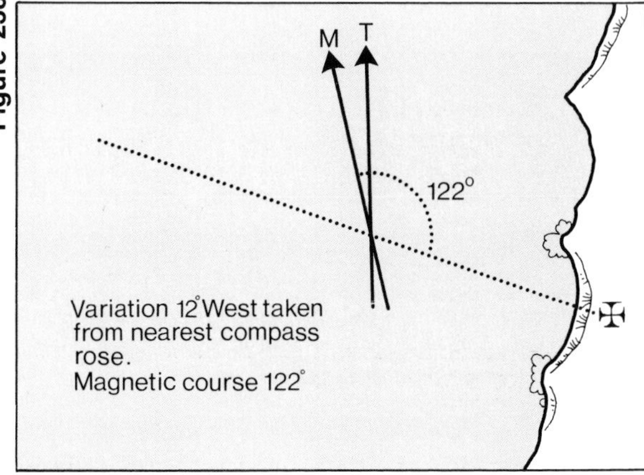

Adjust to True

Transit

When two objects are observed in line they are said to be in transit (Figure 239). This type of position line is also called a fisherman's mark. When the distance from the observer to the nearer object is not more than about three times the distance separating the two objects, the method can be quite accurate and is a popular one for divers to use for locating a favourite dive site.

Figure 239

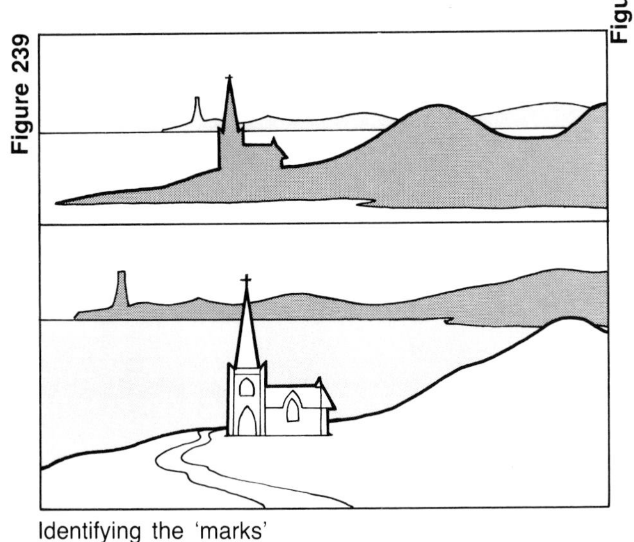

Identifying the 'marks'

Figure 240

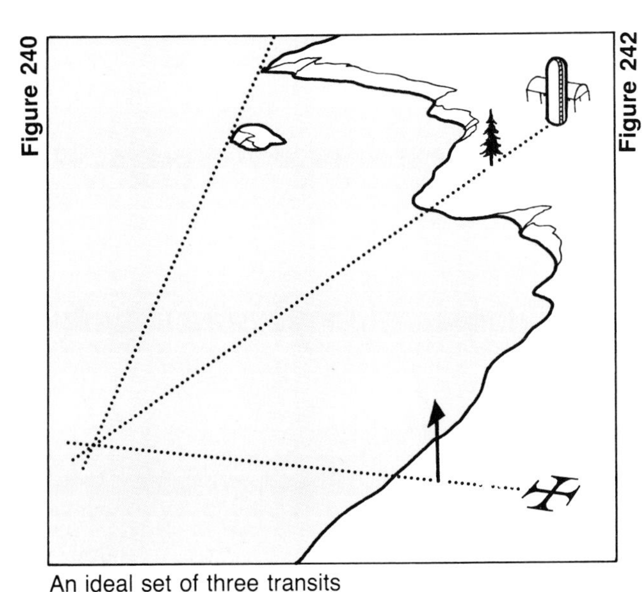

An ideal set of three transits

If the compass bearing of a transit can be compared with the true bearing taken from the chart, the transit can also be used to determine the compass error.

Horizontal angle

By measuring the horizontal angle between two objects which are also shown on the chart, it is possible to produce a position line. In this case the position line will be a circle (Figure 242).

Figure 241

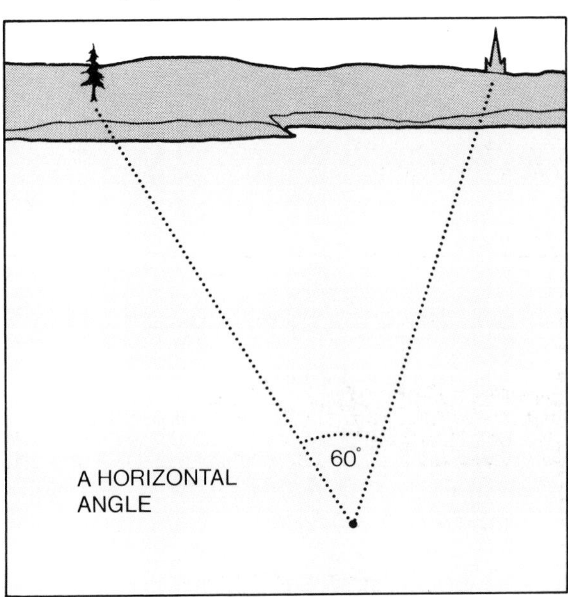

A horizontal angle measured between two points

Figure 242

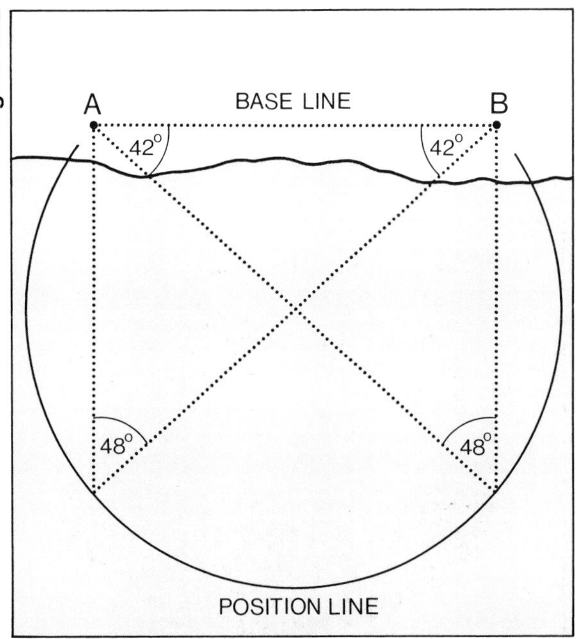

The curved position line given by a single horizontal angle

Figure 243

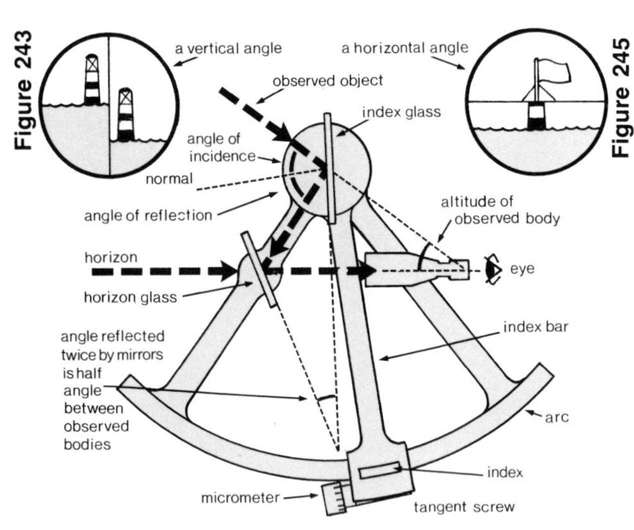

The principle of the sextant

Figure 245

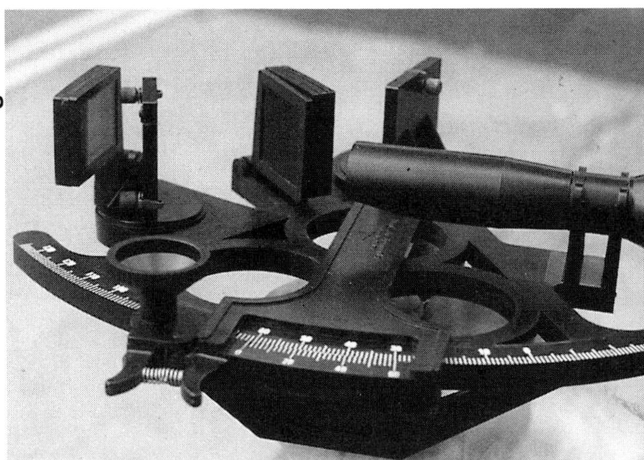

The sextant is held horizontally for horizontal angle fixes, instead of vertically as when measuring the angle between the horizon and the sun

Measuring the angle with a sextant is usually the most accurate method. It can also be measured as the difference between two compass bearings taken with an accurate magnetic compass. In this case there is no need to allow for compass error since it will be the same for both readings. However, even with an accurate compass, the accuracy of measurement is not nearly as good as that possible with a sextant.

The angle can be plotted on the chart using reasonably simple, though long-winded, geometry (Figure 247). Say the angle between the two objects A and B is 48°.

1. On the chart join the two objects A and B with a straight line.
2. From A draw a line at an angle of 42° (i.e. 90° – 48°) to AB.
3. From B draw a line at an angle of 42° (i.e. 90° – 48°) to AB.
4. Where these two lines intersect is the centre of a circle through A and B. This is the position line.

For the mathematically minded, this technique relies on the fact that the angle made by a chord at the centre of a circle is twice the angle made by the chord at the circumference of the circle.

Figure 244

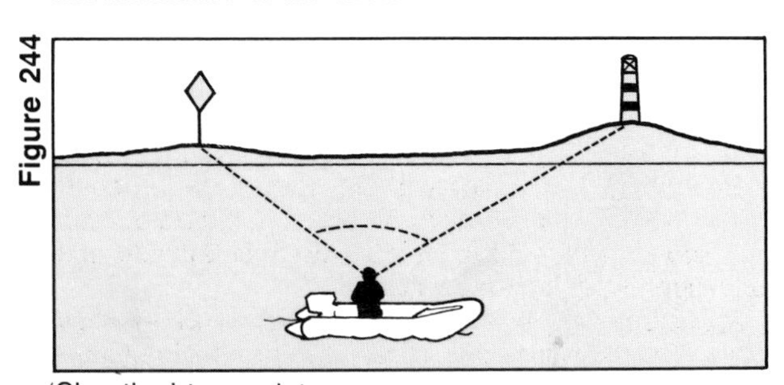

'Shooting' two points

Figure 246

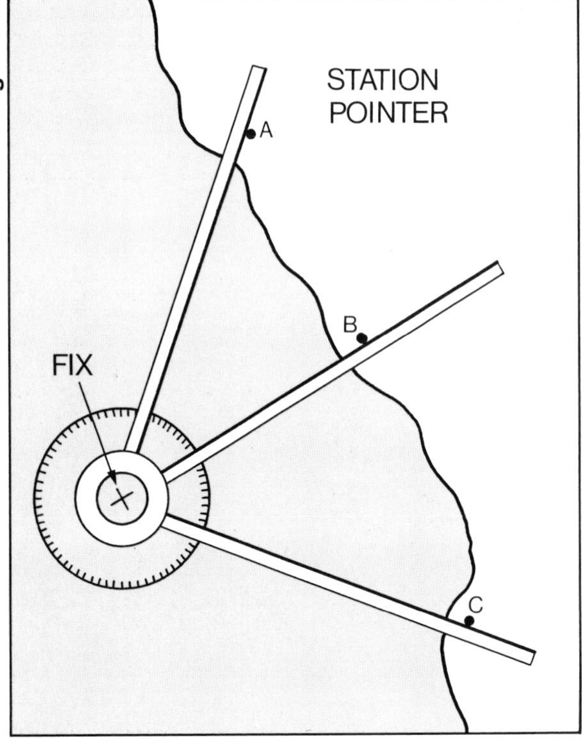

A station pointer allows two angles to be set to fix a point

Figure 247

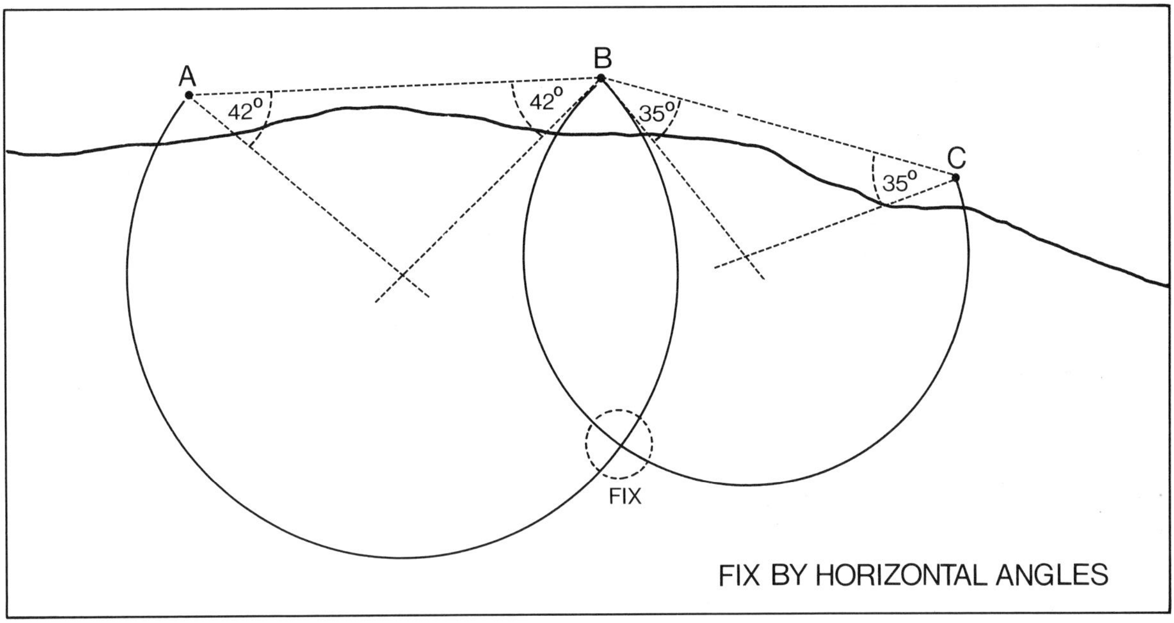

FIX BY HORIZONTAL ANGLES

The geometry of two horizontal angle fixes

Vertical Angle

If the height of a prominent mark is shown on the chart, a sextant can be used to determine the vertical angle between the height of the mark and the mean high-water spring tides (MHWS). The level of MHWS can be found from tide tables and sea level. Again, as in the case of the horizontal angle, the position line resulting from a vertical angle is a circle (Figure 248).

Figure 248

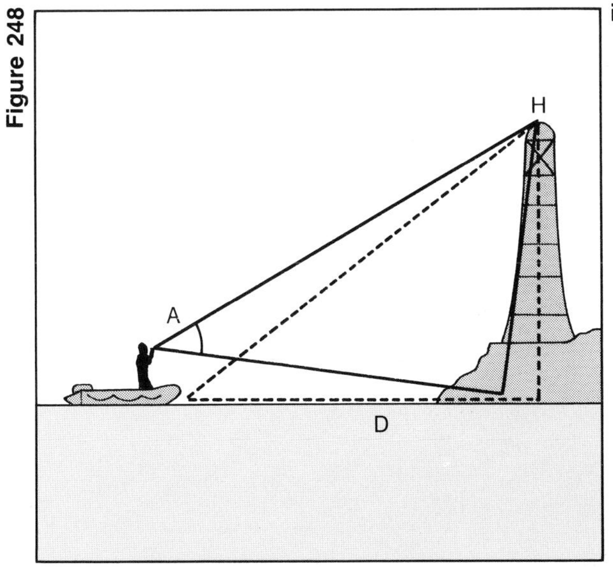

Measuring distance off a known height

Figure 249

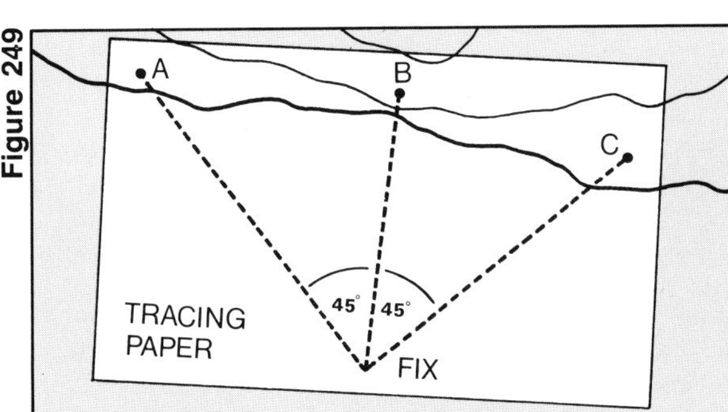

A simple method for transferring a fix to a chart using tracing paper

If the angle is measured as a and the height h of the mark is found from the chart, The distance d from the mark can be found using tables or by trigonometry:

$$d = h \times \text{cotan } a$$

By plotting two or more position lines on the chart using one of these methods, the position of the boat can be fixed. It is then possible to read off the latitude and longitude of the known position.

Position fixing is a useful skill for the diver who wishes to use it not so much for navigation but for making sure that he can return to his favourite dive site.

Compass Bearing

Supposing a compass bearing has to be taken in order to obtain a position line.

If a hand-bearing compass is to be used, try to stand well away from any magnetic influences, such as steel or iron, and, holding the compass up to your eyes horizontally, point it at the object whose bearing you are taking. Wait for the needle to stop swinging – most hand-bearing compasses are filled with liquid and this damps the movement – before taking the reading.

1. Let us suppose that the compass gives a reading of 075° (Figure 250).
2. From the nearest compass rose on the chart of the area, take the reading for the variation (Figure 251).
3. Suppose this says 'Variation 8° 20′ W (1978) decreasing about 5′ annually' and we are in 1986.
4. From 1978 to 1986 is 8 years and 8 × 5′ is 40′.
5. Subtract 40′ from 8° 20′ and we get 7° 40′ W.
6. To convert the bearing to a true reading, subtract the error from the compass reading: 075° − 7° 40′ = 067° 20′. Since we cannot plot lines to an accuracy of minutes, this is rounded down to 067°.
7. Now find the object on the chart and, using parallel rules, draw a line at 067° to the object from the sea (Figure 252).

If the bearing is taken with a boat's compass, perhaps on a larger charter vessel, then it is also necessary to allow for deviation (see p. 112).

Although the above procedure describes how to take a bearing and then plot it on a chart as a position line, the reverse procedure will allow a bearing to be taken from a chart so that it can be used as a compass bearing for position fixing at sea.

Figure 251

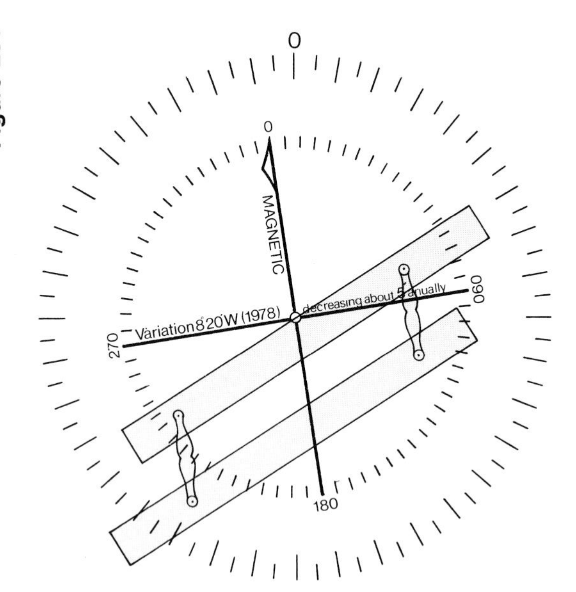

Use compass rose nearest to object

Figure 250

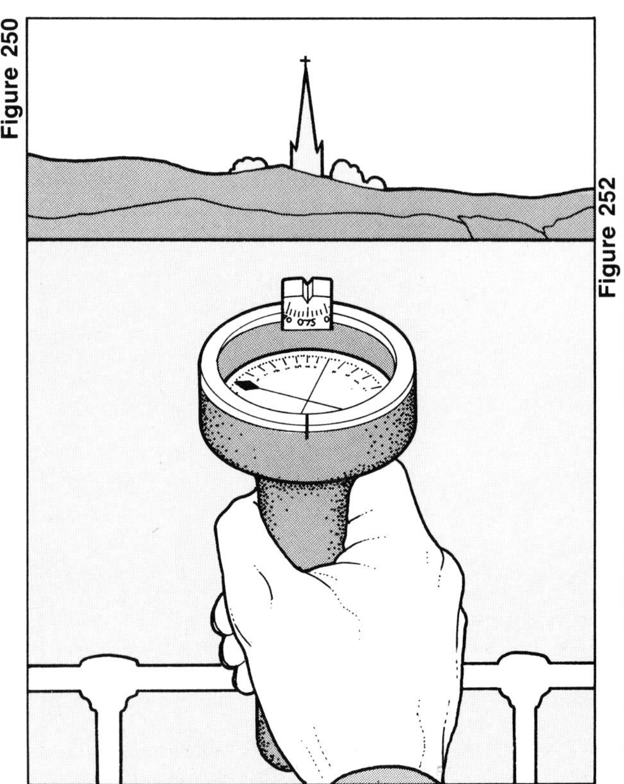

Using the hand-bearing compass

Figure 252

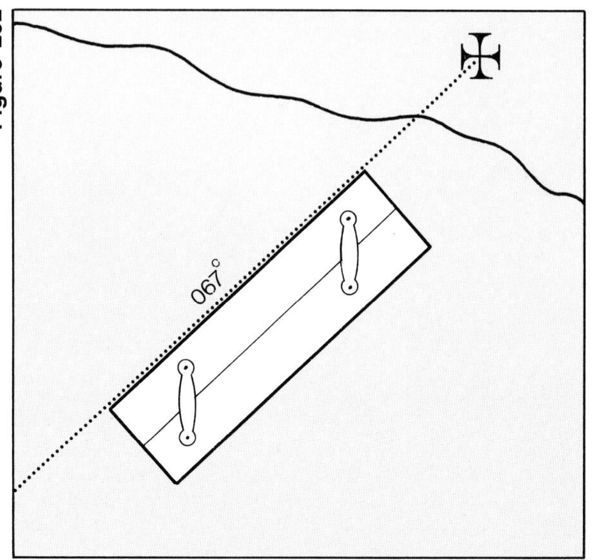

Transferring bearing from compass rose using parallel rules

Transit

Taking a transit and then plotting it on a chart is simplicity itself. One only needs to ensure that the objects that are in line for the transit are also clearly marked on the chart.

Locate the two objects on the chart, making sure that they are the same objects as those used for the transit (it is amazing how many towers, spires and masts can be found in one area), and then draw a line, with a ruler, through both points.

Again the reverse procedure will allow transits to be taken from a chart and used for position fixing at sea.

Figure 253

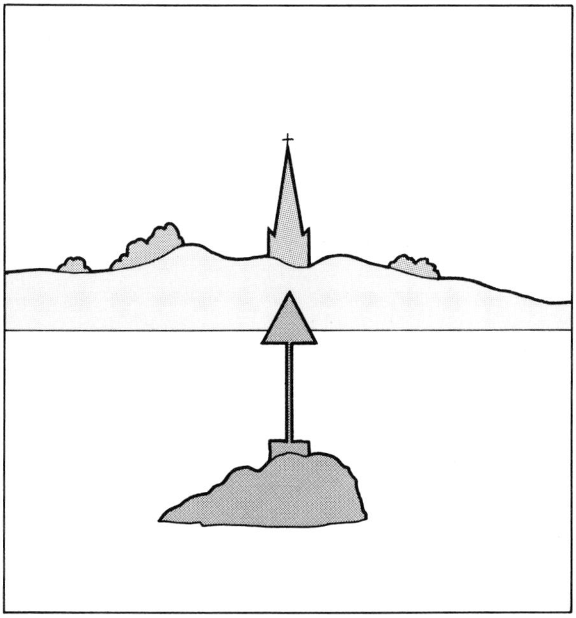

Choose objects identifiable on chart

The methods described above are by far the easiest to use both in a boat and on a chart. In each case the position line is a straight line. The actual position can be fixed by obtaining two such position lines and the fix is where the two lines intersect. If horizontal or vertical angles have been measured then the position line is the arc of a circle. This is more difficult to plot on a chart and is also quite difficult to measure from a boat, especially if the sea is anything but flat calm. Taking a horizontal or vertical angle from a chart and then trying to use this for position fixing is also relatively complicated. Position fixing using *two* circular position lines (i.e. two horizontal/vertical angles) is very difficult since it needs considerable skill and knowledge to know in which direction to steer the boat in order to get *both* angles correct. If we assume that the position lines are from transits or compass bearings, the easiest technique for position fixing is to steer the boat on one of the bearings/transits until the second one comes into line and then quickly drop a marker buoy over the side. The position of the marker buoy can then be checked at leisure.

Figure 254

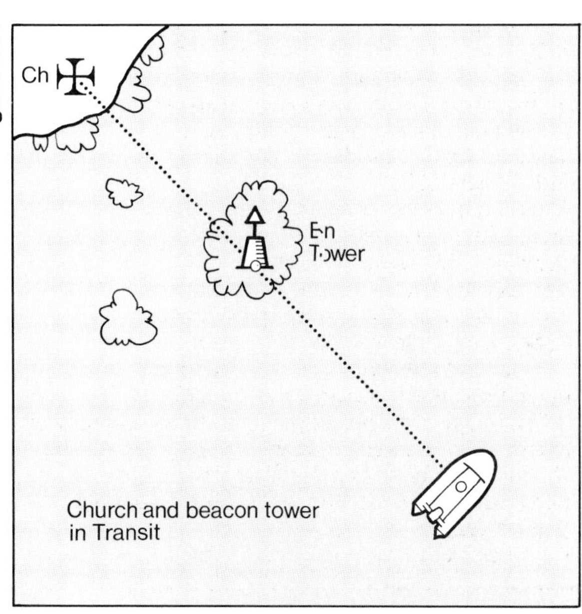

Locate objects on chart and draw position line through them

Figure 255

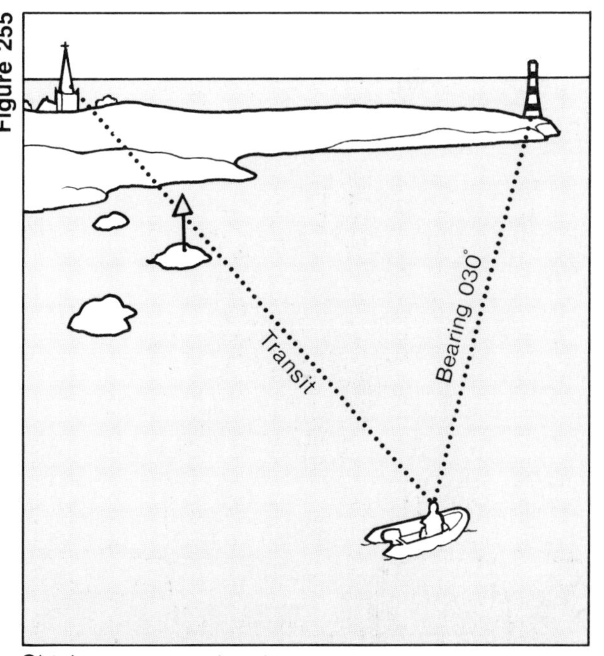

Obtain a compass bearing to give a second position line and thus a position fix at the intersection

Navigation/Wreck Location Equipment

This section covers the types of electronic equipment used for navigating larger vessels, in addition to describing that used specifically for wreck detection.

Radar

Radar operates by sending out a pulse of radiation and detecting the angle of an object and distance over which the ray is reflected back from the object. The display is usually on a circular cathode-ray tube marked with range rings, though digital readout rangefinders are now available. Used carefully, radar can give the distance and the bearing of an object.

The use of radar is almost universal in larger craft. The security and safety that it brings in heavy weather, at night and off unfamiliar coasts are an absolute boon.

Racons are beacons which detect an emitted radar signal and send their own characteristic signal in response. Ramarks are beacons which emit their own radar signal without any external stimulus.

Figure 256

Radar transducer on vessel's mast

Radio Direction Finding

Radio direction finding depends upon detecting, with an appropriate receiver, the bearing of one of a number of special radio transmitters. The bearing of the beacon is then used as a position line on a chart in the normal way.

The bearings are only accurate to about 2 degrees, though this may be of use at an offshore site. It is more likely, however, that Decca equipment will be required.

Figure 257

An electronic Navigator automatically gives boat's position, plus supplementary information

Navigator (Decca)

This is a system of groups of three radio beacons covering Europe (including the UK), India, South Africa, Australia, Japan and the eastern seaboard of Canada and the USA. In the modern version of the equipment a special receiver picks up the three signals and converts them into latitude and longitude. The system is accurate to about 15–100 m, depending on the area and the beam intersection angles.

Older versions of the equipment had to be used with special latticed Decca charts. These had three different coloured grids on them, and the three-coloured readout of the Decca machine enabled the position to be fixed.

To operate a Navigator you must log your initial position into the machine when starting the day. The manual should be studied in detail as modern Navigators are brimming with advanced features.

Most current Navigators allow at least several 'way points' to be entered. These are positions on the chart selected by the skipper as intermediate points in the vessel's course. The instrument will display the distance to the next way point and its direction. This information can be linked into an auto pilot so that the skipper merely has to observe the vessel's automatic progress on its course. If the whole system is also linked to automatic radar collision detection and automatic shallow-depth warnings, then in theory the vessel can find its own way to its destination. In practice it would be a foolhardy skipper who did not monitor his progress.

Figure 258

Echo sounders give an accurate representation of the bottom

Loran/Consol/Omega

These are sophisticated offshore and ocean navigation systems. Loran is accurate to 5 miles, Consol to 5–20 miles and Omega to 1–2 miles. These systems are, therefore, not very useful for inshore navigation or wreck location.

Satellite Navigation

This is an excellent system. A receiver picks up signals from a US Navy navigation satellite passing overhead. Unfortunately this only happens once an hour (and occasionally only every four hours), so you must carefully time your position-fixing attempts. By means of tables, the signals are converted into a position, with accuracy of about 100 m. The equipment is not prohibitively expensive.

Echo Sounding

The principle of echo sounding is simple. A pulse of sound is emitted by a transducer attached to the echo sounder. This sound pulse is reflected back from the seabed or wreck and the total time taken for the pulse to travel both ways is converted into a depth display. The output can be a rotating neon display, a cathode-ray-tube graphical display or a paper record. This latter is the norm on large vessels and is the best type for wreck location.

Cheaper neon-type sounders generally have a wide beam angle of up to 70°. This means that the power is quickly dissipated, and as the sounder detects the nearest object the fine detail in the bottom topography may be missed. Paper-record sounders often have a choice of transducer, offering a beam angle of 8° or 20°. With these the power is more concentrated and the bottom resolution is much improved. In fact, with the narrow-beam transducer the instrument is sampling only a 2-metre-wide section of seabed at a depth of 15 m or a 7–metre section at 50 m depth.

Sonar

The principle of operation is similar to that of the echo sounder, except that the electronics are very much more complicated and are arranged to give a graduated response to the pulse echoes. The area of sweep can extend from several hundred metres to about 2 miles (3,220 metres) around the vessel. The simpler versions are getting cheaper but the larger units are more accurate.

Sonars give a quite superb picture of the seabed which is almost as good as a low-resolution photograph. Wrecks and other seabed features are shown in splendid detail and even the type of wreck can often be determined. The latest versions include colour in a video display.

The transducer is held in a tube mounted vertically through the vessel and is lowered below the hull when the sonar is in use. With older types of sonar (sometimes called side-scan sonar) the transducer head (or 'fish') is towed behind the boat at slow speeds.

Proton Magnetometer

This instrument measures the earth's magnetic field. A large concentration of ferrous metal (e.g. a wreck) will distort this field, and it is this alteration in the magnetic environment that the proton magnetometer detects. The equipment consists of a sensing head which is towed about 15 m behind the search vessel and is connected by a cable to a box of electronics in the boat. Power usually comes from a 12-volt battery.

Tides

Tides are the periodic movement of the level of the sea in response to the various tide generating forces. The main forces that generate tides are the moon and the sun. In the British Isles, *semi-diurnal* tides are the norm. This means that there are two high waters (HW) and two low waters (LW) in each lunar day (about 24 hours 50 minutes). The difference in the height of the water between successive high and low waters is called the *range* of the tide. In the British Isles the range of the tide can vary from as little as 1–2 m up to as much as 10 m in some places. The time beween successive high waters is called the *duration* of the tide and this is about a half of a lunar day (i.e. about 12 hours 24 minutes).

Springs and Neaps

The greatest range of the tide is found at or near the new or full moon (i.e. when the earth, the sun and the moon are all in line). These are called *spring tides* and they occur about every fifteen days throughout the year. About 7½ days after the new or full moon, the sun and the moon are at right angles to the earth and the smallest range of tides is found at or near this time. These are *neap tides* and they also occur every fifteen days – just after the first and third quarters of the moon.

As the time passes from spring to neap tides, the high-water heights gradually decrease and the low-water heights gradually increase. As time progresses from neap tides towards springs, the opposite effect occurs.

Figure 259

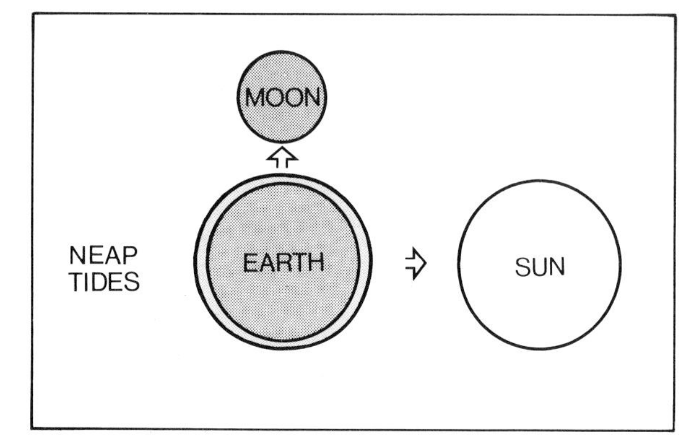

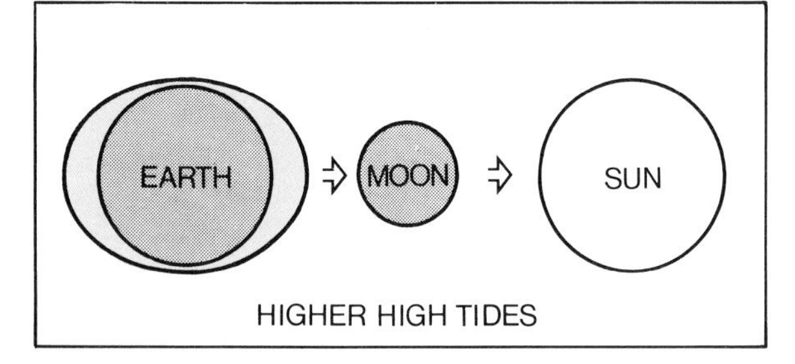

Figure 260

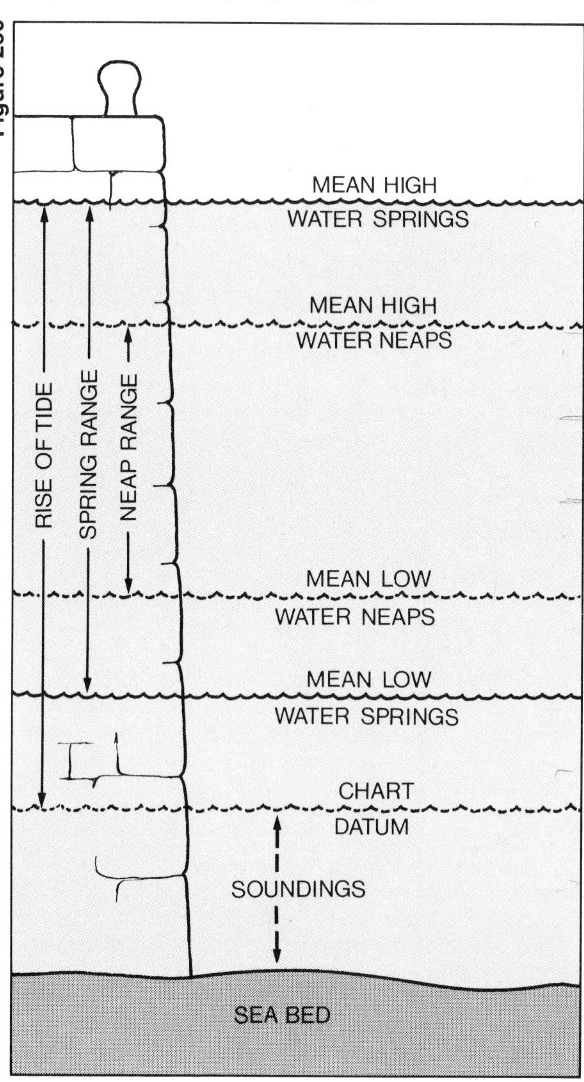

Figure 259
The effect of the sun and the moon on tides

Figure 260
A pictorial representation of tidal height definitions

Tidal Predictions

Admiralty tide tables published every year predict the times of high and low water at certain important ports. *Standard ports* are those for which the times of high and low water have been predicted for every day of the year. *Secondary ports* are other ports and places for which sufficient tidal information is given in the tables to enable the navigator to predict the times of high and low water – usually by reference to a nearby standard port. This information is usually in the form of time and height differences to be added to or subtracted from those of the nearest standard port.

Figure 261

Lat. 53°25'N. Long. 3°00'W. **LIVERPOOL** 473

GMT ADD 1 HOUR MARCH 30–OCTOBER 25 FOR B.S.T. HIGH & LOW WATER 1986

JANUARY

	Time	m		Time	m
1 W	0202	8·5	16 Th	0256	8·3
	0832	2·1		0931	2·2
	1418	8·7		1512	8·6
	2111	1·9		2203	2·1
2 Th	0247	8·3	17 F	0336	7·9
	0915	2·2		1010	2·6
	1504	8·5		1556	8·1
	2157	2·1		2244	2·5
3 F	0336	8·1	18 Sa	0423	7·5
	1004	2·4		1058	3·1
	1555	8·4		1647	7·7
	2249	2·2		2332	2·9
4 Sa	0433	7·9	19 Su	0519	7·1
	1101	2·6		1158	3·4
	1655	8·2		1747	7·3
	2350	2·3			
5 Su	0539	7·9	20 M	0034	3·2
	1208	2·7		0629	7·0
	1803	8·2		1312	3·4
				1900	7·2
6 M	0100	2·3	21 Tu	0144	3·2
	0650	8·0		0744	7·1
	1324	2·5		1423	3·3
	1916	8·2		2011	7·3
7 Tu	0213	2·1	22 W	0247	3·0
	0758	8·2		0846	7·5
	1437	2·3		1524	2·9
	2026	8·5		2110	7·6
8 W	0319	1·9	23 Th	0341	2·7
	0901	8·6		0935	7·9
	1546	1·9		1614	2·5
	2128	8·8		2157	8·0
9 Th	0420	1·6	24 F	0427	2·3
	0957	9·0		1017	8·3
	1647	1·4		1659	2·1
	2226	9·0		2238	8·3
10 F	0513	1·3	25 Sa	0508	2·0
	1049	9·3		1057	8·7
	1742	1·1		1742	1·8
●	2318	9·2		2316	8·6
11 Sa	0603	1·2	26 Su	0547	1·7
	1139	9·5		1133	8·9
	1834	0·9		1821	1·5
				2354	8·9
12	0007	9·3	27	0627	1·5

FEBRUARY

	Time	m		Time	m
1 Sa	0310	8·6	16 Su	0327	7·7
	0938	1·9		0955	2·8
	1527	8·8		1550	7·7
	2214	1·9		2219	2·9
2 Su	0357	8·2	17 M	0412	7·3
	1027	2·2		1041	3·3
	1620	8·4		1644	7·2
	2309	2·3		2313	3·4
3 M	0458	7·9	18 Tu	0515	6·8
	1129	2·6		1156	3·6
	1727	7·9		1800	6·8
4 Tu	0021	2·6	19 W	0038	3·7
	0615	7·6		0646	6·7
	1252	2·7		1334	3·6
	1853	7·7		1933	6·8
5 W	0149	2·6	20 Th	0208	3·5
	0738	7·8		0813	7·0
	1423	2·6		1454	3·2
	2018	7·9		2047	7·2
6 Th	0308	2·3	21 F	0315	3·0
	0851	8·2		0912	7·6
	1542	2·1		1553	2·6
	2128	8·3		2139	7·8
7 F	0414	1·9	22 Sa	0407	2·5
	0953	8·7		0957	8·2
	1647	1·5		1642	2·0
	2226	8·7		2220	8·3
8 Sa	0509	1·5	23 Su	0451	2·0
	1045	9·1		1037	8·7
	1740	1·0		1725	1·5
	2313	9·1		2258	8·8
9 Su	0556	1·2	24 M	0532	1·5
	1130	9·5		1113	9·1
	1827	0·7		1804	1·1
●	2357	9·2		2334	9·1
10 M	0638	1·0	25 Tu	0611	1·1
	1212	9·6		1150	9·4
	1907	0·6		1843	0·7
11 Tu	0036	9·2	26 W	0011	9·4
	0716	1·0		0649	0·8
	1250	9·6		1227	9·6
	1944	0·7		1921	0·6
12	0112	9·1	27	0048	9·5

MARCH

	Time	m		Time	m
1 Sa	0204	9·2	16 Su	0209	8·4
	0837	1·1		0843	2·1
	1419	9·3		1429	8·3
	2107	1·2		2057	2·3
2 Su	0243	8·9	17 M	0240	8·0
	0917	1·5		0914	2·6
	1503	8·9		1504	7·8
	2146	1·8		2131	2·8
3 M	0331	8·4	18 Tu	0319	7·5
	1003	2·0		0956	3·1
	1555	8·3		1550	7·2
	2238	2·4		2217	3·4
4 Tu	0431	7·8	19 W	0413	6·9
	1106	2·6		1058	3·6
	1708	7·6		1704	6·6
	2357	3·0		2333	3·8
5 W	0556	7·4	20 Th	0544	6·6
	1241	2·9		1243	3·7
	1846	7·3		1850	6·6
6 Th	0140	3·0	21 F	0124	3·7
	0730	7·5		0731	6·8
	1423	2·6		1418	3·2
	2019	7·6		2016	7·1
7 F	0305	2·6	22 Sa	0243	3·2
	0849	8·0		0840	7·5
	1543	2·0		1522	2·5
	2128	8·2		2110	7·7
8 Sa	0410	2·0	23 Su	0339	2·5
	0946	8·6		0928	8·1
	1642	1·4		1613	1·9
	2219	8·7		2152	8·4
9 Su	0501	1·5	24 M	0426	1·9
	1034	9·1		1007	8·7
	1730	0·9		1658	1·3
	2301	9·0		2230	8·9
10 M	0542	1·1	25 Tu	0508	1·3
	1115	9·4		1045	9·3
	1810	0·7		1739	0·8
●	2337	9·2		2308	9·3
11 Tu	0618	0·9	26 W	0549	0·8
	1151	9·6		1123	9·6
	1843	0·7		1818	0·4
				2344	9·6
12	0011	9·2	27	0628	0·5

APRIL

	Time	m		Time	m
1 Tu	0312	8·4	16 W	0246	7·7
	0952	2·0		0929	2·9
	1545	8·0		1518	7·3
	2223	2·6		2145	3·3
2 W	0417	7·8	17 Th	0336	7·2
	1102	2·6		1030	3·3
	1705	7·4		1626	6·8
	2349	3·2		2252	3·7
3 Th	0546	7·4	18 F	0457	6·8
	1243	2·8		1158	3·4
	1845	7·2		1801	6·7
4 F	0134	3·1	19 Sa	0034	3·7
	0719	7·6		0635	7·0
	1419	2·4		1331	3·0
	2012	7·6		1927	7·1
5 Sa	0254	2·6	20 Su	0158	3·2
	0833	8·1		0751	7·5
	1529	1·8		1439	2·4
	2112	8·2		2027	7·8
6 Su	0353	2·0	21 M	0300	2·5
	0927	8·6		0844	8·2
	1623	1·3		1535	1·8
	2159	8·6		2114	8·4
7 M	0440	1·5	22 Tu	0350	1·8
	1012	9·0		0929	8·8
	1705	1·0		1623	1·2
	2237	8·9		2156	9·0
8 Tu	0518	1·2	23 W	0437	1·3
	1049	9·2		1012	9·3
	1742	0·9		1708	0·7
	2311	9·0		2237	9·4
9 W	0551	1·1	24 Th	0520	0·8
	1123	9·3		1054	9·7
	1811	0·9		1750	0·4
●	2342	9·1		2316	9·7
10 Th	0621	1·1	25 F	0603	0·5
	1156	9·3		1134	9·9
	1839	1·0		1831	0·3
				2357	9·8
11 F	0011	9·1	26 Sa	0643	0·4
	0650	1·1		1218	9·9
	1227	9·2		1910	0·5
	1906	1·2			
12	0039	8·9	27	0039	9·7

Extracts from a tide table

In Figure 261 it will be seen that *two* high waters and *two* low waters are given for Liverpool, the standard port.

The higher high water is mean high-water springs (MHWS) and the lower low water is mean low-water springs (MLWS). These are derived from a series of observations of high and low water at spring tides. The lower high water is the mean high-water neaps (MHWN) and the higher low water is the mean low-water neaps (MLWN). Both of these are determined also from a series of tidal observations at neap tides. The heights for each of these tide levels are available for all standard ports. Heights for secondary ports can be determined using the tables of tidal differences.

It should be noted that all heights given in tidal information are heights above *chart datum*. This is a level that has been fixed such that the depth of water will hardly ever fall below it.

Figure 262

Terms and Definitions

Chart datum (CD) The level below which the tide never or rarely falls.

Height of tide The height of the sea surface above chart datum at any given instant.

High water (HW) The highest level reached by the sea surface during any one cycle.

Low water (LW) The lowest level reached by the sea surface during any one cycle.

Predicted range of the tide The difference in height between successive high water and low water for one particular cycle.

Spring tides Those tides of maximum range occurring about twice a month at or near new or full moon.

Neap tides Those tides of minimum range occurring about twice a month, at or near the first and last quarters of the moon.

Equinoctial springs Greater than average spring tides occur near the equinoxes (March and September), at new and full moon.

Mean high water springs (MHWS) The average height of high water at spring tides throughout the year.

Mean low water springs (MLWS) The average height of low water at spring tides throughout the year.

Mean high water neaps (MHWN) The average height of high water at neap tides throughout the year.

Mean low water neaps (MLWN) The average height of low water at neap tides throughout the year.

Highest astronomical tide (HAT) and lowest astronomical tide (LAT) These are the highest and lowest predictable tides under average meteorological conditions.

The datums of mean high water springs (MHWS) and chart datum (CD) are used to measure heights of land objects and seabed levels respectively.

Depth of Water

A useful method for determining the depth of water at a site is the Rule of Twelfths. This states that the tide will rise or fall, as appropriate, as follows:

1/12th of the range in the first sixth of its duration
2/12ths of the range in the second sixth of its duration
3/12ths of the range in the third sixth of its duration
3/12ths of the range in the fourth sixth of its duration
2/12ths of the range in the fifth sixth of its duration
1/12th of the range in the final sixth of its duration

Tidal Streams

So far all the tidal information has been concerned with the depth of water at different places and at different times. When a large mass of water moves (i.e. when the tide comes in or goes out), this movement of water gives rise to tidal streams. These are of interest to the navigator, who needs to allow for them when making passage. Tidal streams also affect the diver, since he would prefer to dive when the water is moving as little as possible – that is, at slack water. It should be remembered that, unlike winds where the opposite system is used, tidal streams are described by stating the three-figure notation of the direction, *towards* which the stream is flowing. The tidal stream is also given a rate in knots which is the rate at which the water moves over the seabed.

Again, it is possible to get tidal stream predictions for many areas. One useful method is by using the tidal diamonds on Admiralty charts. These small diamonds are positions on the chart where accurate measurements of tidal stream directions and rates have been determined for six hours before and six hours after high water at a local standard port. Each diamond is lettered for identification and on the tidal stream table it is also identified by its exact latitude and longitude. The table shows the direction (Dir) of the tide and its rate in knots (kn) for both spring (Sp) and neap (Np) tides.

It should be remembered that there may be other factors that will also affect the tidal streams and the heights of the tides. Strong wind conditions can have very marked effects. Local knowledge is thus helpful when trying to determine the best time to dive at a site where tidal streams are complex.

Figure 264

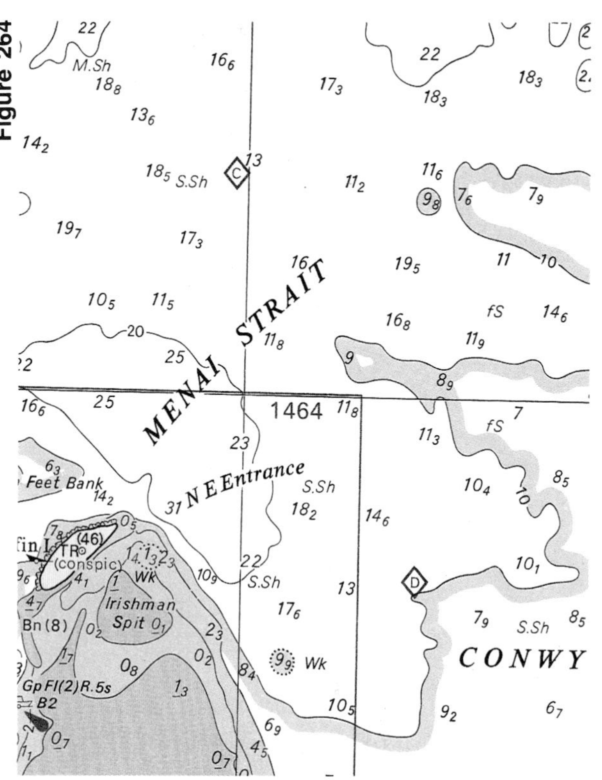

The letters enclosed in diamonds in the chart above (C,D) refer to the data applying to these positions in the information below (Crown Copyright)

Figure 263

van Sands.

Tidal Streams referred to HW at LIVERPOOL

Hours	A 53°29′·0N 4 21·9W Dir	Rate(kn) Sp	Np	B 53°26′·7N 4 20·3W Dir	Rate(kn) Sp	Np	C 53°21′·2N 4 00·1W Dir	Rate(kn) Sp	Np	D 53°19′·0N 3 58·4W Dir	Rate(kn) Sp	Np	E 53°29′0N 3 49·8W Dir	Rate(kn) Sp	Np
Before HW 6	066	0·5	0·2	102	0·6	0·3	115	0·2	0·1	124	0·4	0·2	000	0·2	0·1
5	089	2·2	1·1	099	1·4	0·7	098	0·9	0·5	114	0·8	0·4	098	0·8	0·4
4	095	3·4	1·7	100	2·3	1·2	100	1·5	0·9	127	1·1	0·6	102	1·6	0·9
3	099	3·3	1·6	101	3·3	1·7	111	1·4	0·8	134	1·2	0·6	106	1·7	1·0
2	101	2·4	1·2	101	3·1	1·6	120	0·9	0·5	146	0·9	0·5	105	1·3	0·7
1	121	0·7	0·3	087	0·3	0·2	128	0·3	0·1	164	0·6	0·3	098	0·6	0·4
HW	263	0·8	0·4	278	1·4	0·7	265	0·3	0·2	241	0·3	0·2	Slack		
After HW 1	275	2·2	1·1	276	2·3	1·2	287	0·9	0·5	296	0·7	0·4	280	0·6	0·4
2	276	3·0	1·5	276	2·8	1·5	290	1·4	0·8	311	1·1	0·6	277	1·1	0·6
3	277	2·8	1·4	277	2·4	1·2	296	1·3	0·7	317	1·2	0·6	280	1·5	0·8
4	279	2·2	1·1	277	2·2	1·1	298	0·9	0·5	318	1·0	0·5	287	1·4	0·8
5	283	1·4	0·7	276	1·4	0·7	295	0·3	0·2	337	0·5	0·3	282	0·9	0·5
6	320	0·3	0·1	170	0·1	0·0	114	0·2	0·1	315	0·1	0·0	313	0·3	0·2

Tidal Levels referred to Datum of Soundings

Place	Lat N	Long W	Heights in metres above datum MHWS	MHWN	MLWN	MLWS	Datum and remarks
h Ruffydd	53° 17′	4° 40′	5·0	3·9	1·8	0·6	

Tides – Examples

Example 1

What is the time and height of low water at Plymouth on 21 June 1986 and what is the time and height of the following high water?

1. Page 504 and of Reeds (Figure 265) gives high and low water for Plymouth for May, June and July.
2. Against 21 June (Sa) we see:
   0434 5·2
   1053 1·0
   1706 5·3
   2321 0·9
3. The low water times are 1053 and 2321 (GMT – add one hour for BST). Of these two, 1053 is the one that is most likely to be chosen by the diver (i.e. morning rather than late at night) and the corresponding height of water is 1·0 m.
4. The corresponding following high water time is 1708 and the height of water is 5·3 m.
5. The tidal range is thus 5·3 − 1·0 = 4·3 m.

Example 2

What is the time and height of low water at Salcombe on 24 June 1986 and what is the time and height of the following high water?

1. Page 502 in Reeds (Figure 266) shows a table of tidal differences based on Plymouth, and Salcombe, a secondary port, is the next to last of the places listed.
2. In the column headed MLW (mean low water) we find the time difference (Tm. Diff.) is 0.00 – this means that the time of low water is the same as that for Plymouth. The height difference (Ht. Diff.) is −0·1 m and therefore 0·1 m should be subtracted from the 0.9 m found for low water at Plymouth.
3. Time of low water at Salcombe is 1325 GMT and the height of water 0·8 m.
4. In the column headed MHW (mean high water) we find the time difference is +0.10 and, therefore, 10 minutes should be added to the time of high water at Plymouth. The height difference is −0·2 m and therefore 0·2 m should be subtracted from the height of high water at Plymouth.
5. Time of high water at Salcombe is 2002 GMT and the height of water 5·2 m.

Spring and neap tides are indicated by the differences in tidal heights in the tide tables.

If heights of water at particular times between high and low water need to be calculated, the tidal range can be determined (high water height–low water height) and the duration can be found (time of high water–time of low water) using 'rule of twelfths' (see p. 123). Alternatively, in many almanacs there are tidal graphs available for standard ports. These show the range at different times during the tidal cycle.

Figure 265

504 **PLYMOUTH**

HIGH & LOW WATER 1986 GMT ADD 1 HOUR MARCI

MAY

	TIME	M		TIME	M
1	0440	1.8	16	0344	1.9
	1109	4.2		0948	4.2
TH	1708	2.1	F	1559	2.1
	2333	4.4		2212	4.4
2	0602	2.0	17	0442	2.1
	1234	4.1		1052	4.1
F	1837	2.2	SA	1708	2.3
				2319	4.4
3	0102	4.4	18	0601	2.1
	0733	2.0		1207	4.2
SA	1405	4.3	SU	1835	2.2
	2002	2.0			
4	0225	4.6	19	0032	4.5
	0841	1.7		0724	1.9
SU	1510	4.6	M	1325	4.4
	2103	1.7		1955	1.9
5	0325	4.8	20	0147	4.8
	0932	1.4		0833	1.5
M	1557	4.9	TU	1437	4.8
	2151	1.4		2059	1.5
6	0409	5.1	21	0256	5.1
	1015	1.1		0931	1.2
TU	1635	5.1	W	1538	5.1
	2233	1.1		2155	1.2
7	0447	5.2	22	0357	5.3
	1054	1.0		1024	0.9
W	1709	5.2	TH	1634	5.3
	2312	1.0		2248	0.9
8	0520	5.3	23	0455	5.5
	1131	0.9		1114	0.7
TH	1741	5.3	F	1726	5.5
●	2347	1.0	○	2337	0.7
9	0553	5.3	24	0551	5.5
	1205	0.9		1202	0.6
F	1812	5.3	SA	1818	5.5
10	0022	1.0	25	0026	0.6
	0625	5.2		0646	5.4
SA	1238	1.0	SU	1249	0.7
	1842	5.3		1908	5.5
11	0054	1.0	26	0113	0.6
	0657	5.1		0738	5.3
SU	1309	1.1	M	1334	0.9

JUNE

	TIME	M		TIME	M
1	0019	4.5	16	0525	1.8
	0647	1.8		1127	4.5
SU	1309	4.3	M	1754	2.0
	1914	2.0		2348	4.7
2	0127	4.6	17	0636	1.7
	0752	1.7		1238	4.6
M	1413	4.5	TU	1908	1.8
	2016	1.8			
3	0228	4.7	18	0100	4.8
	0846	1.5		0748	1.5
TU	1506	4.7	W	1352	4.7
	2109	1.6		2019	1.6
4	0319	4.8	19	0215	4.9
	0934	1.4		0855	1.3
W	1549	4.9	TH	1502	4.9
	2156	1.4		2124	1.3
5	0403	5.0	20	0327	5.1
	1018	1.2		0956	1.1
TH	1629	5.1	F	1606	5.1
	2239	1.3		2224	1.1
6	0444	5.0	21	0434	5.2
	1059	1.2		1053	1.0
F	1708	5.1	SA	1706	5.3
	2320	1.2		2321	0.9
7	0524	5.0	22	0538	5.2
	1138	1.1		1146	0.9
SA	1746	5.2	SU	1804	5.4
●	2358	1.2	○		
8	0604	5.0	23	0014	0.7
	1215	1.2		0638	5.2
SU	1823	5.1	M	1237	0.8
				1901	5.4
9	0035	1.2	24	0105	0.7
	0643	4.9		0734	5.1
M	1250	1.3	TU	1325	0.9
	1858	5.1		1952	5.4
10	0110	1.2	25	0153	0.7
	0719	4.8		0825	5.0
TU	1323	1.4	W	1411	1.0
	1931	5.0		2039	5.3
11	0144	1.3	26	0239	0.9
	0751	4.7		0910	4.9
W	1355	1.5	TH	1456	1.2

JULY

	TIME	M		
1	0019	4.5	16	(
	0651	1.8		1
TU	1304	4.4	W	1
	1919	2.0		
2	0123	4.5	17	(
	0753	1.8		(
W	1408	4.5	TH	1
	2022	1.9		1
3	0228	4.5	18	(
	0852	1.7		(
TH	1506	4.7	F	1
	2121	1.7		2
4	0326	4.6	19	C
	0946	1.6		C
F	1557	4.8	SA	1
	2213	1.6		2
5	0418	4.7	20	C
	1034	1.4		1
SA	1643	4.9	SU	1
	2259	1.4		2
6	0505	4.8	21	0
	1117	1.4		1
SU	1727	5.0	M	1
	2342	1.3	○	
7	0549	4.8	22	0
	1157	1.3		0
M	1807	5.1	TU	1
●				1
8	0020	1.2	23	0
	0630	4.8		0
TU	1234	1.3	W	1
	1844	5.1		1
9	0056	1.2	24	0
	0707	4.8		0
W	1309	1.3	TH	1
	1918	5.1		2
10	0131	1.2	25	0
	0740	4.8		0
TH	1343	1.3	F	1
	1948	5.1		2
11	0205	1.2	26	0
	0810	4.8		0
F	1418	1.3	SA	1

Figure 266

TIDAL DIFFERENCES ON PLYMOUTH

PLACE	MHW		MLW		GUIDING DEPTH AT			
	Tm. Diff. h. min.	Ht. Diff. m.	Tm. Diff. h. min.	Ht. Diff. m.	HWS m.	HWN m.	CD m.	POSITION
Mevagissy	−0 10	−0.1	0 00	−0.1	6.3	5.2	0.9	Steps, North Pier
Pentewan	−0 10	−0.1	0 00	−0.1	5.7	4.6	0.3	Sill of Basin
Charlestown	−0 10	−0.1	−0 05	−0.1	4.8	3.7	−0.6	Entrance
Par	−0 10	−0.1	−0 05	−0.2	3.9	2.8	−1.5	Alongside Long Arm
Fowey	−0 05	−0.1	−0 10	−0.2	6.0	4.9	0.6	Whitehouse Pt. Jetty
Polperro	−0 05	−0.1	−0 10	−0.2	4.4	3.2	−1.0	In Harbour
Looe	−0 05	−0.1	−0 05	−0.2	5.1	3.9	−0.3	Steps on breakwater
Whitesand Bay ..	+0 05	0.0	0 00	0.0	25.5	24.5	20.0	Shelving
Plymouth	0 00	0.0	0 00	0.0	7.0	5.9	1.5	Entce. to Sutton Hr.
Devonport	+0 05	0.0	0 00	0.0	28.5	27.4	23.0	Off Ocean Qy. Marina
Tamar River								
Weir Head	+0 45	−3.5	–	–	1.5	–	0.8	Fairway
Calstock	+0 30	−0.8	+2 10	−0.5	3.7	2.4	−1.0	Fairway
Cargreen	+0 15	+0.1	+0 20	−0.1	7.1	5.8	1.4	Fairway
Saltash	+0 15	0.0	+0 15	−0.1	4.6	3.4	−1.0	Saltash Pier head
River Tavy								
Warleigh Quay ..	+0 15	−0.8	–	–	–	–	Dries	
Maristow	+0 15	−2.6	–	–	2.4	1.2	–	Fairway
R. Yealm Entce.	+0 10	−0.1	0 00	−0.1	6.0	4.9	0.6	Bar (Southern point)
River Avon	+0 15	−0.6	0 00	0.0	2.7	1.7	−2.2	Bar
Salcombe River								
Kingsbridge	+0 15	−0.8	–	–	1.3	0.2	−3.4	Squares Quay
Salcombe	+0 10	−0.2	0 00	−0.1	6.2	5.1	0.9	Bar

Tide Rips

In calm surface conditions you may sometimes see a roughening of the water, or at least a break in the surface pattern caused by the meeting of opposing tidal streams and is generally known as a 'tide rip'. Although power boats are largely unaffected by crossing tide rips, you should cross deliberately or at least be aware that you have done so.

Figure 267

A tidal rip showing surface disturbance off a prominent headland

Cross-Currents

In estuaries, harbours and other confined waters there is a possibility of strong cross-currents. For example, in a narrow channel which has sand or mud banks lying parallel to the shore, the flood tide will reach the top of the banks and will start to fill the inner channel. At this moment a surface tidal stream will form which will cause your boat to be drawn towards the shore.

Figure 268

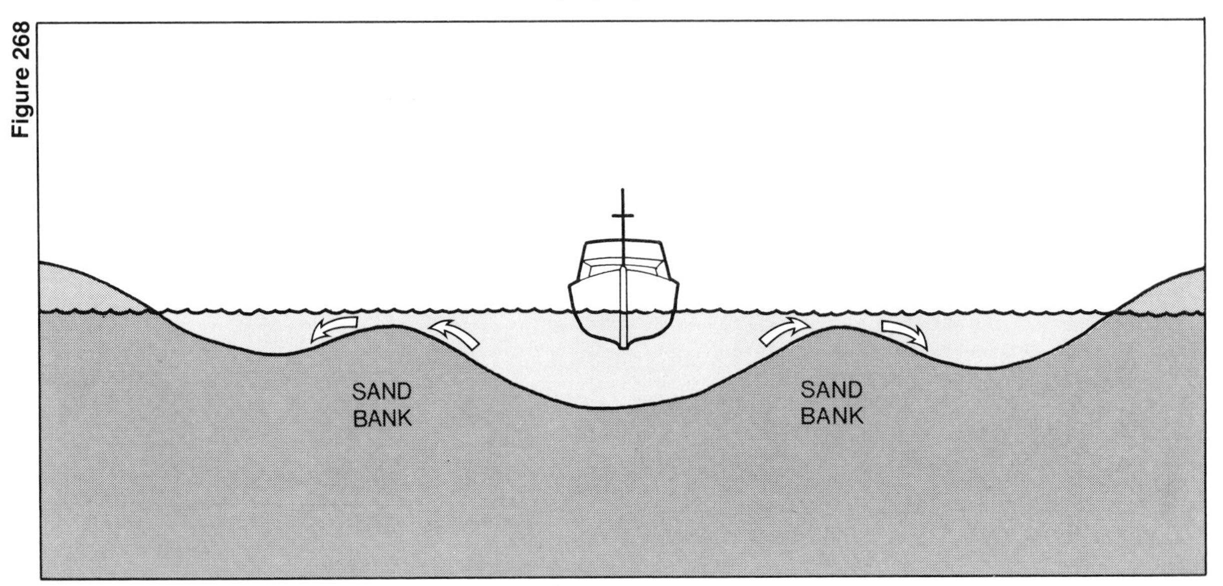

Rip Currents

Rip currents occur when water is driven over a sand bar or reef by a flood tide or adverse weather conditions. The water is then funnelled back through narrow openings in the sand bar or reef, causing a very strong back current. If you find yourself in a rip current, then steer a course parallel to the shore until you are clear of the rip area. Diving in such areas should be approached with caution.

Figure 269

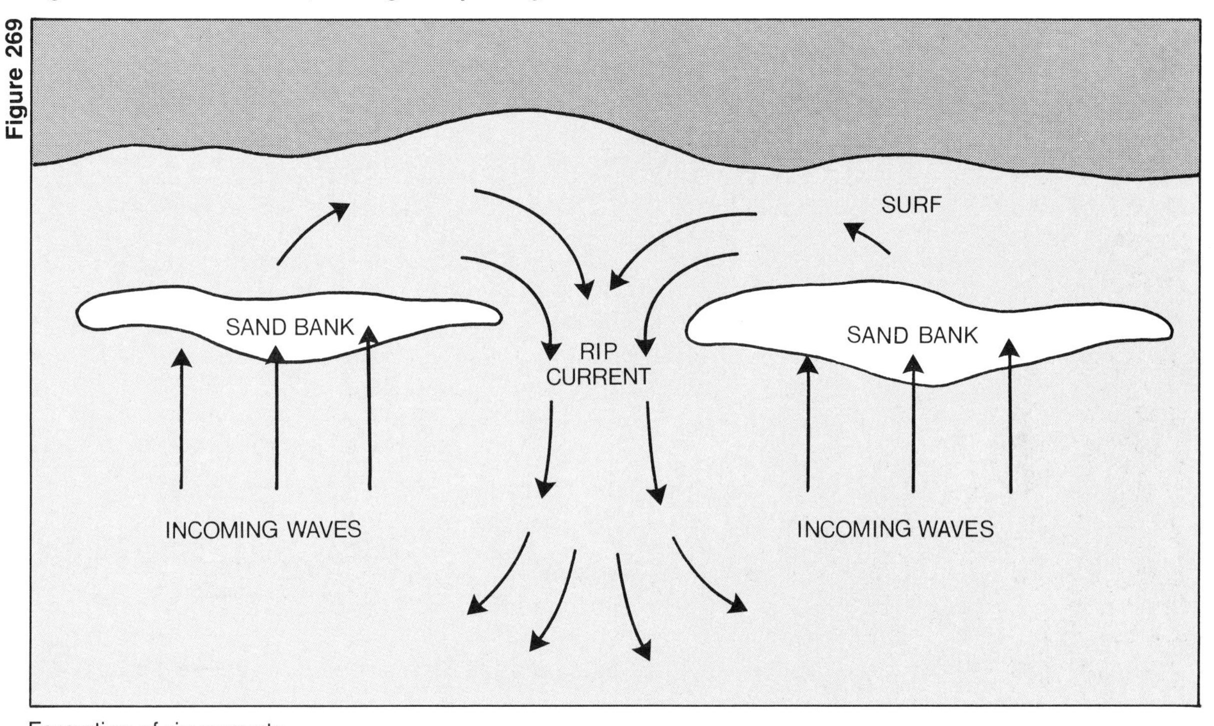

Formation of rip currents

Overfalls

Sometimes depth and the configuration of the seabed, combined with strong localized tidal streams or eddies, create local conditions known as overfalls. These can often be seen as breaking waves caused by a strong tidal stream crossing rapidly shoaling water, an irregular bottom or an underwater obstruction. These conditions can cause loss of control in a small boat.

Figure 270

Overfalls in the Gulf of Corryvreckan

Figure 271

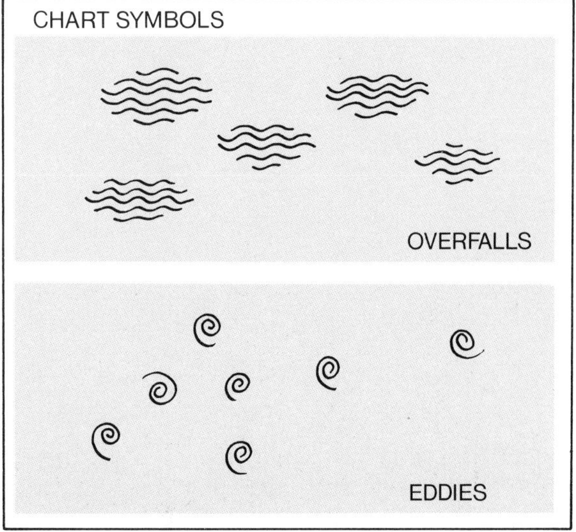

Chart symbols for turbulent water

Figure 272

The Weather

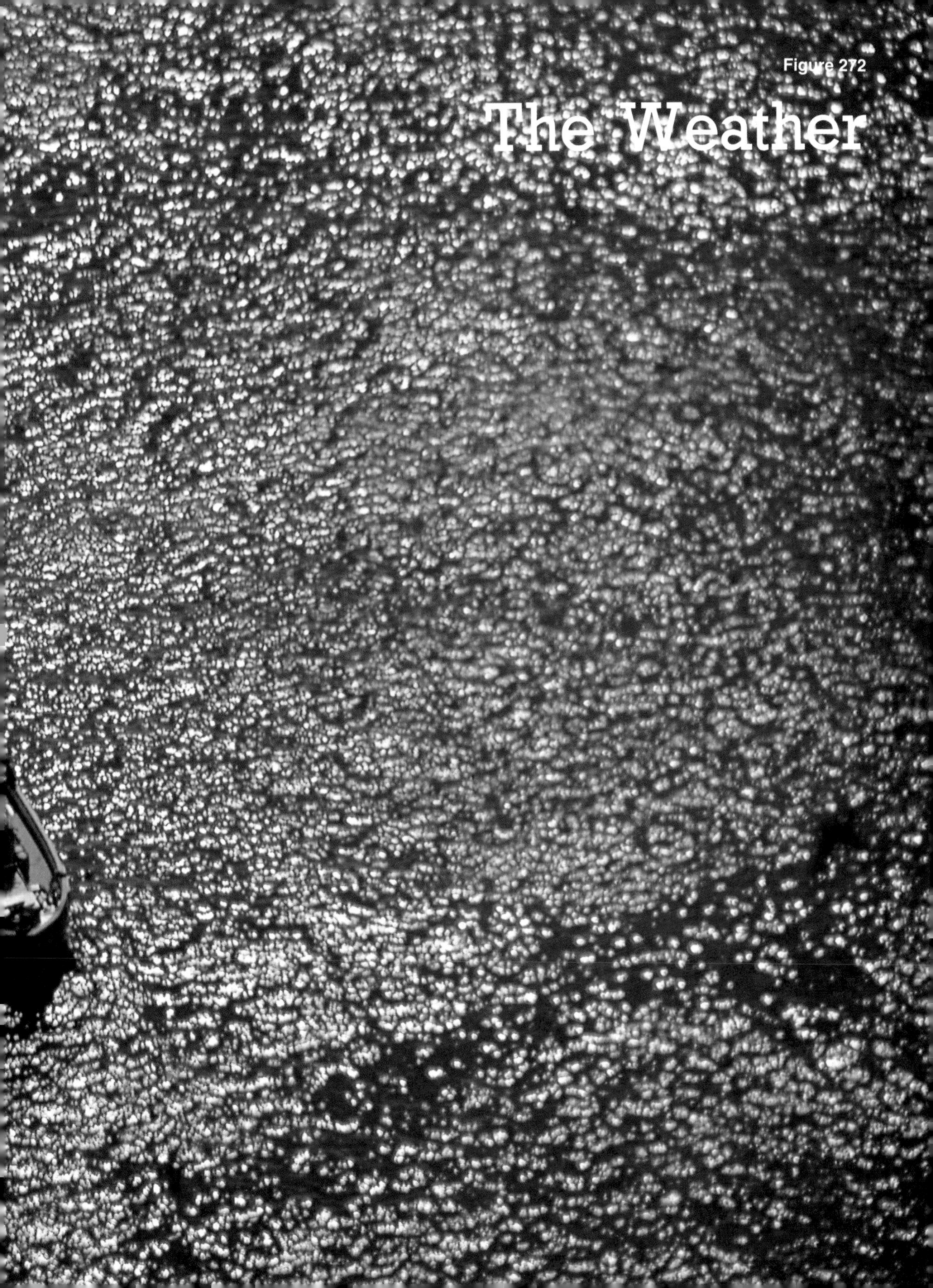

Meteorology

Meteorology, or the science of weather and weather forecasting, was so named because it was once thought that variations in the world's weather were due to the appearance of swarms of meteorites which interfered with the upper atmosphere. We now know that weather phenomena have a more earthly origin.

For divers, weather forecasting is a vital part of any dive plan, especially in areas of the world which have a very variable climate, such as the British Isles. The term 'weather' applies to conditions experienced on a day-to-day basis; the term 'climate' is used to describe weather conditions over a period of at least thirty years in any particular location.

The weather conditions that are of greatest concern to divers are *wind*, *sea fog* and *low surface visibility* caused by low cloud and/or precipitation. Precipitation is the word used to cover rain, sleet, snow, etc. Of all the above, wind is the weather phenomenon which can most easily disrupt the most carefully produced dive plan. Sea fog is very unpredictable, can be extremely localized and can descend very quickly. Low cloud and precipitation are easier to predict but can cause problems if the diving is being carried out at a distance from the coast.

It is hoped that this section will provide enough background information to enable divers to gain a better understanding of the weather and to help them make sensible decisions when organizing dives and, thereby, avoid potential dive problems.

The Atmosphere

To understand why winds blow, why sea fogs form and why rain falls very frequently in some areas and very rarely in others, it is necessary to understand a little about the atmosphere and the influence of the land and the sea.

The life-supporting gases that we call the atmosphere are, in reality, a very thin layer covering the surface of the earth. If one imagines a varnished classroom globe, the relative thickness of the atmosphere is about equal to the thickness of the layer of varnish. However, in spite of its relative thinness, it is in the atmosphere that the weather is created. Apart from the life-supporting gases, air also contains water vapour, the result of *evaporation* of surface water from the oceans, lakes and rivers of the world. The amount of water vapour contained in the atmosphere varies considerably with the temperature. Warm air is able to hold much more water vapour than cold air, and if warm air is cooled the invisible water vapour in it is turned back into a visible form by the process of *condensation*. The most common form of condensation in the atmosphere is seen as clouds. When clouds form at ground (sea) level we know them as fog or mist.

Winds

Wind is simply air which is moving due to a pressure imbalance in the atmosphere. Divers will be familiar with the term 'bar'. The pressure of the atmosphere at sea level is almost one bar. This is, however, the average pressure and often there are wide variations. Air pressure is defined as the weight of a column of air pressing on the earth's surface. The average is 1013 millibars. Variations in pressure on either side of this figure are due to a particular location experiencing air which is rising or air which is falling. Rising air will exert slightly less pressure and there will be an area of *low pressure*. Air which is sinking will exert slightly higher pressure and this will produce a *high pressure* area.

Divers should be familiar with the fact that air pressure tries to equalize whenever there is a pressure difference. Decanting from a high-pressure 'air bank' cylinder into a low-pressure aqualung cylinder demonstrates this principle. In a similar way high-pressure areas in the atmosphere will seek to fill adjoining low-pressure areas. The resulting movement of air is a wind, and the greater the pressure difference between the air masses, the greater the strength of the wind.

Wind can be a particular problem to diving activities because it generates waves. The greater the distance of water over which the wind blows, the greater will be the height and strength of the resultant waves. This distance is known as the *fetch* of the wave. A Force 8 gale on the west coast of the British Isles will produce waves which have had the expanse of the Atlantic Ocean over which to build up. A similar strength wind close to the eastern side of the British Isles will not produce such big waves inshore and conditions may be divable. Thus it is very important for divers to try to predict both the strength of the wind and its direction.

Certain areas of the world experience predominantly high air pressure whereas others have permanent low pressure. Figure one shows the distribution of the earth's pressure belts and their resulting winds. Winds which blow in a certain direction for most of the year are known as *trade winds*, so called because ships' masters, in the days of sail, used them to advantage while engaged in long sea voyages. The fact that the trade winds do not blow directly north or south is due to the deflection caused by the earth's rotation. This is known as the *Coriolis effect*. Those divers who live in the British Isles will know that the predominant wind direction is southwesterly. Most of the weather systems which affect the British Isles travel from west to east.

Figure 273

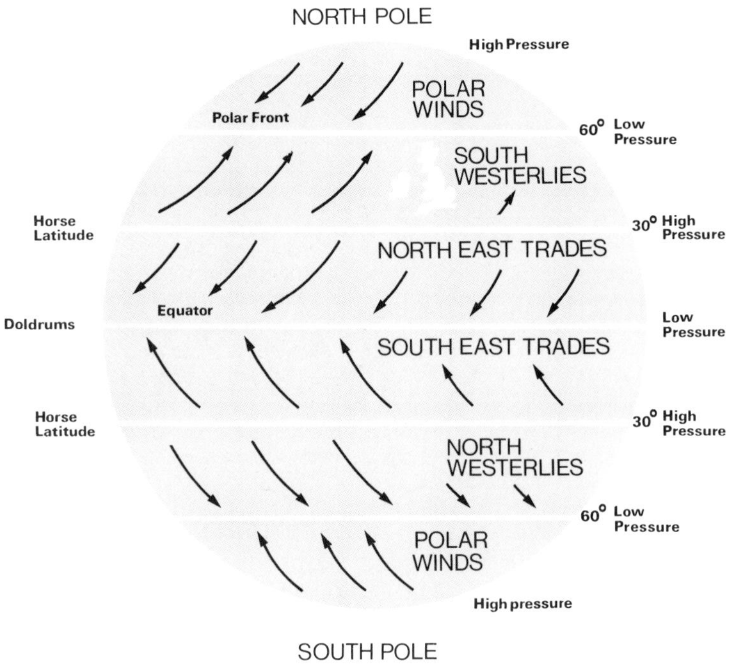

NORTH POLE

High Pressure

POLAR WINDS

Polar Front

60° Low Pressure

SOUTH WESTERLIES

Horse Latitude

30° High Pressure

NORTH EAST TRADES

Equator

Doldrums

Low Pressure

SOUTH EAST TRADES

Horse Latitude

30° High Pressure

NORTH WESTERLIES

60° Low Pressure

POLAR WINDS

High pressure

SOUTH POLE

Weather Systems

Distribution of the Earth's pressure belts and resulting winds

Weather Systems

What is it that makes the weather in the British Isles so unpredictable, and yet other parts of the world have such a constant, everyday pattern that it becomes almost monotonous? The British Isles has changeable weather because it lies in the same latitudes as the dividing line between the warm, tropical air from the south and the cold polar air from the north (see Figure 273). A line which divides warm air from cold is called a *front* and, just as the term refers to a line between two armies, in meteorological terms a front signifies a battle zone between warm and cold air. The polar front, as it is known, provides a constant battle for the dominance of our weather between warm air from the south and colder air from the north. This explains why there are days in the winter when it is almost warm enough for shirtsleeves and in summer there are days when overcoats are necessary. It all depends on which type of air has won the battle at that particular time.

Wherever two air masses meet, a front develops and it is along a front that unsettled weather conditions arise.

Figure 274 shows in more detail the *air masses* which conflict to try to dominate our weather. Air masses are huge areas of air which have the characteristics of the area where they developed. Polar continental air, for example, was born in Siberia and shares the characteristics of that climate. Tropical continental air has the characteristics of northern Africa. All air masses are

Figure 274

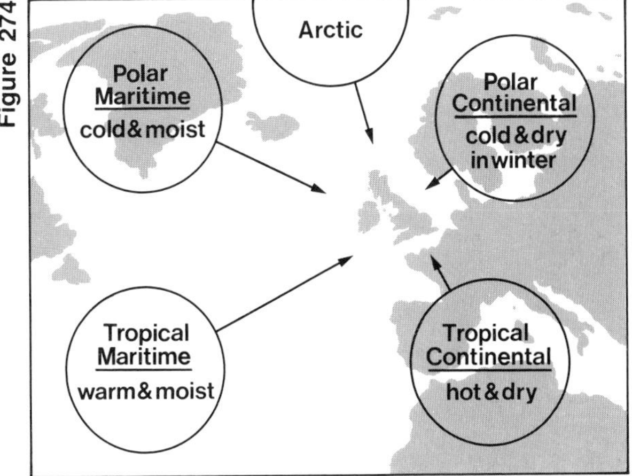

Air masses affecting British Isles weather

changed by their passage over seas and oceans and, depending on their temperature, collect varying amounts of water vapour.

Our most common weather feature is a *depression*. This is a weather system, born in the Atlantic, along the line of the polar front. Warm air from the south drives a wedge into cold, polar air and, as the warm air is less dense, it is forced to rise over the cold air. As it rises it also cools, giving up much of its water vapour and forming clouds. When this occurs a *warm front* develops, bringing with it rain and strong winds. Figure 275 shows a typical depression as seen on the weather map and Figure 276 shows it in cross-section. A *cold front* is formed when cold air tries to undercut the warm air and this often brings strong northwesterly winds and heavy showers. If you follow the passage of a depression you will notice that the cold front gradually advances and catches up with the warm front. This is known as an *occlusion* and is the result of the higher-pressure, colder air trying to equalize and fill the void created by the lower-pressure, warm air. When the cold front catches up completely with the warm front, the system just fizzles out. Unfortunately this normally occurs long after we have suffered it. The whole mass of air, the depression, moves across the Atlantic from west to east, driven by a very strong, upper-atmospheric wind called the *jet stream*. The British Isles lie directly in its path. Unfortunately a depression never creates good diving conditions.

It is useful for divers to know something about depressions since the weather sequence and the wind direction are reasonably predictable. The wind direction and fronts are shown in Figure 275; these form a typical depression. It is quite usual, however, to see warm fronts without cold fronts and vice versa. These never produce settled conditions.

What are the weather conditions that divers can expect as a depression approaches and passes over? Figure 276, a cross-section through a depression, shows the typical cloud type, height and precipitation that can be expected as a depression passes over. The first signs of an approaching warm front are the high white *cirrus* clouds, sometimes known as mares' tails because of their similarity to a horse's tail. These usually approach from the west or the southwest and are often aligned parallel to each other, being whipped along by the jet stream, which blows up to 250 km per hour. Incidentally there is more energy stored in a depression than in a hurricane, the difference being that the energy in the latter is much more concentrated and therefore creates much more environmental damage.

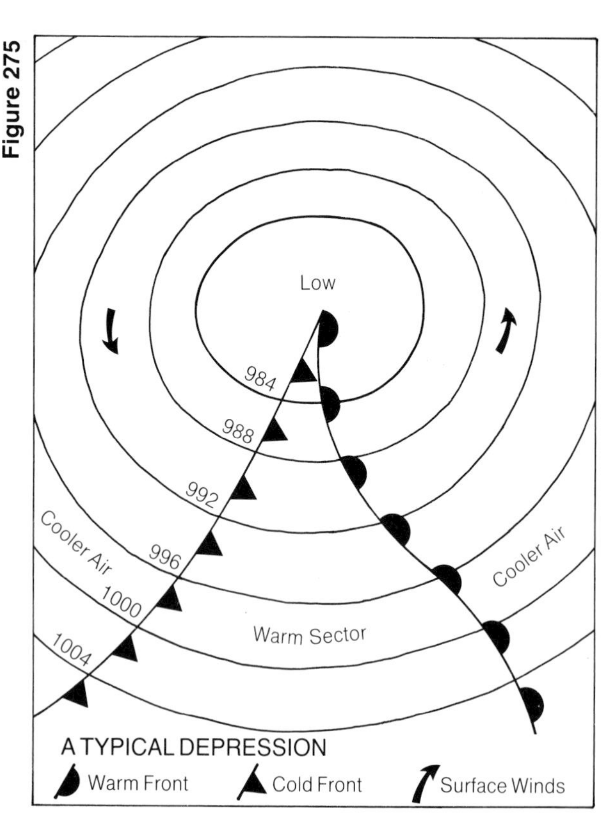

Figure 275
Typical depression

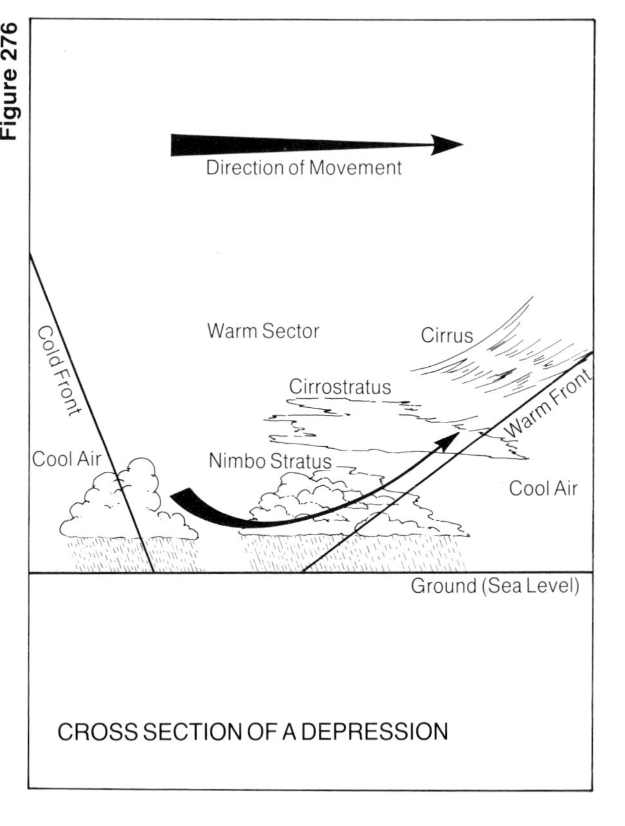

Figure 276
Cross section of a depression

Clouds

There are four basic cloud forms, shown in Figure 277–280. The cirrus clouds are the high white clouds which gradually cover the blueness of the sky and eventually become *cirrostratus*. The higher the cloud the whiter it appears, mainly because it is composed of ice crystals, the water droplets in it having frozen. *Stratus* cloud is any cloud which forms a layer or blanket over the sky. *Cumulus* clouds are the larger cauliflower-shaped clouds which are sometimes a sign of bad weather. *Nimbus* clouds are the dark grey ones associated with periods of rain, particularly on a warm front.

The basic cloud types can be combined. For example, as the warm front of a depression approaches, the cirrus gives way to cirrostratus, while cumulus at high level is known as cirrocumulus. As cirrostratus covers the sky the sun often appears to have a watery halo. As can be seen from Figure 278, the cloud height or base becomes lower as the front approaches. At the same time it is usual for wind strength to increase, so that by the time the cumulonimbus rain clouds appear diving conditions are generally very poor.

Figure 277

Cirrus clouds

Figure 278

Stratus clouds

Figure 279

Cumulus clouds

Figure 280

Nimbus clouds

Depressions

Depressions pass at different speeds and the precipitation associated with a warm front can take between six and twenty-four hours to pass. If the weatherman describes a depression as 'vigorous', one can expect it to be quite fast-moving. Once the warm front passes, this is not necessarily the end of our troubles. The wind may still be quite strong and the surface visibility, although improved, may still not be ideal because of cloud cover. However, the temperature climbs as the warm air passes. The cold front usually brings heavy, perhaps thundery, showers, with huge anvil-shaped cumulonimbus clouds reaching up to 15,000 m. Wind strength increases from the northwest, especially just before and during a rain squall. It is usual for the wind to die appreciably following a squall, only for it to increase as the next one approaches. As the cold front passes a distinct drop in temperature is noticeable as we find ourselves once again in cold-sector air.

The annoying thing about depressions is that, quite often, as soon as one has disappeared another follows on its tail. The pressure belts surrounding the earth generally move with the sun, which tracks continually between the two tropics throughout the year. In the northern hemisphere's summer the sun is closer to the Tropic of Cancer and in winter to the Tropic of Capricorn. In theory this should ensure that the polar front moves north of the British Isles, during our summer, with harmful depressions passing over Iceland and northern Scandinavia. It only takes a shift of a few degrees south, however, for the polar front to be located over the British Isles and then we have a poor, unsettled summer. In a good year the tropical continental air mass from the Sahara Desert and Azores dominates our weather as it does every year throughout the Mediterranean.

Apart from the predictable precipitation and poor surface visibility associated with a depression, one of the useful features for dive planning is that the surface winds tend to blow anticlockwise around its centre in the northern hemisphere (clockwise in the southern hemispere). This means that the winds may start off northwesterly, then go westerly, moving to south-west, south and finally south-easterly as the cold front passes. This information is useful for dive planning as long as you are aware of how far away the depression is and how soon it is expected to pass over your intended dive site. Media weather forecasts should give this information.

Television or newspaper synoptic (weather) maps can also give much information. The lines drawn on a weather map are called *isobars* and they connect all places of equal barometric (air) pressure. Figure 281 shows a typical depression; you will notice that the pressure is given in millibars and that it gets lower towards the centre. The warm front always comes first and is seen as a line with half circles on it. The cold front has small triangles on it. You can remember the difference by imagining the triangles are icicles.

It was mentioned earlier that winds blow from high-pressure areas to low-pressure areas and that the greater the pressure difference, the stronger will be the wind. A weather map demonstrates this in that the closer together the isobars, the stronger the wind. Avoid diving when you can hardly see the map for isobars.

So far it has been nearly all doom and gloom. How do we predict good diving conditions?

Anticyclons

Figure 281 shows a typical weather-map *anticyclone*. This is the opposite of a depression and is an area of stable, high-pressure air. We have already mentioned the effect on our summer weather when it is dominated by the tropical, continental air from North Africa and the Azores. Notice that on the map the isobars are far apart, a sign of very light winds which tend to blow clockwise around its centre. The pressure builds towards the centre of the anticyclone and, once established, is very stable. A much shorter weather phenomenon, but one which usually brings a day or two of fine settled weather, is a *ridge*, which will often be sandwiched between two depressions.

Figure 281

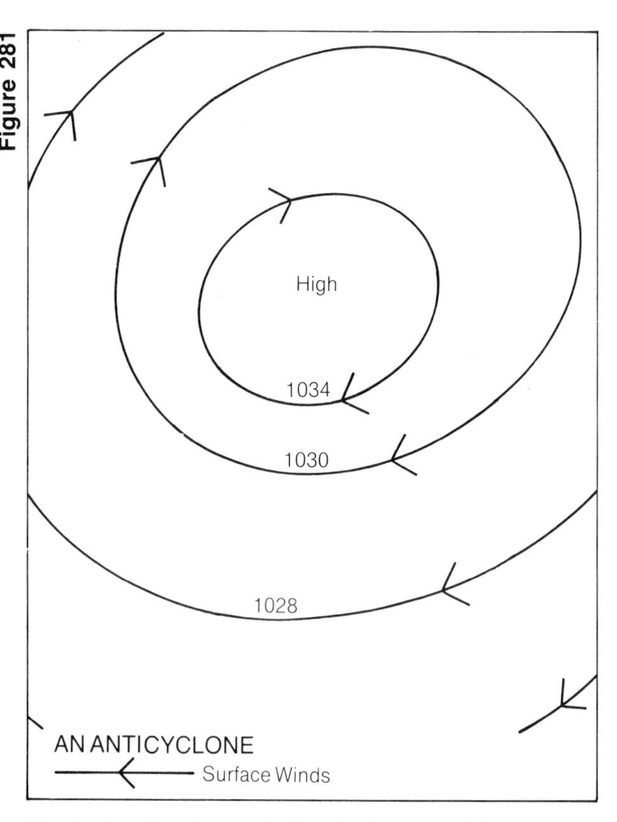

A typical anticyclone with its widely spaced isobars

Fog and Mist Formation

High pressure, however, brings its own problems of poor surface conditions with sea mist and fog. The North Sea coast of the British Isles is notorious for its 'sea fret' or, to give it its correct name, *advection fog*. This occurs anywhere in the world where a warm stream of air passes over a relatively cool sea surface. Warm, continental air coming into contact with the North Sea will condense rapidly and suddenly to give a sea fog which can reduce visibility to a few metres. Inland the sun soon evaporates any mist or fog, but beware when planning any dive on the North Sea coast when the wind is easterly or southeasterly.

The same phenomenon occurs on the Pacific coast of California. California has a Mediterranean-type climate but, unfortunately, has a cold ocean current running along its coastline. San Francisco is famous for its fogs and suffers in much the same way as does the North Sea coastline of the British Isles.

There are certain patterns of weather systems which can greatly exaggerate the wind strength and ensure difficult, if not impossible, diving conditions. Figures 282, 283 and 284 show how to recognize such conditions. You have to remember that winds blow anticlockwise in a depression and clockwise in areas of high pressure. Figure 282 shows a situation in which a depression has moved out into the North Sea and is followed by a ridge of high pressure. You will see from the isobars that there is an area of very strong northerly gales where the two systems meet. Figure 283 shows a similar situation with a depression over northern France and an anticyclone over Scandinavia. The eastern coast of England and Scotland would be rendered undivable in such conditions because the very strong easterly winds would have had the fetch of the North Sea in which to generate large waves. Figure 284 shows a depression over Iceland and high pressure over France. The result is a very strong westerly wind. The west coastline of the British Isles has its own particular problems with rough seas, due to the size of the Atlantic. A storm in the Atlantic can generate such waves that the resultant *ground swell* makes conditions very difficult on shorelines exposed to the Atlantic, even though the storm itself does not reach our waters.

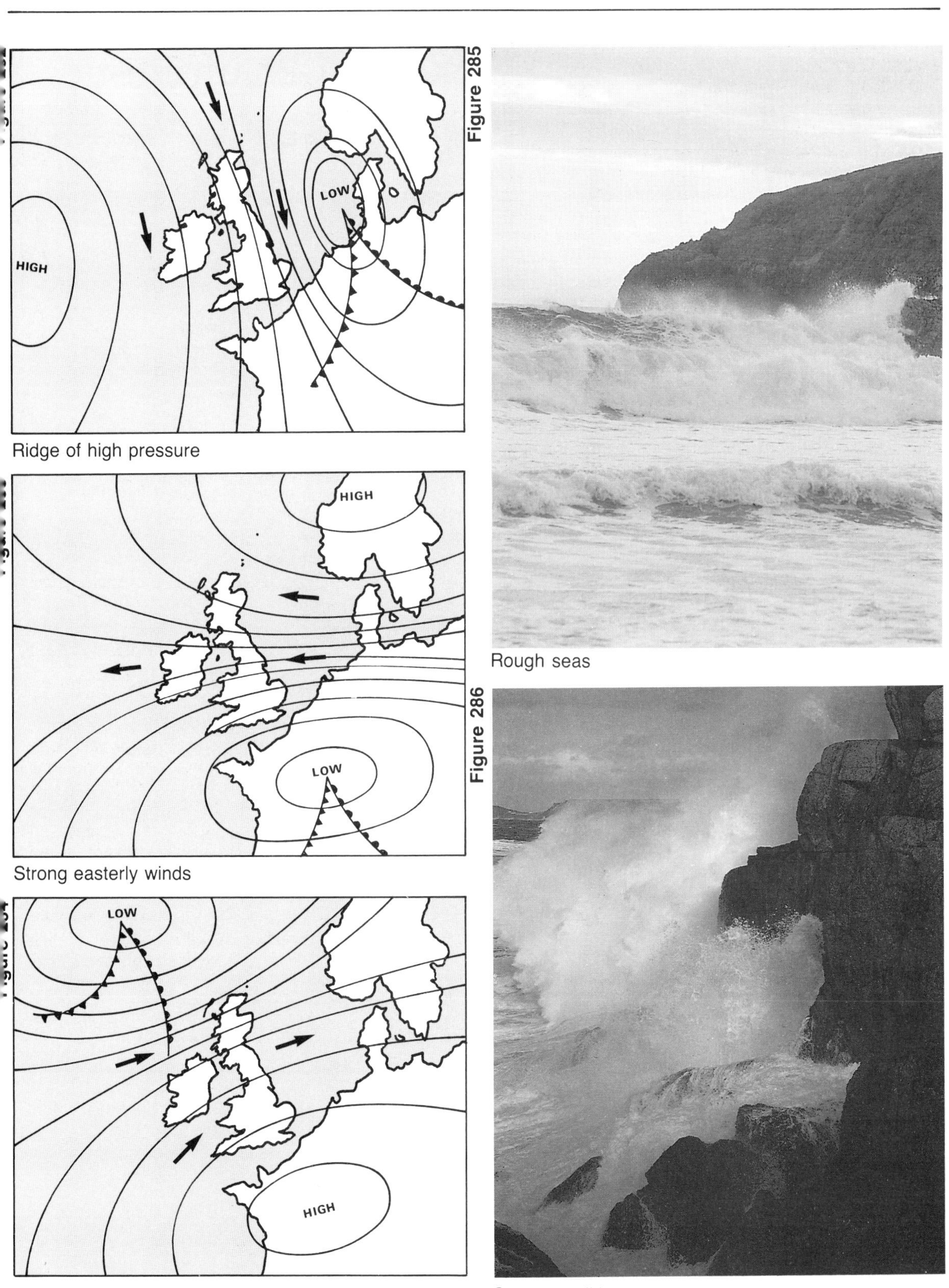

Ridge of high pressure

Strong easterly winds

Strong westerly winds

Rough seas

Storm conditions

Seasickness

Some divers suffer quite badly from seasickness, though most people become accustomed to the motion after a couple of days at sea. This is not the place to discuss fully how to combat the problem, though some tactical suggestions can be offered:

Select a bunk as near the middle of the vessel as possible.

Seasickness preparations can be useful to most people in rough weather. (Everyone suffers from motion sickness if the conditions are rough enough.) All anti-emetic drugs have a sedative effect to some degree and can therefore exacerbate the effects of nitrogen narcosis. Therefore you must test the effect of a particular preparation on yourself before using it in a diving situation. The best drug by far for most people seems to be cinnarizine (trade name Stugeron).

Prepare your diving equipment while the vessel is in calm water.

Avoid intricate physical tasks (i.e. preparing underwater cameras) if at all possible.

If using a dry suit, don your 'woolly bear' before the vessel leaves calm water.

Before leaving calm water, stow your dive gear where it is ready for immediate use.

Avoid ambitious meals or rich food shortly before diving, though a little dry food may help.

Stay in the fresh air or lie on your bunk.

Stay as near to the waterline of the vessel as possible.

Avoid areas with diesel fumes.

Try to avoid using the 'heads' in rough weather.

Take especial care when alone on deck in heavy weather, especially if you are not feeling too well. If you fall in the water in heavy seas it is unlikely that you will be spotted in time to be rescued.

If you have to be sick, do it downwind and with panache.

Do not dive when you feel really sick.

Figure 288

One-man recompression chamber with oxygen supply

Rescue Equipment

There are legal requirements controlling the safety equipment that must be carried on different classes of vessel. In addition it is prudent to include certain extra items.

The classifications appropriate to vessels that divers might use are:

Pleasure yachts under 5.5 m in length
Pleasure yachts 5.5–13.7 m in length
Pleasure yachts 13–21 m in length
Pleasure yachts 21–26 m in length
Pleasure yachts over 26 m in length and vessels of any size of 150 tons gross and over sailing vessels
Passenger vessels with a Load Line Exemption Certificate
Passenger vessels with a Load line Certificate (usually Class II(A) or Class III)

Lists of prescribed or recommended equipment are available for all these classes of vessel.

There are different lists for each of these classes and to give them in all their detail is not appropriate as they appear in full in nautical almanacs and Department of Transport specifications. Instead a brief composite list is given. This is relatively comprehensive, though some small vessels will not need all of the items listed.

Personal Safety Gear

1. A lifejacket for each person aboard.
2. Safety harness for working on the deck of a power vessel in heavy seas.
3. Waterproof clothing.

Rescue Equipment and Provisions

4. Four hand-held distress flares.
5. Four hand-held parachute distress rockets.
6. Two buoyant smoke signals.
7. Two lifebuoys – 12 cm (30 in) in diameter with at least 18·3 metres of buoyant line attached. One should be fitted with a combined self-activating light and smoke lifebuoy marker.
8. Emergency radio transmitter.
9. Heaving line of 30 metres with a rescue quoit.
10. Boathook.
11. Lifelines.
12. Boarding ladder.
13. Bulwarks and/or safety rails of adequate height above deck (e.g. 1 metre).
14. Towrope.

General Equipment

15. Compass plus a spare.
16. Echo sounder.
17. Charts and instruments.
18. Almanacs, pilots.
19. Watch or clock.

20. Barometer.
21. Radio receiver.
22. Sound signalling equipment.
23. Radar reflector.
24. Navigational lights.
25. Water-resistant torch and spares.
26. First-aid box plus anti-seasickness tablets.
27. Anchor of adequate size with chain or warp.
28. Sea anchor and warp.
29. Bilge pumping system.
30. Leak-stopping kit.
31. Engine tool kit.

Fire-Fighting Equipment

32. At least one hand pump with a permanent sea connection, one hose with 10-mm nozzle, producing a jet of water with a throw of at least 6 metres.
33. Two or more extinguishers (2-gallon foam or equivalent dry powder).
34. Two appropriate portable extinguishers in machinery space.
35. Two fire buckets with lanyards.
36. Fire blankets.
37. Either a smothering gas system or an automatic water spraying system.
38. Calor-gas installations must be in a well-ventilated deck compartment.

Survival Equipment:

39. Inflatable life raft of Department of Transport-approved type capable of accommodating everyone on board (two if there are more than eight people aboard).
40. Life raft equipment. The equipment supplied as standard is not adequate for other than a couple of days. Lists born of first-hand experience are detailed in Dougal Robertson's *Sea Survival* (see below).
41. Life raft book(s).

References

Watts (ed.) *Reed's Nautical Almanac*, Reed, 1986.

Hewitt and Lees-Spalding (eds.), Macmillan & Silk Cut Yachtsman's Handbook, Macmillan, 1984.

Cole, *Safety on Small Craft*, HMSO, 1973

Robertson, *Sea Survival*, Elek, 1975.

Bailey and Bailey, *117 Days Adrift*, Nautical Publishing Company, 1974.

Robin, *Survival at Sea*, Stanley Paul, 1981.

Craighead and Craighead, *How to Survive on Land and Sea*, revised by Smith and Jarvis, Naval Institute Press, 1984.

Engine Toolkit and Spares

The following lists are an indication of the tools and spares that may be found useful on a larger vessel.

Tools

A boat toolkit should contain:

- Set of open-ended spanners
- Set of ring spanners
- Set of socket spanners and accessories
- Hexagon wrenches (Allen keys)
- Various screwdrivers
- Various crosspoint screwdrivers
- Engineer's hammer
- 2-lb mallet
- Various pliers
- Mole grips
- Coarse and smooth files
- Hacksaw
- Hydrometer
- Multimeter
- Soldering kit

Spares

A boat spares kit should contain:

- Belts for engine
- Hoses for engine
- Jubilee clamps
- Gaskets for engine
- Gasket sealer
- Filters/filter elements
- Pump impeller and gasket
- Thermostat unit
- Lubricating oil for engine and gearbox (one change each)
- Sparking plugs or injectors
- Points for petrol engine
- Plug leads for petrol engine
- Fuses of all capacities
- Bulbs for all lights
- Electrical cable
- Insulating tape
- Grease for stern tube
- Penetrating oil
- Windscreen-wiper blades
- Distilled water (battery)

Outboard Motors

This section is designed to help people who have little knowledge of outboard motors or their use. It contains some practical tips about the choice of motor, its use and faultfinding at sea. It is not intended to be a detailed, technical maintenance guide.

The modern two-stroke outboard motor is an efficient, reliable machine which will, if properly maintained, provide years of useful service. Sizes of motors are quoted by their horsepower (hp) and range from small 5-hp motors, which may be used as an auxiliary engine, to a 200-hp monster used to drive a large, rigid-hulled boat.

Figure 289

Outboard motor mounted on the transom of an aluminium assault craft

The Controls

Tiller or remote cable steering/gear change is available on motors rated at 40 hp or less. Motors greater than 40 hp in size, because of their power, will normally only be available with remote steering. Motors up to approximately 75 hp are usually fitted with manually adjustable engine tilt/rake devices. Motors larger than this usually have power tilt/rake facilities. Smaller motors are usually started using a recoil pull cord at the front of the motor. Electric-start and automatic-choke facilities are available for most motors but are essential on the larger ones. This is because the compression is far too great for them to be started manually, except in an extreme emergency. Boat electrics normally work from a battery that is recharged by the motor while it is running.

All motors have some form of easily accessible stop button and many incorporate a 'dead man' control. The latter is a clip device which holds the stop button open and is fastened to the cox's wrist with a lanyard. If he falls overboard the button closes and the engine stops.

Choice of Motor

Choice of motor depends on the size and the design of the boat to be powered and the speed required. A small inflatable with a 25-hp motor will plane with four fully kitted divers, whereas the average 4·5-m inflatable will probably need at least a 40-hp motor. A displacement-hull boat is not designed for high speed and perhaps could be powered by a 25-hp motor. It is much more economical in terms of fuel consumption and engine wear to acquire a motor large enough to power the boat's load with ease. Many divers make the mistake of buying, for example, a 25-hp motor in the mistaken belief that smaller motors do not use as much fuel. In reality, with its normal diving load, the boat will only plane at full power. However, a 40-hp motor on the same boat will plane easily, allowing the cox to throttle back to half revs and still maintain speed. Reserve power is available if needed and the motor is far more economical. Engine wear is also reduced. You should remember, when calculating load, that each diver carries equipment whose weight is equivalent to half an adult's weight, so carrying six divers is equivalent to carrying nine ordinary adults. Most boat manufacturers recommend a maximum motor size and to exceed their recommendation may invalidate any insurance claim in the event of an accident.

There is little point in fitting a displacement-hull boat with a large outboard motor since it will achieve its optimum speed with a smaller motor. Indeed, there is a body of opinion which states that one should not fit an outboard to a slow-moving craft, as a two-stroke engine thrives on high revs, not achieved when travelling at slow speed. Steerage is also better at greater speeds and propeller revolutions.

Generally speaking inflatable boats are designed for tiller steering although remotes can be used. The shape of the hull ensures that the farther back one sits, the smoother is the ride. Farther forward, the hull tends to slam in any sort of a rough sea and it is very uncomfortable. Another drawback when using remote steering/ gear change on an inflatable is that the expansion and contraction of the tubes through temperature variations, together with movement over waves, can cause cable lengths to vary and careful adjustments to be altered.

Many divers now use rigid-hulled boats and the design of these usually involves the use of wheel steering and remote controls. Boats with V-shaped hulls tend to slam the water less and cables can be attached to the rigid hull in such a way as to eliminate movement. Once correctly set up, remote cable steering and gear changes on rigid-hulled boats need very little adjustment.

Fitting Your Motor

When choosing a motor it is essential to know the transom depth of the boat. Outboard motors are available with standard or long shafts depending on the depth of the transom. Standard shafts operate where the transom depth does not exceed 38 cm and long-shaft motors are required for a 51-cm transom. Conversions from standard shaft to long shaft are available for some motors. When the motor is fitted correctly the anti-cavitation plate on the lower engine leg should be just above the water when the boat is planing. If it is much lower than this, extra drag will reduce the efficiency and the speed. Any higher and the propeller will cavitate. This means that air is being dragged into the rotary propeller movement. The engine note will rise and the boat slow down and, unless the motor is throttled back there is a danger of damaging it by overrevving.

The rake or engine angle is another important consideration. It is the angle between the engine leg and the transom. Figure 290 shows the correct rake and what will happen if it is wrongly adjusted either way.

Having correctly positioned the motor in the centre of the transom and secured it by means of the engine clamps, it is essential that precautions are taken to avoid it becoming an 'overboard' motor. On smaller motors it is possible to tie the clamp buckles together in order to stop them unscrewing or to chain one of the clamps to the transom. A far superior method is to bolt the motor to the transom, using stainless steel or non-ferrous bolts (see Figure 291). The engine fixing bracket has holes already drilled for this purpose. This can be something of a nuisance if the motor is regularly removed from the boat but it is the only totally safe way of securing the motor, especially if it is a large one. A large motor has tremendous torque and this tends to twist it away from the transom. Bolts fitted through the transom also provide an effective anti-theft device.

Figure 290

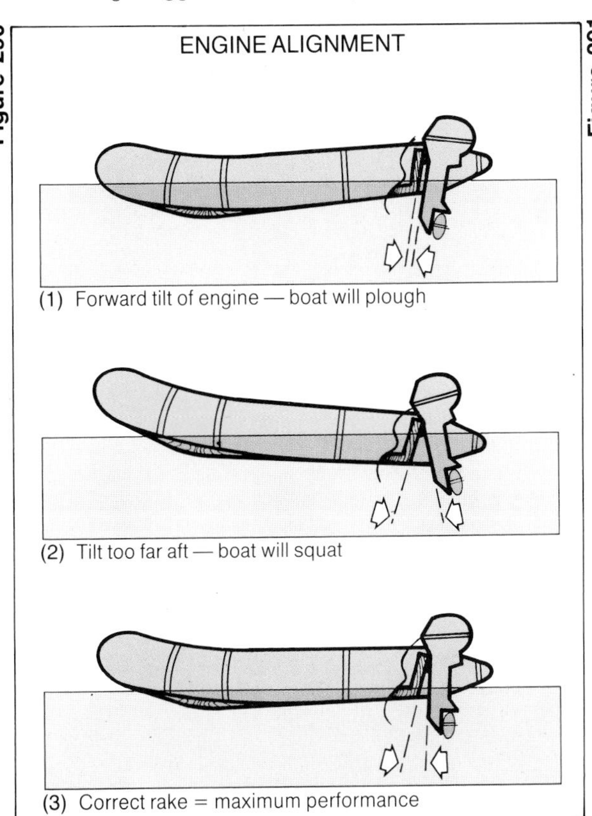

Rake adjustment ensures engine operates at most efficient angle

Figure 291

For maximum safety and security, the motor can be bolted through the transom

Propellers

The propeller is important when determining the efficiency of your motor. All motors have a range of propellers available which have different diameters and *pitches*. The pitch of a propeller is rather like gearing on a car and is defined as the theoretical horizontal distance that the propeller would travel in one revolution. For example, a general-purpose propeller for a 40-hp motor is likely to be 13-in pitch (most propellers are of American manufacture and they still use Imperial measurements). This means that, allowing for no slippage, the propeller travels 13 in through the water with one revolution. For the same motor, propellers of pitches ranging from 10 to 17 in are available. These non-standard propellers will only be supplied on special request.

In general, the coarser the pitch the lighter the boat needs to be, since the boat is effectively being given a higher gear. A coarse-pitch propeller may not allow a 40-hp motor to cause a dive boat to plane because it will not have sufficient power to overcome the bowwave. Conversely, a fine-pitch propeller will overcome this problem but, if the boat carries a light load, there is a danger that the motor can be overrevved inadvertently. A general-purpose, middle-of-the-range propeller pitch is probably the best compromise. The pitch of the propeller is normally stamped on the outside of the boss.

Two types of propeller drive are available. These are known as through-prop exhaust/splined shaft drive and shearpin drive. In recent years the former has become more popular. Figure 292 shows the drive shaft of the splined-drive system. Notice that the propeller centre is designed to fit the splined-drive shaft from the gearbox. It is secured with a castellated nut and splitpin. The centre boss of the propeller (Figure 293) is constructed with a rubber bush so that if the propeller strikes an underwater obstruction the initial impact is taken by the rubber, thus saving damage to the gearbox. In reality the propeller blades will probably chip. The motor's exhaust gases pass through the centre of the propeller and are vented underwater. This leads to quieter operation and fewer exhaust fumes. Figure 294 shows the shearpin drive system. A shearpin is a sacrificial pin, usually made of copper, which holds the propeller onto the drive shaft. As the name implies, it is designed to shear on impact with an obstruction and, thereby, save the propeller blades and the gearbox from damage.

Towing Security

Many motors are permanently fixed to the boat, as described above, and the whole unit is towed on a suitable road trailer. Consideration must be given to the security of the motor while towing. If the boat is towed with the motor in the normal down position there is a risk of serious damage to the skeg and gearbox if the motor strikes the ground while in transit. The use of a high trailer may avoid this but it brings the added problem of finding water deep enough to launch the boat from the trailer. This can be a problem on a flat, shelving beach. With motors with power tilt this problem can be overcome by towing them on half tilt. With motors

Figure 292

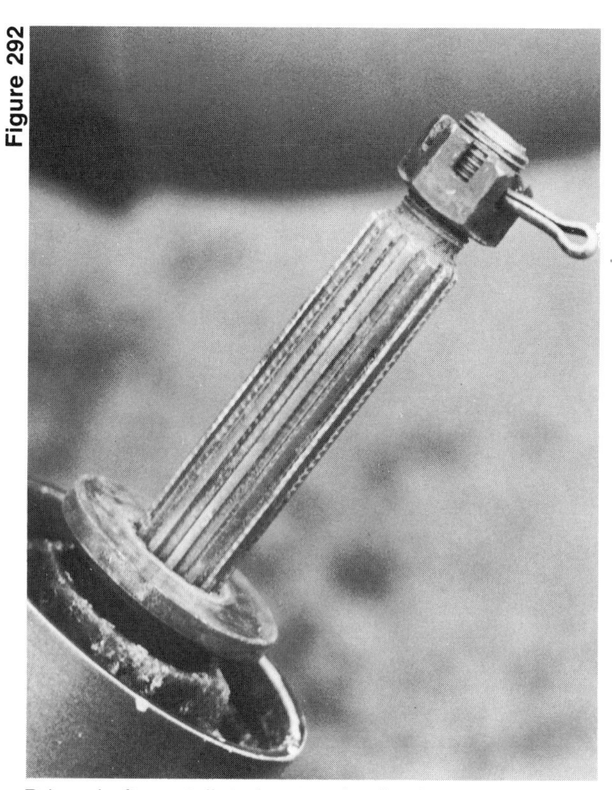

Drive shaft, castellated nut and split pin

Figure 293

Central propeller boss with through-hub exhaust

Figure 294

Shear pin

without power tilt one must rely on the mechanical tilt lock and when towing in this situation one risks the motor coming off tilt on bumpy road surfaces. To overcome this motors can be tied in position. Figure 295 shows another alternative. On this purpose-built trailer the centre spine is constructed from steel box section and a custom-built, angled support leg fits inside the box section and supports the motor at the gear case. This also takes weight off the transom while towing.

It is illegal, while towing, to have any sharp projection at the rear of the trailer. Therefore a stout bag must be tied over the propeller, preferably of a fluorescent colour.

When transporting the motor separately from the boat, ensure that it is packed securely and that the power head is always higher that the gearbox. This is to prevent oil, water, etc., running back into the power block.

Running-In and Fuel Mixture

Manufacturers' recommendations should always be followed when operating any motor. When a motor is brand new or if it has had a major overhaul it is usual to increase the amount of oil in the petrol to give greater lubrication while the motor is run in. *Always* use reputable *outboard motor two-stroke oil* and never that designed for motorcycles or any other air-cooled, two-stroke motor. Outboard motors are designed to run at lower operating temperatures than normal air-cooled engines. Oil designed for the latter may not combust properly if used with an outboard and the likely result will be a rapid spluttering to a halt and fouled sparkplugs. Any grade of petrol can be used as the octane rating becomes irrelevant with the introduction of oil. Some of the larger outboard motors have a separate oil tank from which the oil is automatically added to the petrol and adjusted according to the different throttle openings.

When filling the fuel tank always try to add the correct amount of oil at the same time as the petrol. This ensures that the engine will not seize. The amount of oil per litre of petrol varies between 1:10 and 1:100. It is a good idea to paint the correct ratio on the fuel tank in a position where it cannot be missed by anyone filling the tank. When the tank is full replace the filler cap and ensure that the bleed screw, if fitted, is in the closed position (Figure 297).

The positioning of the fuel tank should be given some consideration. Some boats are designed with space for tank stowage under seat and consoles. In an inflatable some people stow the tank under the bow dodger in order to save space farther aft. If this is the case, care must be taken with the positioning of the fuel line, which can easily be snagged or cut by people or gear inboard. An extra-long fuel line will also be required. Figure 296 shows a useful way of stowing the tank in the more orthodox position next to the transom. The wooden frame screwed to the floorboard holds the tank in position and prevents it moving about in rough seas.

Figure 295

Figure 296

Figure 297

Figure 295
Outboard supported on trailer with special bracket

Figure 296
Fuel tank in fixed position

Figure 297
Air bleed screw

Starting Procedure

Before starting the motor ensure the fuel line ends are free of debris. After unscrewing the bleed screw (see Figure 297), the fuel line must be primed using the bulb shown in Figure 298, squeezing it until it becomes reasonably solid. Ensure that the gear lever is in neutral (Figure 299) and that the choke is operated if necessary. If a 'dead man' control is fitted, ensure it is connected correctly. The motor is now ready for starting either manually or electrically. Once started, release the choke as soon as possible, and always check that the cooling water is flowing from the outlet. Most motors have a 'telltale' jet which shows whether the system is operating correctly. If the water from the telltale becomes very hot, this is a sign that something is wrong and the motor should be stopped immediately.

All motors have a tilt lock (Figure 300) which must be engaged whenever it is necessary to travel in reverse. Without such a lock the engine leg will lift out of the water whenever the engine is in reverse. There are devices which automatically engage once the motor is lowered while others engage once reverse gear is chosen. When going forward in shallow water it is advisable to disengage the tilt lock just in case you hit an obstruction. With the lock disengaged, the engine leg will lift and so minimize damage.

Once on site, if it is decided to keep the motor ticking over in neutral, it is advisable to give the throttle the occasional 'blip' to prevent the sparkplugs from oiling up.

On return to base it is advisable to disengage the tilt lock when approaching shallow water. Before finishing for the day, uncouple the fuel pipe with the motor still running and allow it to run out of fuel. This empties the carburettor and fuel lines and reduces the build-up of residue.

Figure 298

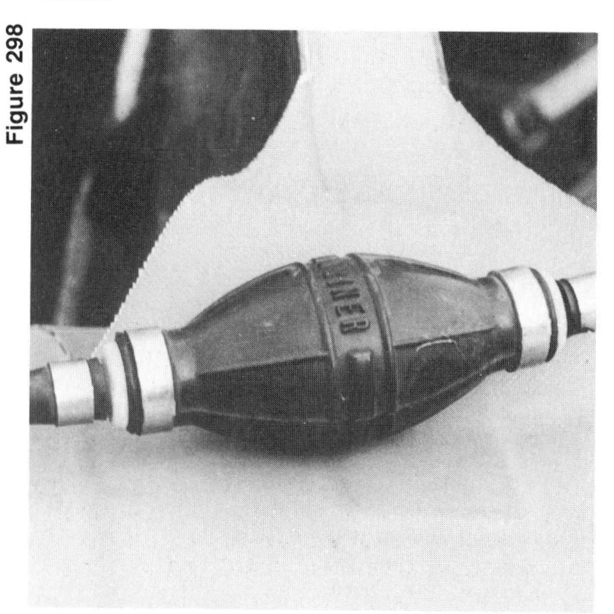

The fuel-line bulb

Figure 299

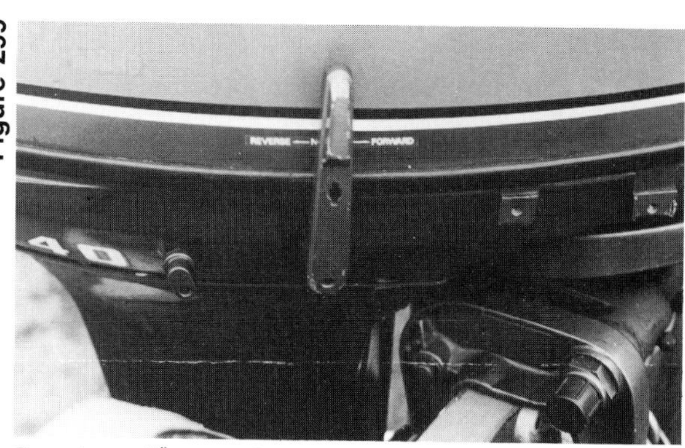

Gear lever in neutral position

Figure 300

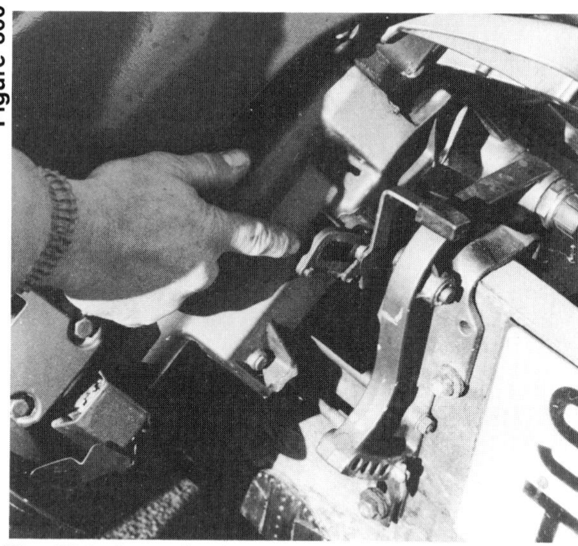

The tilt lock mechanism

Faultfinding at Sea

Ideally a spare motor should be carried for use in an emergency, but this is not always practical. The following procedures are recommended in order to eliminate the most common faults which cause an outboard motor to stop, or fail to start, when at sea.

A toolkit and spares pack in a waterproof container are essential and should contain at least the following items:

1. Spare sparkplugs set at the correct gap, preferably wrapped to prevent contamination and accidental gap adjustment.
2. Plug spanner with lanyard.
3. Shearpin(s) or spare propeller, depending on type fitted. Spanner for propeller nut (splined drive).
4. Pliers and small adjustable spanner.
5. Large and small screwdrivers.
6. Insulation tape.
7. Spare fuel line and/or connector ends.
8. Emergency starting cord.
9. Clean, dry rag.

If the motor stops or fails to start, the chances are that, barring major damage, the fault will be connected with fuel supply or the electrical supply.

Always look for the simple thing before wholeheartedly attacking the motor. It may be nothing more than a disconnected fuel line or a loose wire. Check that you have not run out of fuel!

As with a car, decide whether the engine has stopped mechanically or electrically. This judgement is gained by experience. If the motor splutters to a halt, it is more than likely to be the fuel system which is the cause, whereas a sudden, total loss of life points to an electrical fault. To confuse the situation slightly, one misfiring sparkplug can suggest a fuel problem.

In a small, cramped boat there is little chance of making major repairs and there are only a few options. If you decide that the problem might be fuel, the following points should be checked:

1. Is there fuel in the tank?
2. Is each end of the fuel line connected properly?
3. Is the bleed scew unscrewed?
4. Is the fuel line trapped, cut or blocked?
5. Is the fuel line cracked or perished?

If all the above appear to be satisfactory remove the cowl and check that the fuel filter (Figure 301) is not blocked. This is done by unscrewing the bowl and wiping out any sediment. Check all flexible fuel lines attached to the motor, particularly the ends. Squeeze the priming bulb to check whether fuel is reaching the filter. If the problem is still not found, it could well be the carburettor. Do not attempt to strip the carburettor as this is a specialized job and you may lose vital small components.

If you decide the fault is electrical, first of all check any battery connections. If a 'dead man' control is fitted, ensure that the clip has not become disconnected. Having removed the cowl, check for any loose or broken wires. Next remove the plugs. Figure 302 shows the position of the plugs on a typical outboard motor. Their removal is easy on land but remember that at sea they will be facing out to sea and you will need to lean over the motor. For this reason it is a good idea to secure the plug spanner, or any other tools which may be dropped overboard, to a convenient place, perhaps your wrist, with a lanyard. Having removed the plugs, inspect them to see if they are wet due to unburnt fuel, the electrodes worn or the gap too big. Fit the plug leads to replacement plugs and, while earthing each one in turn to a clean unpainted metal surface, check for a spark by pulling the starter cord or operating the key/switch. If all the plugs spark, replace them and try to start the motor. If they do not spark, the chances are that an ignition coil has malfunctioned (on magneto ignition systems) and there is little that can be done at sea unless you fit a spare. On some modern motors electronic CD ignition has been introduced. If this is the case, take great care that the plugs are properly earthed if removed. Irreparable damage to the electronic ignition unit can occur if this advice is ignored. Do not hold any bare part of the plug lead while testing for a spark or you will receive a small electrical shock. Holding the plug lead with insulated pliers will overcome the problem.

Figure 301

The fuel filter housing and element

Figure 302

The spark plugs and high tension leads

If, while underway, the motor vibrates violently or seems to be erratic, it is possible that the propeller has been damaged and to continue at speed will severely damage the gearbox. If the boat does not move when gear is engaged and it has a shearpin drive, then the shearpin has probably broken. Always practise the changing of a shearpin on land, as it is not an easy job at sea. A diver, working in the water, may provide the easiest option.

If the tiller becomes detached and cannot be refitted for any reason, steerage can be maintained by manoeuvring the whole motor. Alternatively a paddle may be strapped to the motor as an emergency tiller.

Post-Dive Care and 'Wintering'

On many outboard motors one can connect a hosepipe (Figure 303), using a special adaptor, to the cooling system in the engine leg. This allows the motor to be run while not immersed in water. An alternative is to run the motor in a large container of fresh water, preferably with the propeller removed to reduce turbulence (remember not to overrev the motor with the propeller removed). This allows any salt deposits and debris to be flushed out of the system, thus reducing corrosion and wear of the water pump impeller. Ideally this should be done after each time the boat has been used. External surfaces should be washed down with fresh water and the inside of the cowl and power block wiped down. Car wax, applied to external paint surfaces, helps to protect them from salt damage.

If the motor is to be stored over the winter period, apart from the above, the following procedures are recommended as a minimum service:

1. Remove the cowl and thoroughly clean the power head with a degreasing agent and then wipe with a clean cloth.
2. Remove the sparkplugs and introduce two or three squirts of two-stroke oil into each cylinder. Pull the motor over to ensure maximum distribution on the cylinder walls. Fit new plugs.
3. Tighten any loose nuts and bolts with a suitable spanner. Check for loose wiring. Lubricate all cables.
4. Lubricate all greasing points with a recommended waterproof grease.
5. Drain the gearbox of oil and check for any signs of water. A grey emulsified liquid is the sign of water contamination. If satisfactory, replenish with fresh oil. Remember to fill from the lower of the two plugs. The top plug is the 'level' (see Figure 304).
6. Any unused fuel should not be saved. Clean petrol should be used to clean the inside of the fuel tank. Painting the tank is a wise move.

Figure 303

Flushing the cooling system with a special hose

Figure 304

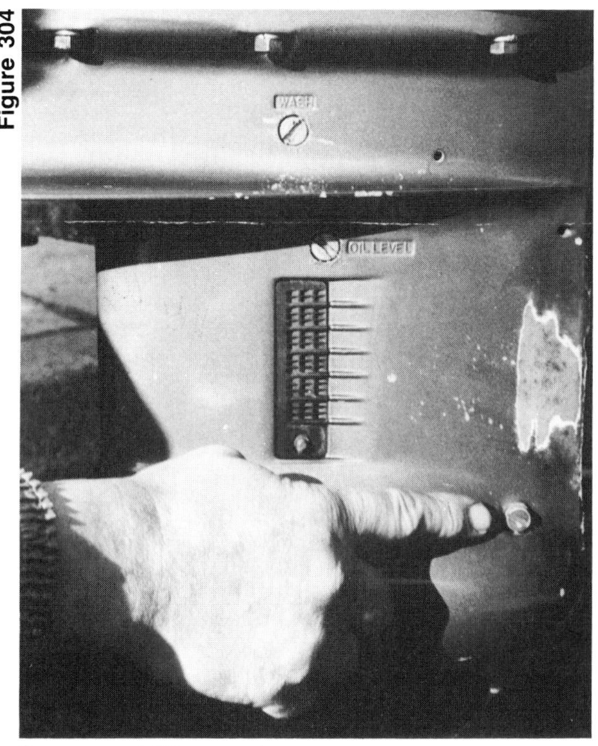

Gear box oil filling point

Figure 305

Twin outboard motors with twinned controls

Boat Trailers

There are several designs of boat trailer, ranging from those similar to a camping trailer, which hold a deflated inflatable, motor and safety equipment, to those that carry a boat and engine ready to launch direct from the trailer.

The type choosen depends on the type of boat, the launching facilities and the number of personnel available at the launch site. For example, a 7-m dory-type, rigid-hulled boat will probably need a double-axle trailer and a concrete slipway or very firm beach for it to be launched with ease. A vehicle, preferably a tractor, will be required to deliver the boat to the water's edge and several people will be needed to steady it once it is off the trailer. A 4-m inflatable, on the other hand, may be carried shoulder high by four people and launched in places that are impossible to reach by trailer.

Before choosing a trailer several factors have to be taken into consideration:

1. The type of boat (rigid, rigid-hull or inflatable).
2. Whether an inflatable has a rigid or an inflatable keel.
3. The length of the boat and motor (if the boat is carried with the motor attached).
4. The weight of the boat and its equipment.
5. The size and weight of the towing vehicle(s).
6. Whether or not the launch will be dry or wet.
7. Road type and surface (rougher roads demand robuster trailers).
8. Launch site access (large wheels facilitate rougher launches).

Many people buy a custom-built trailer with their boat and in many cases it will have been designed for that particular boat. It will usually have galvanized metal components and satisfy legal requirements for towing, for example, in regard to lighting and braking.

Bearing in mind this list, the choice of trailer should be guided as follows:

Type of Boat

A rigid or rigid-hull boat requires a trailer with supports which follow the contours of the centre of the hull. This is usually achieved with a central section of sturdy design, often with rollers to enable the boat to be launched and retrieved with minimum friction. In addition, outriggers of some description are used to stabilize the hull, minimize sideways rolling and help distribute the weight. Sometimes the outriggers also incorporate rollers, particularly on trailers designed for heavier boats. Inflatables, by design, do not need the same type of support and, being much lighter, often do not require any rollers. Much more of the weight is taken by the side tubes and most trailers use flat boards, contoured to the shape of the keel, and the tubes in order to distribute this weight safely. This type of trailer weighs less and is easier to manhandle.

Inflatables – Keel Design

The trailer contours will be decided by keel design. With an inflatable keel, usually deflated while on the trailer, the load-bearing sections (i.e. the central spine) can be flat and horizontal. A complete flat-bottomed trailer gives ideal weight distribution. With a rigid-keeled inflatable the side tube supports should be flat and horizontal. The centre spine should be flat but angled to suit the rake of the keel. This design keeps the boat in level, horizontal trim for towing and distributes the weight evenly.

Figure 306

Trailer for an inflatable

Length of Boat and Engine

The trailer should be long enough to accommodate both the boat and the engine. There should be enough clearance between the boat and the tow hitch to allow a complete reverse turn without the boat colliding with the side or rear of the towing vehicle. The rear of the hull should, ideally, not overhang the trailer.

Weight of Boat, Motor and Equipment

Many boats are towed complete with boat equipment, motor, full fuel tank and diving equipment. It is essential that the trailer suspension units are sufficiently sturdy to handle the total towed weight. Double axles may be needed if the towed weight exceeds the capacity of the sturdiest single-axle unit. Double-axle trailers are usually used for larger, rigid-hulled boats; they are more difficult to manhandle, especially when trying to turn.

Size and Weight of Towing Vehicle

There is a legislated weight-to-weight ratio for the towing vehicle and the laden trailer which must be observed. On heavier units it is illegal to tow on public roads without fitted trailer brakes which operate independently of the towing vehicle's braking system.

Dry or Wet launch

Some trailers are designed to have their wheels submerged in order to facilitate launching and retrieval of the boat. Immersion in salt water has led to special hub designs which, if efficient, completely seal the wheel bearings from the water. With trailers with unprotected wheel bearings, it is prudent to allow the wheels to cool down before immersion. Maintenance and frequent replacement of bearings are essential with this system since salt water displaces the grease and rapid deterioration of the bearings occurs. Braked trailers have their own problems if the wheels are immersed when launching or retrieving. After immersion drive carefully until you are satisfied that the brake drums are dry. Some heavier trailers have a 'break-back' facility which allows the rear half of the trailer to be lowered to ground level in order to facilitate launching and retrieval. They may also incorporate a winch for retrieval.

The above applies to trailers that are available for purchase. Many people have the experience and technical capability to build their own trailer. Plans for different types of trailer are readily available and can save the purchaser a considerable amount of money. There are strict legal requirements regarding the weight, size and lighting systems. Some motoring organizations publish up-to-date literature on this subject. The local police should also be able to help.

Trailer Maintenance

Before the diving season begins the trailer should be checked over. Particular attention should be given to wheel-bearing wear and lubrication. If the trailer is constructed from non-galvanized ferrous metal, it should be wire-brushed and any welding checked for cracks. These should be repaired and then painted. Any deteriorating timbers should be replaced and varnished. Tyres should be checked for wear.

In the event of a punctured trailer wheel one will need a correctly inflated spare wheel and a suitable jack. Spare wheel bearings should be part of the spares kit, especially when travelling to remote regions.

Figure 307

A four-wheeled, close-coupled trailer

Appendix 1: Wind Speed and Sea States

Beaufort Wind Scale

Beaufort Number	Mean Velocity Knots	m/s	Descriptive Term	Deep sea criterion	Probable height of waves in metres*
0	Less than 1	0–0·2	**Calm**	Sea like a mirror	—
1	1–3	0·3–1·5	**Light air**	Ripples with the appearance of scales are formed but without foam crests	0·1 (0·1)
2	4–6	1·6–3·3	**Light breeze**	Small wavelets, still short but more pronounced. Crests have a glassy appearance and do not break	0·2 (0·3)
3	7–10	3·4–5·4	**Gentle breeze**	Large wavelets. Crests begin to break. Foam of glassy appearance. Perhaps scattered white horses	0·6 (1)
4	11–16	5·5–7·9	**Moderate breeze**	Small waves, becoming longer; fairly frequent horses	1 (1·5)
5	17–21	8·0–10·7	**Fresh breeze**	Moderate waves, taking a more pronounced long form; many white horses are formed. (Chance of some spray)	2 (2·5)
6	22–27	10·8–13·8	**Strong breeze**	Large waves begin to form; the white foam crests are more extensive everywhere. (Probably some spray)	3 (4)
7	28–33	13·9–17·1	**Near gale**	Sea heaps up and white foam from breaking waves begins to be blown in streaks along the direction of the wind	4 (5·5)
8	34–40	17·2–20·7	**Gale**	Moderately high waves of greater length; edges of crests begin to break into spindrift. The foam is blown in well-marked streaks along the direction of the wind	5·5 (7·5)
9	41–47	20·8–24·4	**Strong gale**	High waves. Dense streaks of foam along the direction of the wind. Crests of waves begin to topple, tumble and roll over. Spray may affect visibility	7 (10)
10	48–55	24·5–28·4	**Storm**	Very high waves with long overhanging crests. The resulting foam in great patches is blown in dense white streaks along the direction of the wind. On the whole the surface of the sea takes a white appearance. The tumbling of the sea becomes heavy and shocklike. Visibility affected	9 (12·5)
11	56–63	28·5–32·6	**Violent storm**	Exceptionally high waves. (Small and medium-sized ships might be for a time lost to view behind the waves.) The sea is completely covered with long white patches of foam lying along the direction of the wind. Everywhere the edges of the wave crests are blown into froth. Visibility affected	11·5 (16)
12	64+	32·7+	**Hurricane**	The air is filled with foam and spray. Sea completely white with driving spray; visibility very seriously affected	14 (–)

Notes

1. It must be realized that it will be difficult at night to estimate wind force by the sea criterion.
2. The lag effect between increase of wind and increase of sea should be borne in mind.
3. Fetch, depth, swell, heavy rain and tide effects should be considered when estimating the wind force from the appearance of the sea.

*This table is intended only as a guide to show roughly what may be expected in the open sea, remote from land. In enclosed waters, or when near land with an off-shore wind, wave heights will be smaller, and the waves steeper. Figures in brackets indicate probable maximum height of waves.

Warning: for a given wind force, sea conditions can be more dangerous near land than in the open sea. In many tidal waters wave heights are liable to increase considerably in a matter of minutes.

Conversion Table for Wind Speed

Knots	Metres/second
2	1
5	2·6
10	5·1
15	7·7
20	10·3
25	12·9
30	15·4
40	20·6
50	25·7
60	30·9

1 knot = 0·514 m/s
1 m/s = 1·943 knots

Table of Sea States

1. Swell Wavelength

	Metres
Short	0–100
Average	100–200
Long	over 200

2. Swell Wave Height

	Metres
Low	0–2
Moderate	2–4
Heavy	over 4

3. Sea Wave Height

Code Description	Metres*
0 Calm, glassy	0
1 Calm, rippled	0–0·1
2 Smooth wavelets	0·1–0·5
3 Slight	0·5–1·25
4 Moderate	1·25–2·5
5 Rough	2·5–4
6 Very rough	4–6
7 High	6–9
8 Very high	9–14
9 Phenomenal	over 14

Note: In each case the exact boundary of length or height is included in the lower category, e.g. a sea of 4 m/s described as 'Rough'.
*Average wave height

Coastal Weather Forecasts

The Meteorological Office provide special services for shipmasters, fishermen and yachtsmen operating in the North Sea, the English Channel, the Irish Sea and the North Atlantic seaboard. These include regular transmissions by radio at scheduled times from the BBC and from coastal stations. Gale warnings are issued on each of these channels and special forecasts are available on request.

Extracts from

Appendix 2: International Regulations for Preventing Collisions at Sea, 1972

Part A – General

Rule 1 Application

(a) These rules shall apply to all vessels upon the high seas and in all waters connected therewith navigable by seagoing vessels.

(b) Nothing in these rules shall interfere with the operation of special rules made by an appropriate authority for roadsteads, harbours, rivers, lakes or inland waterways connected with the high seas and navigable by seagoing vessels. Such special rules shall conform as closely as possible to these rules.

(c) Nothing in these rules shall interfere with the operation of any special rules made by the Government of any State with respect to additional station or signal lights, shapes or whistle signals for ships of war and vessels proceeding under convoy, or with respect to additional station or signal lights or shapes for fishing vessels engaged in fishing as a fleet. These additional station or signal lights, shapes or whistle signals shall, so far as possible, be such that they cannot be mistaken for any light, shape or signal authorised elsewhere under these Rules.

(d) Traffic separation schemes may be adopted by the Organisation for the purpose of these Rules.

(e) Whenever the Government concerned shall have determined that a vessel of special construction or purpose cannot comply fully with the provisions of any of these Rules with respect to the number, position, range or arc of visibility of lights or shapes, as well as to the disposition and characteristics of sound-signalling appliances, without interfering with the special function of the vessel, such vessel shall comply with such other provisions in regard to the number, position, range or arc of visibility of lights or shapes, as well as to the disposition and characteristics of sound-signalling appliances, as her Government shall have determined to be the closest possible compliance with these Rules in respect of that vessel.

Rule 2 Responsibility

(a) Nothing in these Rules shall exonerate any vessel, or the owner, master or crew thereof, from the consequences of any neglect to comply with these Rules or of the neglect of any precaution which may be required by the ordinary practice of seamen, or by the special circumstances of the case.

Part B – Steering and Sailing Rules

Section I – Conduct or Vessels in Any Condition of Visibility

Rule 5 Lookout

Every vessel shall at all times maintain a proper lookout by sight and hearing as well as by all available means appropriate in the prevailing circumstances and conditions so as to make full appraisal of the situation and of risk of collision.

Rule 6 Safe Speed

Every vessel shall at all times proceed at a safe speed so that she can take proper and effective action to avoid collision and be stopped within a distance appropriate to the prevailing circumstances and conditions.

In determining a safe speed the following factors shall be among those taken into account:

(a) By all vessels:

(i) the state of visibility

(ii) the traffic density including concentrations of fishing vessels or any other vessels;

(iii) the manoeuvrability of the vessel with special reference to stopping distance and turning ability in the prevailing conditions:

(iv) at night the presence of background light such as from shore lights or from back scatter of her own lights;

(v) the state of wind, sea and current, and the proximity of navigational hazards;

(vi) the draught in relation to the available depth of water.

(b) Additionally, by vessels with operational radar:

(i) the characteristics, efficiency and limitations of the radar equipment;

(ii) any constraints imposed by the radar range scale in use;

(iii) the effect on radar detection of the sea state, weather and other sources of interference;

(iv) the possibility that small vessels, ice and other floating objects may not be detected at an adequate range;

(v) the number, location and movement of vessels detected by radar;

(vi) the more exact assessment of the visibility that may be possible when radar is used to determine the range of vessels or other objects in the vicinity.

Rule 7 Risk of Collision

(a) Every vessel shall use all available means appropriate to the prevailing circumstances and conditions to determine if risk of collision exists. If there is any doubt such risk shall be deemed to exist.

(b) Proper use shall be made of radar equipment if fitted and operational, including long-range scanning to obtain early warning of risk of collision and radar plotting or equivalent systematic observation of detected objects.

(c) Assumptions shall not be made on the basis of scanty information, especially scanty radar information.

(d) In determining if risk of collision exists the following considerations shall be among those taken into account:

(i) such risk shall be deemed to exist if the compass bearing of any approaching vessel does not appreciably change;

(ii) such risk may sometimes exist even when an appreciable bearing change is evident, particularly when approaching a very large vessel or a tow or when approaching a vessel at close range.

Rule 8 Action to Avoid Collision

(a) Any action taken to avoid collision shall, if the circumstances of the case admit, be positive, made in ample time and with due regard to the observance of good seamanship.

(b) Any alteration of course and/or speed to avoid collision shall, if the circumstances of the case admit, be large enough to be readily apparent to another vessel observing visually by radar; a succession of small alterations of course and/or speed should be avoided.

(c) If there is sufficient sea room, alteration of course alone may be the most effective action to avoid a close-quarters situation provided that it is made in good time, is substantial and does not result in another close-quarters situation.

(d) Action taken to avoid collision with another vessel shall be such as to result in passing at a safe distance. The effectiveness of the action shall be carefully checked until the other vessel is finally past and clear.

(e) If necessary to avoid collision or allow more time to assess the situation, a vessel shall slacken her speed or take all way off by stopping or reversing her means of propulsion.

Rule 9 Narrow Channels

(a) A vessel proceeding along the course of a narrow channel or fairway shall keep as near to the outer limit of the channel or fairway on her starboard side as is safe and practicable.

(b) A vessel of less than 20 metres in length or a sailing vessel shall not impede the passage of a vessel which can safely navigate only within a narrow channel or fairway.

(c) A vessel engaged in fishing shall not impede the passage of any other vessel navigating within a narrow channel or fairway.

(d) A vessel shall not cross a narrow channel or fairway if such crossing impedes the passage of a vessel which can safely navigate only within such channel or fairway. The latter vessel may use the sound signal prescribed in Rule 34(d) if in doubt as to the intention of the crossing vessel.

(e)

(i) In a narrow channel or fairway when overtaking can take place if the vessel to be overtaken has to take action to permit safe passing, the vessel intending to overtake shall indicate her intention by sounding the appropriate signal prescribed in Rule 43(c) (i). The vessel to be overtaken shall, if an agreement, sound the appropriate signal prescribed in Rule 34(c) (ii) and take steps to permit safe passing. If in doubt she may sound the signals prescribed in Rule 34(d).

(ii) This Rule does not relieve the overtaking vessel of her obligation under Rule 13.

(f) A vessel nearing a bend or an area of a narrow channel or fairway where other vessels may be obsured by an intervening obstruction shall navigate with particular alertness and caution and shall sound the appropriate signal prescribed in Rule 34(e).

(g) Any vessel shall, if the circumstances of the case admit, avoid anchoring in a narrow channel.

Rule 10 Traffic Separation Schemes

(j) A vessel of less than 20 metres in length or a sailing vessel shall not impede the safe passage of a power-driven vessel following a traffic lane.

Section II – Conduct of Vessels in Sight of One Another

Rule 11 Application

Rules in this section apply to vessels in sight of one another.

Rule 12 Sailing Vessels

(a) When two sailing vessels are approaching one another, so as to involve risk of collision, one of them shall keep out of the way of the other as follows:

(i) when each has the wind on a different side, the vessel which has the wind on the port side shall keep out of the way of the other.

(ii) when both have the wind on the same side, the vessel which is to windward shall keep out of the way of the vessel which is to leeward.

(iii) if a vessel with the wind on the port side sees a vessel to windward and cannot determine with certainty whether the other vessel has the wind on the port or on the starboard side, she shall keep out of the way of the other.

(b) For the purposes of this Rule the windward side shall be deemed to be the side opposite to that on which the mainsail is carried or, in the case of a square-rigged vessel, the side opposite to that on which the largest fore-and-aft sail is carried.

Rule 13 Overtaking

(a) Notwithstanding anything contained in the Rules of Part B, Sections I and II any vessel overtaking any other shall keep out of the way of the vessel being overtaken.

Rule 14 Head-on Situation

(a) When two power-driven vessels are meeting on reciprocal or nearly reciprocal courses so as to involve risk of collision each shall alter her course to starboard so that each shall pass on the port side of the other.

Rule 15 Crossing Situation

When two power-driven vessels are crossing so as to involve risk of collision, the vessel which has the other on her own starboard side shall keep out of the way and shall, if the circumstances of the case admit, avoid crossing ahead of the other vessel.

Rule 18 Responsibilities between Vessels

Except where Rules 9, 10 and 13 otherwise require:

(a) A power-driven vessel underway shall keep out of the way of:

(i) a vessel not under command;
(ii) a vessel restricted in her ability to manoeuvre;
(iii) a vessel engaged in fishing;
(iv) a sailing vessel.

(b) A sailing vessel underway shall keep out of the way of:

(i) a vessel not under command;
(ii) a vessel restricted in her ability to manoeuvre;
(iii) a vessel engaged in fishing.

(c) A vessel engaged in fishing when underway shall, so far as possible, keep out of the way of:

(i) a vessel not under command;
(ii) a vessel restricted in her ability to manoeuvre.

(d)

(i) Any vessel other than a vessel not under command or a vessel restricted in her ability to manoeuvre shall, if the circumstances of the case admit, avoid impeding the safe passage of a vessel constrained by her draught, exhibiting the signals in Rule 28.

(ii) A vessel constrained by her draught shall navigate with particular caution having full regard to her special condition.

Rule 22 Visibility of Lights

The lights prescribed in these Rules shall have an intensity as specified in Section 8 of Annex I to these regulations so as to be visible at the following minimum ranges:

(a) In vessels of 50 metres or more in length:

- a masthead light, 6 miles;
- a sidelight, 3 miles;
- a sternlight, 3 miles;
- a towing light, 3 miles;
- a white, red, green or yellow all-round light, 3 miles.

(b) In vessels of 12 metres or more in length but less than 50 metres in length:

- a masthead light, 5 miles; except that where the length of the vessel is less than 20 metres, 3 miles;
- a sidelight, 3 miles;
- a sternlight, 2 miles;
- a towing light, 2 miles;
- a white, red, green or yellow all-round light, 2 miles.

(c) In vessels of less than 12 metres in length:

- a masthead light, 2 miles;
- a sidelight, 1 mile;
- a sternlight, 2 miles;
- a towing light, 2 miles;
- a white, red, green or yellow all-round light, 2 miles.

(d) In inconspicuous, partly submerged vessels or objects being towed:

- a white all-round light, 3 miles.

Rule 23 Power-driven Vessel Underway

(a) A power-driven vessel underway shall exhibit:

(i) a masthead light forward;
(ii) a second masthead light abaft of and higher than the forward one; except that a vessel of less than 50 metres in length shall not be obliged to exhibit such light but may do so.
(iii) sidelights;
(iv) a sternlight.

(b) An air-cushion vessel when operating in the non-displacement mode shall, in addition to the lights prescribed in paragraph (a) of this Rule, exhibit an all-round flashing yellow light.

(c)

(i) A power-driven vessel of less than 12 metres in length may, in lieu of the lights prescribed in paragraph (a) of this Rule exhibit an all-round white light and sidelights;

(ii) a power-driven vessel of less than 7 metres in length, whose maximum speed does not exceed 7 knots may in lieu of the lights prescribed in paragraph (a) of this Rule exhibit an all-round white light and shall, if practicable, also exhibit sidelights;

(iii) the masthead light or all-round white light on a power-driven vessel of less than 12 metres in length may be displaced from the fore and aft centreline of the vessel if centreline fitting is not practicable, provided that the sidelights are combined in one lantern which shall be carried on the fore and aft centreline of the vessel or located as nearly as practicable in the same fore and aft line as the masthead light or the all-round white light.

Rule 28 Vessels constrained by their Draught

A vessel constrained by her draught may, in addition to the lights prescribed for power-driven vessels in Rule 23, exhibit where they can best be seen three all-round red lights in a vertical line, or a cylinder.

Rule 30 Anchored Vessels and Vessels Aground

(a) A vessel at anchor shall exhibit where it can best be seen:

(i) in the fore part, an all-round white light or one ball;

(ii) at or near the stern and at a lower level than the light prescribed in subparagraph (i) an all-round white light.

(b) A vessel of less than 50 metres in length may exhibit an all-round white light where it can best be seen instead of the lights prescribed in paragraph (a) of this Rule.

(c) A vessel at anchor may, and a vessel of 100 metres and more in length shall, also use the available working or equivalent lights to illuminate her decks.

(d) A vessel aground shall exhibit the lights prescribed in paragraph (a) or (b) of this Rule and in addition, where they can best be seen:

(i) two all-round red lights in a vertical line;
(ii) three balls in a vertical line.

(e) a vessel of less than 7 metres in length, when at anchor, not in or near a narrow channel, fairway or anchorage, or where other vessels normally navigate, shall not be required to exhibit the lights or shapes prescribed in paragraphs (a) or (b) of this Rule.

(f) A vessel of less than 12 metres in length, when aground, shall not be required to exhibit the lights or shapes prescribed in subparagraphs (d) (i) and (ii) of this Rule.

Part D – Sound and Light Signals

Rule 34 Manoeuvring and Warning Signals

(a) When vessels are in sight of one another, a power-driven vessel underway, when manoeuvring as authorised or required by these Rules, shall indicate that manoeuvre by the following signals on her whistle:

- one short blast to mean 'I am altering my course to starboard';
- two short blasts to mean 'I am altering my course to port';
- three short blasts to mean 'I am operating astern propulsion'.

(b) Any vessel may supplement the whistle signals prescribed in paragraph (a) of this Rule by light signals, repeated as appropriate, whilst the manoeuvre is being carried out:

(i) these lights shall have the following significance:

- one flash to mean 'I am altering my course to starboard';
- two flashes to mean 'I am altering my course to port';
- three flashes to mean 'I am operating astern propulsion';

(ii) the duration of each flash shall be about one second, the interval between flashes shall be about one second, and the interval between successive signals shall not be less than ten seconds;

(iii) the light used for this signal shall, if fitted, be an all-round white light, visible at a minimum range of 5 miles.

(c) When in sight of one another in a narrow channel or fairway:

(i) a vessel intending to overtake another shall in compliance with Rule 9(e) (i) indicate her intention by the following signals on her whistle:

- two prolonged blasts followed by one short blast to mean 'I intend to overtake you on your starboard side';
- two prolonged blasts followed by two short blasts to mean 'I intend to overtake you on your port side';

(ii) the vessel about to be overtaken when acting in accordance with Rule 9(e) (i) shall indicate her agreement by the following signal on her whistle:

- one prolonged, one short, one prolonged and one short blast, in that order.

(d) When vessels in sight of one another are approaching each other and from any cause either vessel fails to understand the intentions or actions of the other, or is in doubt whether sufficient action is being taken by the other to avoid collision, the vessel in doubt shall immediately indicate such doubt by giving at least five short and rapid blasts on the whistle. Such signals may be supplemented by a light signal of at least five short and rapid flashes.

(e) A vessel nearing a bend or an area of a channel of fairway where other vessels may be obscured by an intervening obstruction shall sound one prolonged blast. Such signal shall be answered with a prolonged blast by any approaching vessel that may be within hearing around the bend or behind the intervening obstruction.

(f) If whistles are fitted on a vessel at a distance apart of more than 100 metres, one whistle only shall be used for giving manoeuvring and warning signals.

Annex IV Distress Signals

1. The following signals, used or exhibited either together or separately, indicate distress and need of assistance.

(a) a gun or other explosive signal fired at intervals of about 1 minute;
(b) continuous sounding with any fog-signalling apparatus;
(c) rockets or shells, throwing red stars fired one at a time at short intervals;
(d) a signal made by radiotelegraphy or by other signalling method consisting of the group ...---... (SOS) in the Morse Code;
(e) a signal sent by radiotelephony consisting of the spoken word 'Mayday';
(f) the International Code Signal of distress indicated by N.C.;
(g) a signal consisting of a square flag having above or below it a ball or anything resembling a ball;
(h) flames on a vessel (as from a burning tar barrel, oil barrel, etc.);
(i) a rocket parachute flare or a hand flare showing a red light;
(j) a smoke signal giving off orange-coloured smoke;
(k) slowly and repeatedly raising and lowering arms outstretched to each side;
(l) the radiotelegraph alarm signal.;
(m) the radiotelephone alarm signal;
(n) signals transmitted by emergency position-indicating radio beacons.

2. The use or exhibition of any of the foregoing signals except for the purpose of indicating distress and need of assistance and the use of other signals which may be confused with any of the above signals is prohibited.

3. Attention is drawn to the relevant sections of the International Code of Signals, the Merchant Ship Search and Rescue Manual and the following signals:

(a) a piece of orange-coloured canvas with either a black square and circle or other appropriate symbol (for identification from the air);
(b) a dye marker.

Some Common Nautical Terms Relating to Small Boats

Abaft Towards the stern.
Astern Behind the boat.
Beam Widest point of the boat.
Bilges Bottom of the boat where water collects.
Bow Forward part of the boat.
Draught The depth of water occupied by the boat.
Fairlead A channel for leading a rope over the side of a boat to avoid friction.
Forward Towards the bow.
Freeboard Distance from the waterline to the deck outboard edge.
Gunwale Top rail of the boat.
Hull Structure of the boat below deck level.
Keel Backbone of the boat from front to back.
Lee side Side of the boat away from the wind direction.
Pay out To ease a chain or rope.
Port Left-hand side of the boat looking forward.
Starboard Right-hand side of the boat looking forward.
Stern Rear of the boat.
Tiller Lever for turning the rudder.
Transom Flat stern of a boat on which an outboard engine can be mounted.
Weather side Side of the boat upon which the wind is blowing.

Gale Warnings

Gale warnings are issued only when winds of at least Force 8 or gusts reaching 43 knots are expected. The date and time of origin are given with each message. The term 'severe gale implies winds of a least Force 9 or gusts reaching 52 knots. The terms 'imminent', 'soon' and 'later' indicate gales within six hours, between six and twelve hours, and more than twelve hours from the time of issue respectively.

Radio Broadcasts

BBC Radio 4 – 200 kHz (1500 m) – broadcast gale warnings as soon as possible after receiving them and repeat them on the hour immediately following.

Appendix 3: Department of Transport Regulations

The regulatory body for passenger vessels in the UK is the Department of Transport (DoT). It recognizes the types of craft used by divers for one-day diving trips and it has some perfectly reasonable guidelines to follow when judging the seaworthiness of such vessels.

A difficulty arises for the DoT because the government has not applied its mind to the class of vessel used for extended diving cruises. Typically these vessels are 20 m long and proceed some considerable distance to sea. The full regulations intended for ocean passenger liners are clearly inappropriate, as are the guidelines laid down for open-decked dayboats, which are typically about 10 m long. This lack of appropriate legislation has contributed to a difficult situation, with local DoT officials varying somewhat in the way in which they interpret their guidelines. New legislation in the form of the Small Ships' Regulations is due in late 1987. It is hoped that this will clarify matters.

Meanwhile the details below are necessary so that the organizers of diving parties who charter hard boats can ensure that the vessel complies with appropriate government safety legislation. In the long term it is in the interests of both charterers and boat owners that this happens. Divers must also recognize that it requires considerable finance to comply with some of the regulations. It is obviously in their own interests to be prepared to pay somewhat higher charter fees to live aboard a safer vessel.

Extracts from Department of Transport Regulations

Classes of Passenger Vessels

A vessel carrying *more* than twelve passengers, regardless of the service, is subject to the Merchant Shipping (Passenger Ship Construction and Survey) Regulations 1984.

The following classes are categorized as passenger vessels:

Class I: Ships engaged on long international voyages.
Class II: Ships engaged on short international voyages
Class II(A): Ships not engaged on international voyages
Class III: Ships on voyages within 70 miles by sea from their point of departure and not more than 18 miles from the UK coast.
Class IV: Ships used only on smooth and partly smooth waters.
Class V: Ships used only on smooth waters.
Class VI: Ships, in favourable weather and during restricted periods, with not more than 250 passengers on smooth or partly smooth waters, or not more than 15 miles from their departure point and 3 miles from land.
Class VI(A): Ships carrying not more than fifty passengers not more than 6 miles to UK island communities, and not more than 3 miles from land.

The following classes are not categorized as passenger vessels:

Class X: Fishing vessels.
Class XI: Sailing ships which proceed to sea.
Class XII: Pleasure craft of 13.7 m in length and over.

The Merchant Shipping (Load Line) Rules

Any boat which is used on a *commercial basis* to take parties of passengers to sea for the purposes of leisure pursuits (including sport diving) must comply with the Merchant Shipping (Load Line) Rules 1968, SI 1968, No. 1053 as amended, unless exempted by the Merchant Shipping (Load Line) (Exemption) Order 1968, SI 1968, No. 1116. These rules are to be revised in 1986.

Where compliance with the Load Line Rules is required, it is necessary for the owner to obtain a Load Line Certificate to permit the boat to be operated. To comply with the Load Line Rules the boat must meet specific constructional standards.

Any vessel used by divers would be likely to fall into either Class II(A) or Class III, though vessels in these classes are generally much bigger than those employed by divers.

Very few (if any) diving charter boats can comply fully with these Load Line Rules as these are intended primarily for vessels making international and ocean voyages in all weathers, rather than boats designed for operation in coastal waters in relatively good weather conditions.

The Merchant Shipping (Load Line) (Exemption) Order

The DoT acknowledges these difficulties by issuing a United Kingdom Load Line Exemption Certificate for any boat attaining certain minimum constructional standards, having an efficient engine and being suitably equipped. This Exemption Certificate permits the boat, when not carrying cargo or more than twelve passengers, to be used in favourable weather within defined coastal limits.

To gain a Load Line Exemption Certificate a vessel must be less than 80 registered tons and must not:

1. Carry cargo.
2. Carry more than twelve passengers.
3. Undertake voyages which are more than 15 miles (exclusive of any officially defined smooth waters) from the point of departure nor more than 3 miles from land.

Such a boat is also subject to appropriate ancillary equipment requirements and may also be subject to control by a local authority. There is currently no prescribed scale of safety equipment.

A passenger is defined as any person on the ship except:

1. Someone employed or engaged in any capacity on board the ship on the business of the ship. (In DoT Merchant Shipping Notice M1194 the expression 'employed or engaged in any capacity on the business of the ship' has been defined as either having a contractually binding agreement to serve on the ship in some defined capacity and which could include carrying out such duties under training, or having been duly signed on as a member of the crew.)
2. A person on board the ship either resulting from the master's obligation to lend aid to shipwrecked or distressed mariners or because of circumstances beyond the control of the master or charterer.
3. A child under one year of age. The definition of 'smooth waters' is set out in the Merchant Shipping (Smooth and Partially Smooth Waters) Rules 1977, SI 1977, No. 252 as amended in SI 1978, No. 801, and SI 1984, No. 955. These rules designate which of the coastal waters of Britain are considered sufficiently sheltered to be classed as smooth or partially smooth waters.

'Land' is defined as a portion of coast upon which landing can reasonably be expected. This would normally be interpreted as an area on which a boat could be set down, such as a beach. It would not normally include a coast consisting of broken rocks or cliffs.

'Favourable weather' is when the visibility is good and when the combined effects of wind, sea or swell upon the ship under consideration are never greater than those which would cause moderate rolling or pitching, or result in the shipping of green seas onto the weather deck, or, in the case of open boats, over the gunwale.

The skippers of exempt vessels must be in possession of at least a Boatman's Licence, issued by the DoT. This is described in DoT Merchant Shipping Notice M1036. The requirements are not too stiff and persons holding at least a DoT certificate of competency as second mate, mate (home trade), second hand, yachtmaster (coastal), or a Deck Officer Class 5 Certificate, or a Royal Yachting Association Coastal Skipper Award, or any higher awards, are not required to undergo the tests.

The DoT specify operating conditions which enable vessels to qualify for Load Line Exemption Certificates. These state:

1. The period of validity of the Exemption Certificate varies between two and five years, depending on the mode of construction of the vessel.
2. There must be an annual survey by a DoT surveyor.
3. The number of passengers will be stated on the Certificate; it will never exceed 12.
4. The above weather restriction applies. The interpretation of the favourable weather clause will vary appreciably according to the size, type and sea-handling capabilities of the boat and also upon the force, direction, fetch and duration of the wind in the intended area of operation. Thus the skipper must have a sound working knowledge of his boat and the intended area of operation.
5. Boats will be limited to a specified radius of operation from their place of departure. This is 20 miles for fully decked or well-decked boats and 10 miles for open-cockpit boats.
6. Additionally, any fully decked or well-decked boat having a freeboard of not less than one-tenth of the vessel's beam, and having a high standard of subdivision or a high degree of internal buoyancy, may be permitted to operate within a greater radius than 20 miles. In no case, however, will a boat be allowed to operate more than 40 miles from its point of departure.
7. The areas of operation must be agreed with the Chief Surveyor of the Marine Office of the district concerned.
8. The Chief Surveyor may restrict the number of passengers which may be carried at night in summer and at any time during the winter.

The contradiction between the 15-mile rule and the above 10-mile/20-mile/40-mile rule should be noted.

The DoT also issues guidelines for constructional standards of the vessel enabling a Load Line Exemption Certificate to be issued. They also specify bilge-pumping arrangements, stability, machinery, fuel arrangements, radio, life-saving appliances and fire-fighting arrangements.

Exempted Vessels

Certain boats are exempted from the regulations so far described. These are sailing vessels, club boats and privately owned yachts.

Sailing vessels are defined as vessels that are capable of operating under sail alone. This apparently means that they can use power alone for long periods if they wish – they only must *possess* a sailing capability. Such sailing vessels must still only carry twelve passengers or less, they must be under 24 m in length, carry no cargo, limit themselves to UK coasts and are subject to a general inspection concerning their seaworthiness. They are also subject to the relevant sections of the Lifesaving Appliances and Fire Appliances Regulations.

Club boats are those owned and operated by a club or group for the sole benefit of its members; no financial gain must accrue to anyone, although club members can contribute to running costs. The term 'private yachts' is largely self-explanatory, although it appears to apply to virtually any vessel that you own yourself and do not use for financial gain.

For your own safety and peace of mind you should be very cautious before engaging such classes of vessels for diving charter work. Some, of course, are quite genuine, but others are merely attempting to slip through loopholes in the present regulations.

Vessels Going Overseas

Vessels proceeding overseas (for example, to the Mediterranean or Caribbean) for commercial charter must comply with the full rules of the Merchant Shipping (Passenger Ship Construction and Survey) Regulations 1984. Only if they go as private pleasure vessels are they exempt. In this case cost-sharing co-crew members are allowed, but as soon as a profit is made the full Load Line Certificate is required. It is most unlikely that any charter vessel intended for coastal work could gain this.

Registration

A vessel has to be registered somewhere. Among charter vessels operating in British waters it is usual to be registered as a British ship. Details can be had from the Registrar of British Ships, c/o Customs House at the intended port of registry.

Summary of British Regulations

A normal diving charter vessel operating legally in British waters must have either a Load Line Certificate (very unlikely); or a Load Line Exemption Certificate (most likely, and desirable); or be a club boat operated only for club members; or be a sailing vessel; or be a private yacht.

Small Vessels Regulations in Other Countries

The position obviously varies in the different countries in which a sport diver is likely to operate, making it difficult to generalize. The United States, Canada and Scandinavia have regulations quite similar to Britain. Australia has quite strict rules, as does New Zealand, which has a specific set of Sports Vessels Rules.

For your own and your party's safety, it is important to check the details with the marine authorities in the countries concerned.

Legal Responsibilities of Skipper (or Deputy)

The skipper is legally responsible for the safety of the vessel and all who are aboard her. This means that he is the final judge as to what weather conditions are safe for his vessel and where it is safe for the boat to go.

This is, of course, a statement of the obvious and, provided that a hired skipper is reasonable, it should not lead to difficulty.

Appendix 4: Safety at Sea

Weather-Wise

An up-to-date weather forecast is essential for divers – bad weather probably causes about 80 per cent of all incidents. So, if you are shore diving or taking a boat out, be sure to get the latest forecast and remember – it is often rougher than it looks from shore!

Details of weather services in the British Isles can be obtained via the press, radio, television and coastal stations. Most local authorities and harbour masters post local forecasts outside their officies. You can get forecasts from the nearest meteorological office or dial the telephone weather service (number in the local telephone directory). You can find out about local sea conditions by telephoning the local coastguard.

Sea and Swell

Sea Waves caused by wind at a given place.

Swell Waves formed by past wind, or wind at a distance.

Short swell The length or distance between each successive wave is small.

Long swell The length or distance between each successive wave is large.

Low swell The height between the lowest and highest part of a wave is small.

Heavy swell The height between the lowest and highest part of a wave is great.

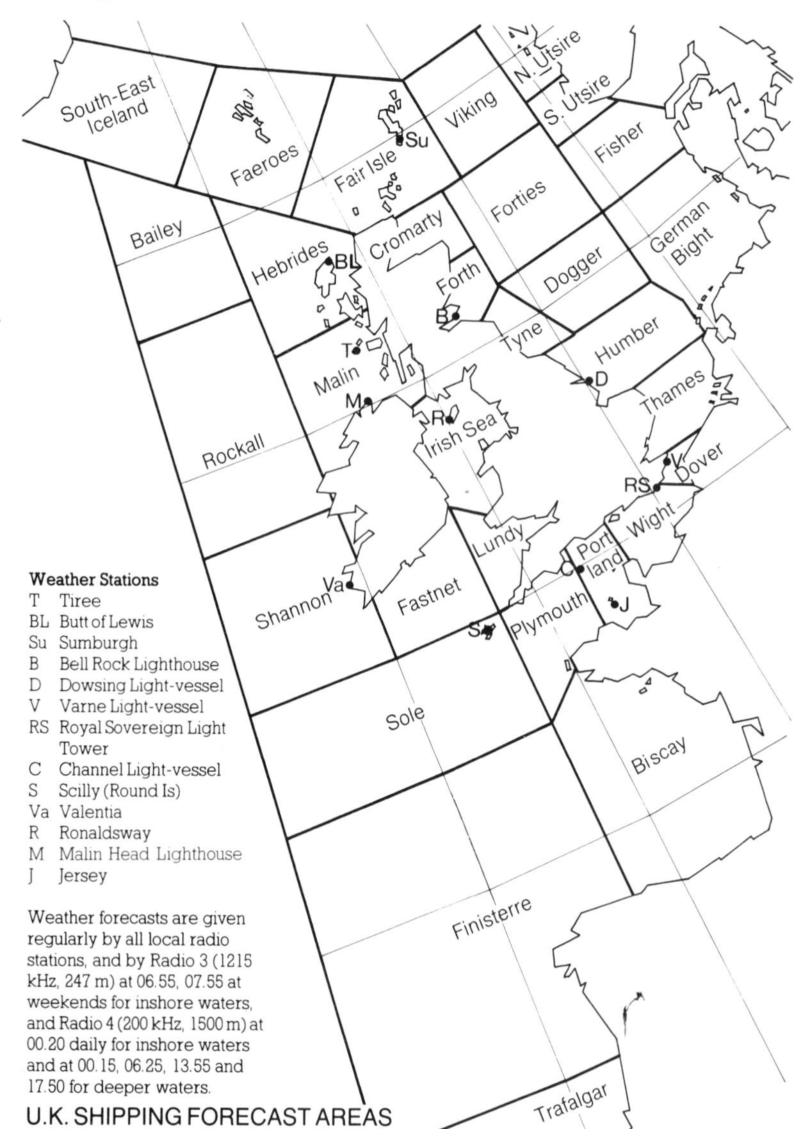

Weather Stations

T Tiree
BL Butt of Lewis
Su Sumburgh
B Bell Rock Lighthouse
D Dowsing Light-vessel
V Varne Light-vessel
RS Royal Sovereign Light Tower
C Channel Light-vessel
S Scilly (Round Is)
Va Valentia
R Ronaldsway
M Malin Head Lighthouse
J Jersey

Weather forecasts are given regularly by all local radio stations, and by Radio 3 (1215 kHz, 247 m) at 06.55, 07.55 at weekends for inshore waters, and Radio 4 (200 kHz, 1500 m) at 00.20 daily for inshore waters and at 00.15, 06.25, 13.55 and 17.50 for deeper waters.

U.K. SHIPPING FORECAST AREAS

INTERNATIONAL SWELL SCALE

Code figure	State of the swell in the open sea
0	None
1	Short or average length; low
2	Long
3	Short
4	Average length; moderate height
5	Long
6	Short
7	Average length; heavy
8	Long
9	Confused

FOG AND VISIBILITY SCALE FOR SHIPS AT SEA

Code number	Description	Definition
0	Dense fog	Objects not visible at 5 m
1	Thick fog	Objects not visible at 200 m
2	Fog	Objects not visible at 400 m
3	Moderate fog	Objects not visible at ½ ml
4	Mist or haze or very poor visibility	Objects not visible at 1 ml
5	Poor visibility	Objects not visible at 2 ml
6	Moderate visibility	Objects not visible at 5 ml
7	Good visibility	Objects not visible at 10 ml
8	Very good visibility	Objects not visible at 30 ml
9	Excellent visibility	Objects visible at more than 30 ml

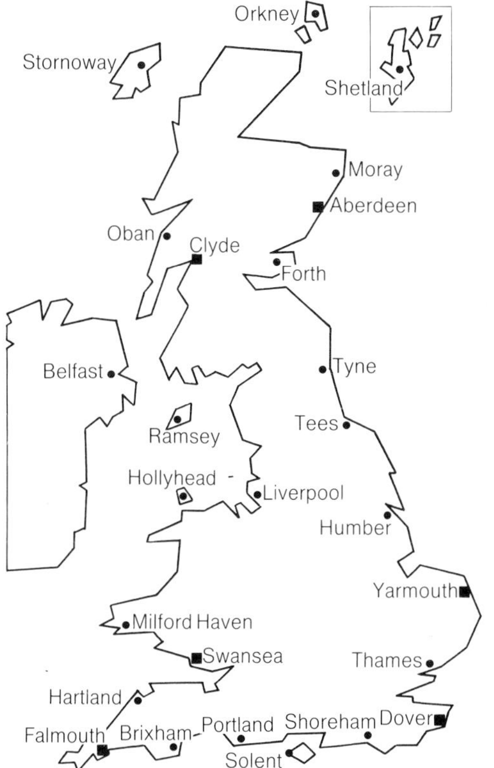

Coastguard Rescue Centres and Telephone Numbers

ABERDEEN	0224-52334
Shetland	0595-2976
Orkney	0856-3268
Wick	0955-2332
Moray	0779-4278
Forth	03335-666
YARMOUTH	0493-51338
Tyne	0632-572691
Tees	0642-474639
Humber	09646-351
DOVER	0304-210008
Thames	02556-5518
Shoreham	07917-2226
BRIXHAM	08045-2156
Solent	0983-752265
Portland	0305-820441
Falmouth	0326-314481
Land's End	073687-351
SWANSEA	0792-66534
Hartland	02374-235
Milford Haven	06465-218
Holyhead	0407-2051
Liverpool	07048-72903
CLYDE	0475-29988
Ramsey	0624-813255
Belfast	024784-284
Oban	0631-63720
Stornoway	0851-2013

In an emergency for coastal or sea rescue, dial 999 and ask for 'Coastguard'.

The above list may change from time to time.

Appendix 5: Small Boat insurance

Small boat insurance, unlike motor insurance, is not a legal requirement. However, most reputable organizations, including the BSAC, require a minimum level of insurance, usually third party liability, which covers only injury and damage to others and their property. Boat owners would be wise to take out more insurance than this, in which case an all-risks policy, which covers all damage, injury or loss that is currently insurable, will give a greater degree of protection.

In general only the craft itself and the equipment necessary for its safety are insurable; in many cases sensitive equipment, such as marine radios, can only be insured against certain types of accident. Diving equipment cannot be covered as part of the boat's equipment and should be insured separately.

Marine insurance is not as straightforward as household or personal accident insurance. With marine insurance it is possible unwittingly to invalidate your policy by doing something with the boat for which it is not covered. For example, leaving it unattended while at anchor is in most cases not allowed. In marine insurance 'the principal of the business' is the most important factor and, provided that you act as 'prudent owner uninsured' (that is, sensibly and in your own best interests, as if you were not insured), you should not have any problems should a claim be necessary. This, it should be emphasized, does not give you a licence to use your insurance policy as a cheap way of replacing old boats or equipment, a practice that only serves to increase the cost of the insurance and the hostility of your underwriter (insurer).

Be selective about which insurance policy you choose. The one which suits your pocket best is unlikely to be the one which gives you the best cover. Before choosing it is essential to obtain a copy of the policy, called a policy wording, which should be studied carefully. It is equally important that you make a complete declaration of what 'risks or adventures' you wish to insure when you obtain a quotation. Many proposal forms do not ask enough questions and a separate sheet attached to the proposal form may well be necessary in order for you to make a full declaration of the risk.

Some, but not all, of the questions you should answer, whether or not they are asked on the proposal form, are:

Is the boat to be used for water-skiing?

What will be the standard or ability of the person or persons who will generally be in charge (rather than physically in control) of the craft?

Will the craft be used for instruction?

Is member-to-member cover required? A club, being a legal entity made up of its members, cannot claim against itself; in other words, should an accident occur through negligence causing injury to a member or damage to his property, this would not be an insured risk unless you have member-to-member (cross-member) cover.

Where will the boat be stored?

Any other point which you may feel to be at all unusual.

Some of these points will incur an additional premium, a matter your broker will be able to advise you on. Additional premiums are often levied because of: a lack of basic cover in the original policy; a lack of understanding on behalf of the underwriter; or a genuine increase in the risk. It is therefore worth requesting clarification and negotiating with the underwriter to reduce, or even remove, any additional premium, except perhaps in the first instance, where a more suitable policy should be sought.

You must also inform your underwriter of any changes in circumstance or events that affect the risk, or the underwriter's position under that risk. Like all insurance, failure to make a full declaration or to keep your underwriter informed may result in forfeiture of the policy; no matter what you have already paid, you will be uninsured.

As a rule it is safer to use a qualified insurance broker, if possible the one recommended by your own organization, as he is more likely to understand your position.

Index

Page numbers in *italic* refer to illustrations

Illustration Acknowledgements

Thanks are due to the following for allowing the use of copyright photographs:

Mike Busuttili, figures 0, 2–57, 82, 85, 105–109, 112, 117, 121, 122, 124, 126, 128, 130, 132, 135, 136, 139–141, 146, 147, 148, 150, 157, 163, 169–171, 173, 184, 194, 195, 202, 206, 207, 212, 213, 256, 267, 289, 306;
Dave Gillette-Inglis, figures 25, 257;
Jerry Hazzard, figures 87, 104, 110, 113, 137, 138, 143–145, 307;
Mike Holbrook, figures 92, 100, 126, 129, 180;
Humber Inflatables, figure 125;
Mariner, figure 305;
Howard Painter, figures 102, 103;
Gordon Ridley, figures 118, 164, 178, 183, 193, 270, 272, 285, 286, 288;
Royal National Lifeboat Institution, figure 211;
Dave Shaw, figures 67, 71, 72, 88, 90, 91, 93, 94, 97–99, 111, 114, 198, 201, 204, 205, 208–210, 243, 277–280, 291–304;
Barry Winfield, figures 75, 191, 192, 224.

Figures 196, 219, 220, 223, 225 and 264 are Crown Copyright, reproduced from Admiralty Chart No. 1977 (Figure 196, Admiralty Chart No. L1977), with the permission of the Controller of Her Majesty's Stationery Office.

Figures 261, 265 and 266 are reproduced with the permission of Reed's Nautical Almanac.

All the artwork for this book was specially commissioned from Rico Oldfield.